Making Nursery Rhyme Toys

By the same author:
The Great Soft Toy Cat and Kitten Book
Crafts and the Disabled
The Techniques of Soft Toymaking
Patterns for Soft Toys – Applying Soft Toy Techniques

Making Nursery Rhyme Toys

ENID ANDERSON

*With 21 colour photographs
and 109 line illustrations*

David & Charles
Newton Abbot   London   North Pomfret (Vt)

To Joyce and Cecilia

Photography by Jonathon Bosley

British Library Cataloguing in Publication Data
Anderson, Enid
 Making nursery rhyme toys.
 1. Soft toy making
 I. Title
 745.592'4   TT174.3

ISBN 0-7153-8653-0

Phototypeset by ABM Typographics Limited Hull
and printed in Great Britain
by Redwood Burn Ltd Trowbridge
for David & Charles Publishers plc
Brunel House   Newton Abbot   Devon

Published in the United States of America
by David & Charles Inc
North Pomfret   Vermont 05053   USA

CONTENTS

INTRODUCTION

Nursery rhymes are deeply interwoven in our traditions and history. We are taught nursery rhymes as infants, and in turn pass this knowledge on to our children, and so it continues and has done through the ages. I greatly enjoyed the research for this project, spending many happy hours in libraries and bookshops, often receiving strange looks from the younger generation as I sat on tiny chairs in the children's section reading nursery rhymes. I found many delightful books, some of which are listed in the Bibliography, and would like to thank the authors who inspired me to create the toys. There is a wide variety and scope in these toys, which should result in the reader learning, or experiencing, many different toymaking techniques. The overall 'soft-toy' image has been extended however to include puppetry, a pull-along toy, a mobile and a musical box.

Many magazines include patterns for soft toys, and most people at some time have 'had a go' at making toys without any formal training, often with disappointing results. As with any craft, there are great rewards to be had if the basic techniques are learned first, then the more intricate techniques will follow with ease, so I have included a comprehensive section on the techniques required. However, space is at a premium here when so many designs want inclusion so it would help to read my previous book on toymaking techniques (see Bibliography).

Soft toymaking is a great therapy, so relax and enjoy making the toys; this will be reflected in the finished articles and the subsequent praise you receive.

ACKNOWLEDGEMENTS

My sincere thanks to the following: Valerie Dawson for her valuable help; Tina Stubbs for typing the manuscript; Margaret Annand of Mea Crafts for proving the manuscript; Maureen Poyser and Elizabeth Holland for making the knitted strip toys possible. Also to Anne Dyer for the hen in 'I had a little hen', based on her original design. 'There was a monkey' developed as a result of a body design by Pamela Peake. 'The Teddy Bears' Picnic' © 1907 M. Witmark & Sons, reproduced by permission of B. Feldman & Co. Ltd, London WC2H 0LD. 'Horsey Horsey' © 1937, reproduced by permission of Frances Day and Hunter Ltd., London WC 2H 0LD.

SOFT TOYMAKING TECHNIQUES

The following sections should enable the reader, whether accustomed to soft toymaking or not, to make the nursery rhyme toys in this book with few problems. Before enlarging the patterns, always carefully read through the instructions, studying the pattern at the same time, then any possible doubts or problems will occur prior to cutting out and you will avoid wastage. If a technique is new to you, practise it on an oddment of material before commencing the real thing. Allow plenty of time for your toymaking and work in a tidy and organised way; fewer mistakes will occur then. If a disaster happens, do not be too hasty in discarding the toy; it may well be that it can be rescued with a few minor adjustments. Look for further potential in the given patterns: possibly with the addition of a few different accessories the toys could become other nursery rhyme characters.

Basic Tools and Materials
Sewing needles, assorted sizes and thicknesses including a curved needle
Scissors
Dressmaking pins
Variety of sewing threads
Tape measure
Ruler
Tailor's chalk
Teasel brush
Stuffing sticks
Tracing paper
Graph paper
White card
Pencils
Pair of compasses
Strong wire
Adhesive tape
Lampshade tape
Thin round-nosed pliers
Wire cutters
All purpose adhesive (eg, Copydex or
    Elmer's Glue-all)

Fabrics
Toymaking patterns rarely stipulate the colouring of the toy, usually giving the type of materials required and leaving the final colour choice to the maker. This book is the exception; since specific nursery rhyme characters have been designed and in many cases the material choice and colouring have a definite bearing on the portrayal of the toy. The colouring should be adhered to whenever possible. There are many exciting fabrics around, so if the material type stated is not readily available it should not be too difficult to substitute an alternative, but still keeping to the given colouring. Some of the glove puppets, however, will allow freedom of choice as they are a useful way of using up oddments of material.
NOTE: For information on the stockists of any specialist materials used in the pattern please refer to the Appendix.

Take care when choosing fur-fabric – it is not always the most expensive which is the best. Avoid those fabrics which have a poor pile covering as it will be impossible to hide the seams in the finished toy. Test by running the thumb and first finger against the pile of the fabric. If it is thick and springy it should make up well. Polished fur-fabric has a smooth shiny pile which lies flat on the backing, and you should make sure the pile covers the backing adequately. Try to choose a fur-fabric which has a firm backing; if this is not available, and the backing of the fabric is of a knitted texture or very soft, then it may be necessary to add a piece of

Velcro behind those areas where features are to be applied, in order to give extra 'body' to the fabric backing. It is not economical to purchase the smallest amount of material available (eg, 0.25m); the larger the amount of material the proportionately greater is the quantity of toy production.

Felt is not a woven material; it consists of fibres matted under pressure and therefore has no warp or weft. Felt varies considerably in quality. Test it by holding a piece up to the light and weak areas will show as lighter patches. Use a felt which has a fairly even texture. Felt is an exciting medium in toymaking as it has such a wide range of colours.

For sock toys, it is essential to use socks which have a firm texture and preferably a plain or ribbed pattern; avoid fancy patterned socks. Terylene, nylon and cotton are suitable.

You may want to economise on dolls' clothes by using materials already to hand, rather than those recommended. However, do bear in mind the wear the clothes will receive in relation to the toy type; a flimsy material will not withstand constant pulling by small fingers. Try always to use new materials; it is false economy to make a doll to a high standard and then dress it using poor materials. This may seem obvious, but it is surprising how many students at toymaking classes turn up with bags of well-worn materials to dress their toys. Colouring is most important: for example, cream-coloured underclothes and a brown-toned dress on a rag doll with a pale-cream or natural body fabric looks most effective. Likewise, a pale-pink doll skin with a pink or blue toned dress fabric and white underclothes looks very pretty. Trimmings consisting of lace or ribbons should tone, and the feature colouring should also be connected with the general ensemble.

Enlarging a Pattern

All patterns on grids must be enlarged to the required size before making the toy. Each square represents 2.5cm (1in), so graph paper of that size must be used. The pattern is then simply drawn by hand on to the larger squares, following each line and shape exactly from square to square. Meticulous care at this stage will be reflected in a perfectly fitted toy.

Then, add all the annotations – pile line arrows, name of toy, part of toy, number of pieces, materials to be used, etc. It is a good policy to paste the pattern pieces on to strong card as they will wear better, and give a more accurate outline when drawing round them on to the fabric. After mounting the patterns on card it is helpful to mark on the back those pieces which need to be reversed, or to have a second copy of the pattern piece cut out and marked in the reverse position. Where a pattern piece states, for example, 'cut two in fur-fabric one reversed', make sure that you do reverse the pattern for the second half, otherwise you will have two matching pieces with the pile on the same side.

Understanding the Patterns and Instructions

Unless stated otherwise, a 0.7cm (1/4in) seam allowance has been allowed on all patterns, and the outline of each pattern

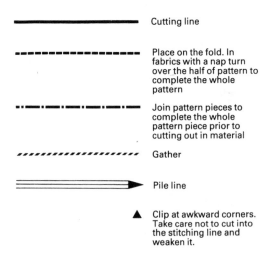

————————	Cutting line
■ ■ ■ ■ ■ ■ ■ ■ ■	Place on the fold. In fabrics with a nap turn over the half of pattern to complete the whole pattern
■ ▪ ■ ▪ ■ ▪ ■ ▪ ■	Join pattern pieces to complete the whole pattern piece prior to cutting out in material
//////////////////	Gather
═══════►	Pile line
▲	Clip at awkward corners. Take care not to cut into the stitching line and weaken it.

Fig 1 Pattern Markings

piece is the actual cutting line. Certain conventions have been used when drawing the patterns to save valuable space – see Fig 1. The arrows on the patterns indicate the pile lines.

Wherever possible, the pattern instructions have been kept to a similar form and layout, which should enable the reader to progress from one design to another with ease. The degree of difficulty is not given as this is, of course, relative to the expertise of the individual toymaker. There are very few complicated processes involved, so if the instructions are followed carefully, step by step, with any necessary reference to the techniques section, few problems should occur.

Storing the Patterns

Once the patterns are enlarged, the toymaker should have some system of filing so that they are available at a glance when required. Some toymakers make a hole in the centre of the pattern pieces and thread them on to pipe cleaners, putting all the pieces relating to one subject together, then twisting the pipe cleaner ends to hold them in place. Large A4 size office ring-binders are useful if they have clear plastic pockets into which individual patterns can be placed and filed under alphabetical order. Plain brown office-type pocket folders can be used and placed upright in a box in alphabetical order according to the toy types.

Choose the method you prefer and carefully keep your patterns in order as you progress.

Marking Out

Always mark out clearly and close to the pattern templates, holding the pencil or dressmaker's chalk in a vertical position. If the material will not allow a continuous smooth line, draw broken lines close together. Never use a ballpoint pen which would stain the fabric.

On fur-fabrics, note the pile line indicated by the arrowing on the patterns – it is

the way the pile lies when smooth. Stroke it with your hand and the pile line is soon determined. As an added guide, fur-fabric toys must have their pile lying as it would on a real animal – from head down to tail, from ear base to top of ears, from tail base to tail end, from top of legs to base of legs and from under chin, down stomach to rear end.

Next, turn the fabric on to a smooth surface with the backing uppermost and mark the pile line on the selvedge in pencil or tailor's chalk. This will assist you in lining up the arrows on the pattern pieces. (The selvedge is soft and should be avoided.) Lay the pattern pieces on to the firm backing, noting the arrows carefully at all times.

Cutting Out

Dress materials can be cut out with more than one thickness at a time. Make sure before cutting that you have ironed the materials which can be ironed. An accurate pattern cannot be cut from creased material. Take note of any pattern lines or designs which require continuation from one piece to another.

Sharp scissors are essential for felt, otherwise it will twist within the blades and simply drag the impacted fibres apart. It is very important to cut the felt pattern pieces out evenly, using long cuts and the full length of the blades where possible to produce a smooth outline.

With fur-fabric, place the pile side to the table and the backing uppermost. Cut carefully by snipping around the marked pattern shape, cutting the backing only and threading the under-blade of the scissors through the pile to part it. If fur-fabric is cut as ordinary dressmaking material, the pile will be cut. If a curve is required, turn the material to the scissors as the backing is cut, keeping the scissors facing directly to the front at 12 o'clock. Never turn the scissors at an angle; this would result in the pile also being cut at an angle and spoiled.

Pinning

After cutting out dress materials, pin together with the right sides facing. It may be necessary to tack (baste) together areas which are too small to pin easily.

Fur-fabric pieces should be pinned together right sides facing (colour headed pins are very suitable). As the toy is pinned together, push all the pile inside with your finger so that only the edges of the fabric show with no pile caught between. With all the toys, especially fur-fabric ones, it is advisable to count the number of pins inserted into the shapes and then count them again on removal, to prevent a pin being left in a toy and hurting a child. All the pattern pieces of the toys, other than the string puppet circle cat, are pinned prior to stitching, after which the pins are removed. Some toymakers find it easier to remove the pins as they stitch. From time to time in the following patterns you will be reminded to remove the pins, although this should be done automatically.

Felt adheres easily to itself, so if two pieces are placed together they require very few pins.

Stitching

The word 'thread' in the patterns refers to any sewing medium used.

If the clothes are made of dress materials and designed to be removed from the toy, it is essential to make sure that all the seaming is sound and will withstand constant pulling. Whilst hand stitching is desirable for a great proportion of soft toymaking, a sewing machine often makes for greater strength with less effort, especially on cotton dresses, pantaloons and petticoats, etc. Velcro is very useful as a fastening, neatly stitched in place. Snap fasteners can also be used. The clothes in this book have been specially designed to suit specific toys, so do study this as a guide to future toymaking.

For fur-fabric, backstitch 0.7cm (¼in) from the outside edges unless stated otherwise, using a strong sewing thread. After stitching remove the pins. After the stuffing process, ladder stitch to close the openings.

With felt, when overstitching around the

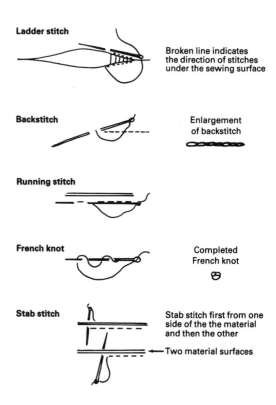

Fig 2 Stitches

outside edges of the toys, use a matching thread. Three strands of six-strand composition Anchor stranded embroidery cotton is suitable (a sharp thin cotton or sewing thread may cut through the felt when pressure is placed on the seams). Three strands also makes a neat continuous edge to the toy, whereas single-strand cotton can result in bulges forming along the edges between the stitches. However, a neatly stitched edge will not hide any snags along the edges caused by poor cutting out. Close any stuffing openings with the same kind of stitch as used for the seams.

Stuffing

Once the toy has been cut out, pinned and stitched, turn all pieces to the right side, paying careful attention to any extremities. Cut a snip at any tight corners to ease the seaming. (A material like felt may have

10

been top stitched so will not require turning.)

There are many different types of toy filling, used for a variety of purposes, but a good quality lightweight terylene toy filling in white is suitable for all the toys in this book. Do not use foam chips, cut-up ladies' nylon stockings or tights, or any heavy filling. Exact quantities of filling are not stated with the individual patterns because fabrics vary so much in 'stretchability', and the reader's toy materials may not be the same as the author's. If the exact quantities were given it could result in poorly stuffed toys. Almost without exception, students of toymaking will inflict on the toys vast quantities of toy filling, as one might push straw into a sack, and the result is misshapen articles and disappointment. A toy should be moulded from within to the toy skin shape. To achieve this, take a small quantity of toy filling at a time, tease it out between the thumbs and first fingers of both hands, then insert into the toy, building it up to the shape. The teasing-out process is to remove any lumps which would show through the toy skin, and to produce a good even texture to the filling. As you stuff the toy, hold it in the left hand and use this hand to assist with the shaping (reverse if left-handed). Dowel rods or wooden knitting needles are useful as stuffing sticks to help reach any awkward areas.

A toy should be very firmly and evenly stuffed. If inadequately stuffed, a soft cuddly toy can quickly end up as an almost empty skin once the toy has been handled – the filling settles as the air is expelled. When stuffing a large toy, for example Goosey, Goosey, Gander, it is advisable to leave it for a few hours or overnight before closing the stuffing opening; it is surprising how much more filling can then be inserted. As the stuffing opening on any toy is closed, add more toy filling behind the line of stitching until the opening is completely closed.

With the felt toys, carefully stuff and shape without adding too much stress on the seaming; felt tears very easily, especially if a poor quality is used.

Features

It is the features which make the toy. These do not necessarily need to be complicated in design except where being used for a very stylised toy. Often a more simple approach, well executed, produces a more satisfactory end-result. All features should be applied carefully, using either neat stitching or, on rare occasions, glue. A toy can quickly be spoiled if the features are glued on using the wrong type of adhesive and are easily removed by small fingers. If gluing in place, use a latex-based adhesive, eg, Copydex which will bond together the whole thickness of the felt.

Placing of features can sometimes be a difficult task. Whilst feature placing may be given on a pattern, it should be used as an approximate indication only, as variations to the toy can occur during construction. Do not be in a hurry to place the features. Move them around until you are really satisfied that they are placed correctly. Look through books on anatomy and animal encyclopedias as these can provide a good guide to feature placing.

Painting features There are many mediums for painting the features on a toy. Taking into consideration the cost involved – if, for example, only one toy is to be made using painting as the method – I would advise the reader to use whatever materials are available, always testing them well first on a scrap of the material. Make sure that the colouring is suitable for the recipient. Do not give painted toys to a young child who may suck them.

With food colouring, eg, cochineal, lightly wet the area where the colouring is required and apply it with a soft paintbrush. The colour will spread, so only wet where it is required.

When applying wax crayons, seal them by covering with a clean rag and pressing with a warm iron.

Use lipstick very carefully, bearing in

mind that with all colouring of this type you can add more but cannot take away. Dab lipstick on to the required place then treat as for wax crayons.

Fabric printing dyes are suitable for cotton, linen and soft leather. Use Dylon Paint and Dylon Cold Dye – the paint thickens the dye so that it can applied with a brush. Rowney fabric painting dye is another liquid paint which is suitable for cotton, linen and some synthetic materials.

Nail polishes, if well applied, can be most effective, and face powder (loose or compacted) produces a nice soft blush to a rag doll's cheek.

Water colours should be artist's quality not student's, as the latter are synthetic. Water colours mixed with white emulsion can produce very useful colours.

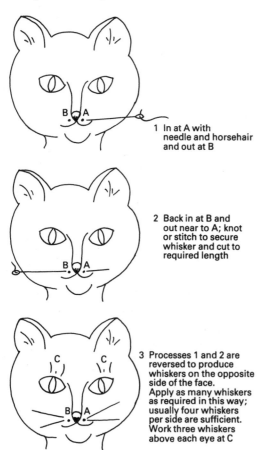

1 In at A with needle and horsehair and out at B

2 Back in at B and out near to A; knot or stitch to secure whisker and cut to required length

3 Processes 1 and 2 are reversed to produce whiskers on the opposite side of the face. Apply as many whiskers as required in this way; usually four whiskers per side are sufficient. Work three whiskers above each eye at C

Fig 3 I Love Little Pussy: Whisker application

Painting eyes on a felt mask Paint the eye bases white and allow to dry thoroughly. Then apply the iris and allow this to dry before the pupil is added. When the whole eye combination is dry, add the highlights to give depth to the expression. A small pink or red dot at each end of the eye, at the corners, adds realism.

Freckles Freckles are usually added across the bridge of the nose. Pay careful attention to their colouring in relation to the rest of the toy. They can be painted, or worked in French knots (see Fig 2).

Whiskers Thread a long needle with horsehair which has been previously washed in disinfectant (ie if you collect your own). Horsehair is available from commercial outlets already prepared. Insert the needle into one side of the face where the whisker is required; take it through to the opposite side. Work a few stitches to hold and take the threaded needle back to the same side it entered previously, bringing the needle out at the required placing of the second whisker. Remove the needle. Thread the needle with another strand of horsehair and reverse the process starting at the opposite side of the face. As many whiskers as required can be inserted using this method. Take care to balance the whiskers evenly on both sides of the face. Trim as required.

Needle-modelling

Students of toymaking are often rather hesitant about using needle-modelling, but with practice it quickly becomes a most exciting process. The technique consists of taking stitches through the stuffed toy from one place to another, pulling on the (strong) thread to form recesses, dimpling, and perhaps ridges and fuller areas.

It can be useful at the outset to make and stuff a doll's head in fabric, secure it at the base and practise needle-modelling, to discover what can be created with a few stitches. To create a nose, the threaded needle is inserted in one side and brought out at the other to form a ridge.

To create dimpling, sew either from one

side of the head or limb to the opposite side or from the front to the back and pull up firmly. Chin dimples are made by taking the thread at an angle from the back of the head, bringing the needle and thread through at the exact place where the dimple is required at the front of the head, and then taking the needle back again almost through the same place to the back of the head, and fastening off.

Wiring a Toy

The Cock-a-Doodle Doo cockerel is wired. The following points should be observed when constructing the wire armature shape; the actual wire sizes are given with the pattern instructions.

Bend any cut ends of wire back on to themselves. Completely bind the wires using adhesive tape. Wrap toy filling around the taped wires and hold this in place with thread. Lampshade tape or strips of old sheeting are then wound over the toy filling and stitched to hold in place. Always imagine that the wire armature shape is the skeleton of the toy and this should provide a good indication of where the wires should be placed, according to the work they are required to do.

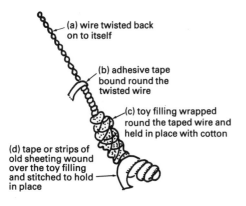

(a) wire twisted back on to itself

(b) adhesive tape bound round the twisted wire

(c) toy filling wrapped round the taped wire and held in place with cotton

(d) tape or strips of old sheeting wound over the toy filling and stitched to hold in place

Fig 4 Cock a Doodle Doo: Preparation of wire for wiring a toy

Laminating a mask

There are different methods of laminating a mask; the one used for the head of the Lavender's Blue doll is as follows. Grease the mould or mask being used – Vaseline is suitable. If using a hollow doll mask, it is necessary to fill it with Plasticine to give it extra stability; make sure it is not distorted in any way. Measure the mask and cut out two pieces of muslin large enough to cover it completely, taking into account the indentations of the features. Using mixed Polycell wallpaper paste, soak the materials thoroughly. Cut a piece of felt to the same size and soak this in the wallpaper paste. If the felt will not readily absorb the paste, soak it in warm water first. Remove one piece of the soaked muslin and squeeze to remove the excess paste. Lay over the mould and press the material well into the features. Treat the second piece of muslin in the same way. A knitting needle, cocktail stick or wooden modelling tool is useful for pressing the soaked layers into the feature indentations. Lastly, take the felt layer, remove excess paste and lay it diagonally on to the mask and press to the features.

Place the covered mask in a warm place to dry slowly; do not try to hasten the drying process. During the drying time it will be necessary to press the material layers back into the feature indentations from time to time. When dry, prise off the material layers and trim excess material to a good shape. The various layers add strength to the mask, but you should take great care when stuffing the toy that the toy filling supports all the raised areas, for example the nose and cheeks, otherwise the mask could easily be flattened in play.

The back head patterns are given for Lavender's Blue although adjustment may be necessary if the mask used is not exactly the same size as the original. To check the size, measure the mask or head sideways and also the depth of the mask side view, then adjust the patterns accordingly.

Musical Units

Sound can add charm to many toys. A musical unit will turn an ordinary toy into a special gift. Most units of the musical box type are either key-wind, as used in The

Teddy Bears' Picnic, or pull-wind. When used in a soft toy, the unit is inserted when the toy is partially stuffed, and the key- or pull-wind protrudes from the back of the toy through the stuffing opening. The final filling is then added, taking care that it can in no way interfere with the key or cord movement, and the opening is closed using ladder stitching. If the unit seems rather heavy for the toy skin, or if it does not appear to be well supported by the toy filling and there is a possibility of it moving, then it is advisable to enclose it in a net bag which is then stitched to the inside of the toy skin prior to closing the stuffing opening.

Glove Puppets

Glove puppetry can be very versatile and of great play (and educational) value. The gloves designed for the subjects in this book can be used as a basis for other toy designs. If more characters are required, the toymaker can often make use of the heads of other toy patterns already in their files – sometimes the only adjustment required is to the scale.

Whilst material types can be mixed, attention must be paid to the actual glove material as this will have hard use and if too flimsy a material is used it will quickly wear out. It is best to make a strong glove and dress it appropriately if the subject requires a light flimsy image. Take care also that the head weight is not too great for the glove construction. It may be necessary to adjust the actual glove or finger size in relation to the size of the puppeteer – a well fitting glove is essential. Puppets can be frustrating to work with if they are too large, and the resulting performance is disappointing.

Unlike string puppets, which are usually operated at a distance from the audience, glove puppets are often used in a booth or small theatre (ie close to their audience), so their features can be less exaggerated.

String Puppets

Little Miss Muffet and Pussycat, Pussycat are string-puppet characters. String pup-

petry is a completely different subject to soft toymaking, but is a useful extension of a toymaker's repertoire. Some of the techniques may even be adapted for other toys.

The most important factor is the stuffing. A soft toy needs to be firm and well stuffed: a string puppet requires lightness and flexibility. If a string puppet is firmly stuffed, it will be stiff and incapable of the soft movements required – at the neck where arms connect to the shoulders, at the elbows, wrists, at the top of the legs where they join the body, and at the knees and ankles. String puppets vary in their design, and the areas where movement is required are incorporated in the individual patterns. The stuffing must be lightweight. Features may well have to be exaggerated. Colouring chosen for the clothes and any accessories should be clear. It assists in the presentation of the puppet if the puppeteer wears a long dark skirt or apron which will show the subject more clearly and avoid distraction from the background details.

Glove puppets are straightforward for children to use, but the strings on string puppets can be a problem. The main criterion is to choose a suitable recipient for the puppet – do not expect very young children to be able to cope. With the Pussycat, Pussycat puppet there is a mouse with simple stringing, which is very useful if a younger member of a family wishes to help with the puppets. The mouse can be displayed in conjunction with an older child working the more difficult stringing. Little Miss Muffet has the addition of the spider and can also be a shared situation. Instructions for manipulating the puppets are included with the patterns, where necessary.

When it is necessary to store the puppet away until the next display, hold the controls steady with the puppet hanging straight down to its fullest extent just off the floor, then twist the puppet until the strings are joined together. Tie round the top of the strings just under the controls with a ribbon, adding a loose bow. Place the puppet carefully in a lightweight bag, with the controls remaining outside; secure the neck of the bag to hold it in place and, if possible, hang the puppet from a hook or similar. When required again, remove the puppet from the bag, untie the ribbon and holding the controls steady in a horizontal position, let the puppet hang down as before and naturally unwind. It is then ready for use.

Knitted Strip Toys

Because these toys appear easy to make, there is a danger that the end product may not do justice to the toy subject. Poorly made soft toys are often displayed at craft shows, but the greater number of faults are usually found amongst the knitted exhibits. Beautiful knitting is ruined by being stuffed with cut-up ladies' tights or nylon stockings. Features are glued in place on the toys with very little detail in the finishing off. Knitted toys are often simple in design, and this simplicity should be accentuated and complemented. Here are a few guidelines.

Tension is very important, as the knitted toy skin requires firmness. Use wool of the same ply throughout the toy unless stated to the contrary.

Whilst the strip designs are an excellent way of using up oddments of wool, do pay attention to the colouring of the toy; if different colours are substituted for those stated, carefully plan ahead what colour tones are to be worked.

To join the seams, work overstitching, with the same yarn as used for the knitting if practical. Ladder stitching is suitable for applying limbs.

If choosing felt features, these should tone with and complement the rest of the toy. Stitch the features to the knitted toy skin using a single-strand thread. A variety of stitches can be employed, depending on the requirement – for example, stab or running stitch, overstitching, blanket stitch and many others which may be suitable.

The filling is very important. Try if possible to use a terylene or similar lightweight toy filling, which has a 'springy' texture to

enable it to expand to the toy skin. Never insert filling in large quantities. This is a common fault: the student sees an empty knitted toy skin and starts to fill it with large handfuls of toy filling, the knitted skin expands and attains the most peculiar dimensions, and holes and gaps are left in-between the large lumps. It is far more difficult to stuff a knitted toy skin than, for example, a fur-fabric one. The correct method is to take a small quantity of the filling, tease it well to even out the texture, then insert it into the toy skin, carefully building the shape from within the toy. It helps with the shaping if the part being stuffed is cupped or held in the hand to contain the shape.

When stuffing legs made in fur-fabric or material, the shape is held by the strength of the material, but this does not occur with knitted toys as the skin has great elasticity. Always make sure therefore, that legs and arms are stuffed to the same thickness. Balance the toy throughout with the filling.

Mobiles

Mobiles need to be lightweight and well balanced so that they move easily in the faintest currents of air. The Fiddle De Dee mobile cannot be described as flimsy; however, provided the toy filling and materials used are as light as possible and the whole construction is well balanced, there should be plenty of movement. The best places to hang a mobile are near a window, in a doorway or from a ceiling. Avoid at all times hanging one from an electric light or near a fire. The cross bars can be either specially purchased mobile wires – which are available in sets according to the number of wires required for a particular type of construction – or light sticks, for example thin dowelling. Strong thread is required to suspend the subjects – nylon thread is excellent as it is almost transparent.

Mobiles require careful balancing to enable them to function properly. For each rod or wire used, the point of balance has to be found. To practise finding this point of balance, obtain a rod or wire and tie a different length thread on either end, attaching an object to the end of each thread. Then tie another thread tightly to the centre of the wire. Suspend, and move the central thread across the wire until the point of balance has been found; add a spot of glue to the thread to secure. The point of balance is not always at the centre – it depends on the lengths of the threads and the weights of the objects.

Finishing Touches
The finish to a toy can make all the difference between an ordinary article and something really attractive. Fur-fabric toys need careful grooming. During the making process, when they are handled continuously, oddments of stuffing may adhere to the toy skin. Fur pile can be caught between the seams, leaving the pile in disarray. Teasel brushes are available from craft stockists. First pay attention to all the seaming, teasing out the pile to hide the seams, then brush the pile in the way of the pile line. When satisfied that the toy is well groomed and pristine, add any accessories, making sure, where applicable, that they are ironed first, eg, ribbons.

Clothes should be ironed if the material permits. Any cotton ends should be removed. Snap fasteners and buttons should be checked to make sure they are securely applied.

Safety Factors
The importance of safety factors in toys cannot be stressed strongly enough. However carefully toy designers may adhere to the British and European Safety Standards and consider any possible dangers in their toy designs, problems can still occur if an unsuitable toy is given to a child without taking into consideration its age and development. The final decision and responsibility has to be placed with the individual toymakers and parents, so be careful.

Here is an example of the type of danger which could occur. Goosey, Goosey, Gander is a pull-along or sit-and-ride toy. In the latter context, it is designed for use by a child indoors, the child's feet to be firmly on the floor on either side of the goose; in this situation it is perfectly safe. However, a very small child whose feet do not touch the floor is not so safe. Put the toy outside in the garden without adult supervision, with no means of controlling the castors on the toy, and it immediately becomes dangerous. You may find that only part of a toy subject is unsuitable for a particular child; then alter that part and substitute an alternative.

I love Little Pussy

SOFT TOYS

Chook, Chook, Chook

Chook, chook, chook, chook, chook,
Good morning Mrs Hen,
How many chickens have you got?
Madam, I've got ten,
Four of them are yellow,
And four of them are brown,
And two of them are white as milk –
The nicest in the town.

* * *

Toy type: Felt mother hen and chicks (colour picture page 72)

Size of toy: Mother Hen length 22.9cm (9in) Chicks vary in size from height approximately 9.6cm (3¾in) to height 10.3cm (4in)

Mother Hen

White felt for the body, wings and neck piece, 48.2 x 53.3cm (19 x 21in)

Red felt for the comb and throttle, 9 x 9cm (3½ x 3½in)

Yellow felt for the legs and feet, 22.9 x 15.3cm (9 x 6in)

8 pipe cleaners

Orange felt for the beak, 5 x 5cm (2 x 2in)

Body trimming: this can be made up entirely from oddments of white lace, broderie anglaise or similar. However if purchas-

---

Mary Had a Little Lamb, and Wee Willie Winkie

ing the trimming the following amounts are required: 1m (39½in) of 2.5cm (1in) wide pre-gathered white broderie anglaise trimming

1m (39½in) narrow white broderie anglaise trimming, the type with a firm texture and hooped design edge

Approximately 5m (197½in) of 2.5cm (1in) wide white pre-gathered lace

A piece of broderie anglaise material for the pantaloons, 10.3 x 12.7cm (4 x 5in)

Toy filling

One pair of brown 10mm safety-lock eyes

Cut out all the pattern pieces. Place the two side body pieces together. Stab stitch together from A round the top of the head and along the back, inserting the comb piece at B–C, and continue to D at the tail end. Starting at D on the underbody gusset, apply the pre-gathered lace trimming in strips across the gusset from side to side,

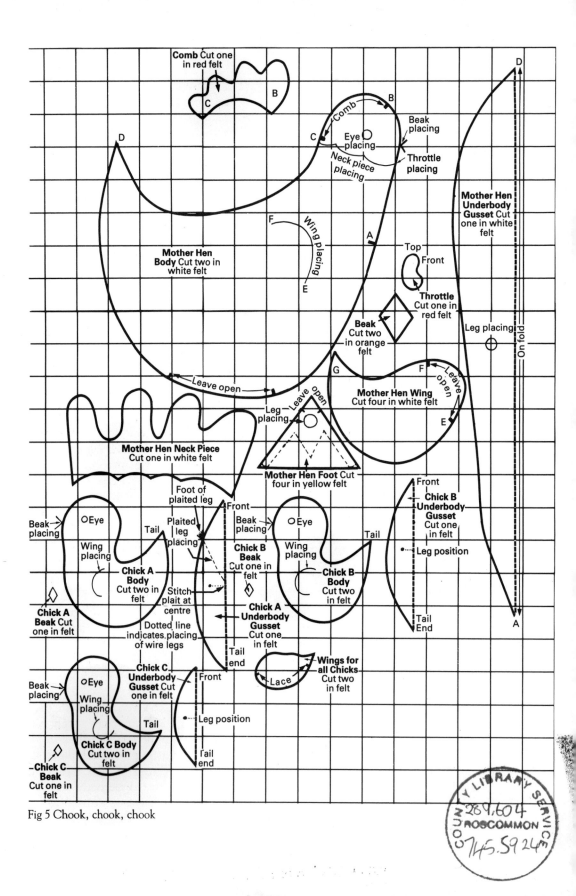

Fig 5 Chook, chook, chook

stitching the gathered edges and frilling out each layer to cover the previously sewn edge. The lace frills should face towards the tail end. Continue in this manner until point A on the gusset is reached and the underbody is completely covered. Insert the underbody gusset into the body, matching A to A and D to D. Pin then stab stitch one side of the gusset first, then return to A and stab stitch the opposite side into place, leaving open where indicated on the body pattern. Insert the safety-lock eyes where indicated. Stuff the body firmly, paying careful attention to obtaining a smooth outer surface to the toy skin. Take care not to stretch the edges of the felt on the stuffing opening; the impacted fibres of the felt fray easily and this could spoil the outline of the toy. Stab stitch the opening to close, matching the previous body stitching.

Cut two pieces of the pre-gathered broderie anglaise trimming to measure 30.5cm (12in) each. Pin then stitch a piece to either side of the body from the tail end and following the body shaping to the base of the chest. Cut one 30.5cm (12in) piece of the narrow broderie anglaise trimming with the hooped design and stitch this in place from where the previously applied broderie anglaise terminated, following the gusset outline to the opposite side. These trimmings following the body seam encase the lace frills. Gather a strip of the broderie anglaise trimming and pull up to make a small fan shape of approximately 5cm (2in) diameter, and stitch to the tail tip, joining the two raw edges of the body broderie anglaise trimming to the back of the fan shape. Stitch to secure at the base to the top seam of the body. Put the felt neck piece in place where indicated and stitch to secure at the back of the neck. If this neck piece is too large, and the size of the neck will vary slightly according to the degree of stuffing, it may be necessary to trim the ends slightly prior to stitching to obtain a firm fit.

Wings Take two wing pieces. Stab stitch together inserting a piece of the pre-gathered lace E–G on the lower curve and leaving open where indicated for stuffing. Stuff lightly, but evenly, and close the stuffing opening with stab stitching. Make the second wing in the same way. Stitch a wing either side of the body at E–F.

Beak Stab stitch the two beak pieces together and stitch across the centre to apply to the head where indicated.

Throttle Place the two throttle pieces, one on either side of the head seam; stitch the top curve only, to attach.

Legs Place three 7.6cm (3in) lengths of pipe cleaner together, and bind to join. Cover with an oblong of yellow felt, stab stitching to join down the seam. Make the second leg in the same way.

Feet Place two of the foot pieces together and stab stitch to join, leaving open where indicated. The easiest way to make the feet is to sew where indicated on the pattern triangle, then after the stitching is completed, cut out the foot shape. Insert 5cm (2in) pieces of pipe cleaner into each long toe, then close the opening using stab stitching. Make a second foot in the same way. Place a foot on to each leg and ladder stitch to join where indicated, making sure the seam on each leg is in line with the back point of each foot.

Pantaloons Cut a piece of the broderie anglaise material, 9 x 6.4cm (3½ x 2½in). Trim one long edge with lace. With the right sides facing, fold in half and join the short edges together. Turn to the right side. Fold in the top raw edge and gather. Place on the leg and pull up the gathering to fit the top of the leg and, with the seam at the back, stitch to the leg and fasten off. Make the second pantaloon piece in the same way and attach to the second leg. Ladder stitch each leg in place on the underbody gusset where indicated, parting the lace frills to enable the legs to be sewn to the felt underbody; the legs should be facing to the front of the body.

Chicks
The chicks consist of 4 in yellow felt, 4 in brown felt and 2 in white felt. They are

21

designed in three sizes so that the reader has a choice of pattern and can adjust to materials which may be available. The standing chicks have wired legs; but if the chicks are intended for a young child, the design with plaited legs should be used.

Chick A: 22.9 x 14cm (9 x 5½in) of felt
Chick B: 22.9 x 14cm (9 x 5½in) of felt
Chick C: 20.4 x 15.3cm (8 x 6in) of felt
Body trimming: each girl chick requires approximately 30.5cm (12in) of narrow white, pre-gathered lace; and each boy chick requires approximately 17.8cm (7in) of narrow white, flat lace
Scraps of orange felt for the beaks
Small circles of black felt for the eyes
Toy filling
Plaited legs: each chick requires nine 12.7cm (5in) lengths of either stranded embroidery cotton or fine knitting yarn
Wired legs: each chick requires a piece of strong thin wire 28cm (11in) long and thin yarn or similar for the top binding

The chicks are constructed in the same way as the Mother Hen with the following exceptions. For the girl chicks, apply the pre-gathered lace from the tail tip down the underbody gusset for approximately 4.5cm (1¾in); and in three flat rows of narrow lace from the tail tip for the boy chicks. The frills, or unsewn edges, of the lace should face the tail tip. The wings are single, not double as for the Mother Hen. The beak is a single piece also. The eyes are two small circles of black felt stitched to the head where indicated.

For plaited legs, lay nine 12.7cm (5in) lengths of stranded embroidery cotton together, parallel. Lay these across the underbody gusset where indicated and stitch at the centre to attach to the underbody gusset. Plait one side first, secure 0.7cm (¼in) from the end and fasten off. Cut the ends level. The plaited parts are the legs, the cut ends the feet. Treat the opposite side in the same way. Stitch at the end of each plait to secure to the underbody gusset where indicated on the pattern.

For wired legs, cut a 7.6cm (3in) length of the wire. Fold into an arch at the centre. Place the ends of the wires through the holes in the underbody gusset where indicated (before constructing the chick), pulling the arch to meet the underbody surface. Cut eight 2.5cm (1in) pieces of the wire. Turn each piece in half to form an 'L' shape and bind to the ends of the leg wire. Use three pieces for the front toes of each foot and one piece for the back of each foot. Add a spot of glue to each end of the wires to help mask the sharp ends. Allow to dry then bind the toes and legs firmly using either stranded embroidery cotton or fine knitting yarn. (This is not the wiring method used for larger toys, but thicker binding would not be suitable for such small toys.)

22

I Love Little Pussy

I love little pussy,
Her coat is so warm,
And if I don't hurt her,
She'll do me no harm.
So I'll not pull her tail,
Nor drive her away,
But pussy and I,
Very gently will play.

* * *

Toy type: Lying down fur-fabric soft-toy cat and kittens (colour picture page 17)
Size of toy: Cat height 20.4cm (8in); length not including tail 33cm (13in)

These toys are designed to be washable, and are suitable for most age groups. The body of the Mother Cat has not adhered to the correct fullness of a lying down cat's body, but has been slimmed down slightly to provide a more hollow curve which will enable it to be used as a head cushion on a teenager's bed if required. Care should be taken when stuffing a lying down toy not to overstuff the underleg as this would result in the top leg lying too high. Cats are difficult subjects to portray as soft toys; many designs are caricatures to overcome this problem. This toy was designed to look realistic, so needlemodelling was used on the face to produce the desired effect. Whilst the nursery rhyme refers to cat in the singular, patterns are included for two kittens as an extension to the design and appeal of this toy.

Usually people are attracted to a fluffy cat, but bearing in mind the emotional need of 'touch' and the wording of the nursery rhyme, a polished fur-fabric was used. This is smooth and pleasant to stroke, and it added line and shaping to the body. Fluffiness was added in the form of an acrylic long-pile shaggy fur-fabric tail. As it is to be washable, use terylene or nylon toy filling. Beware that the word 'soft' in the toy description does not mean understuffed, as this would result in the toy quickly becoming an empty skin. If the cat is to be used as a head cushion, it is advisable to use a nylon filling of a more compacted texture where the head will be laid; encase this in the terylene filling to ensure an even texture throughout the body surface. The pads, nose and eyes are in Furmofelt which has been previously washed. (Traditionally, felt was not used on washable toys, but this is bonded on to a backing, so it is much more versatile.)

Mother Cat
White polished fur-fabric 53.3 x 53.3cm (21 x 21in) for the body
White shaggy-pile acrylic fur-fabric 6.4 x 28cm (2½ x 11in) for the tail
Pale-pink felt 22.9 x 22.9cm (9 x 9in) for the ear linings, nose and pad markings
Oddments of blue, white and black felt for the eyes
10.3 x 14cm (4 x 5½in) white felt for the foot pads
1m (39½in) of 2.5cm (1in) wide pink ribbon for the neck bow
White terylene or nylon toy filling
Horsehair for the whiskers

Cut out all the pattern pieces.
Head Sew the head darts first using backstitch. With the right sides of the two head pieces facing, pin then stitch from A to B. Insert the head gusset piece evenly between the head pieces, matching B on the gusset

23

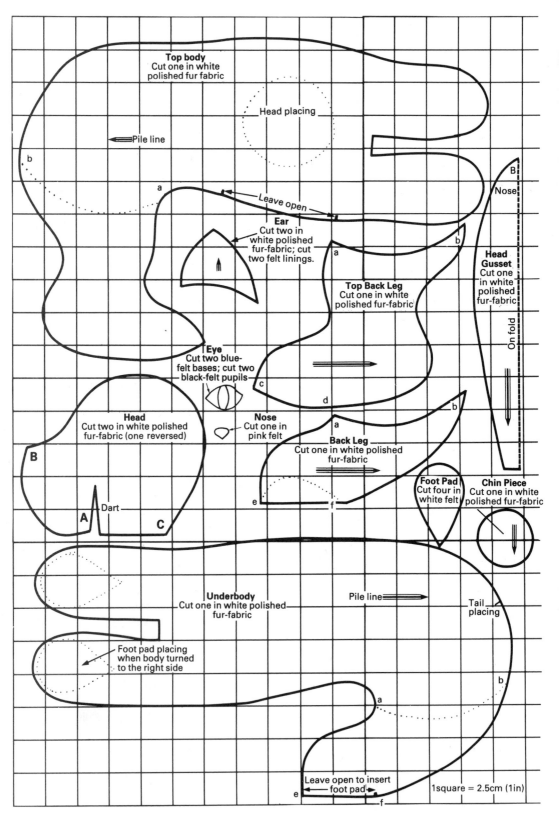

Fig 6 I love Little Pussy

to B at the nose tip, pin and then backstitch the gusset in place. Turn to the right side, remove the pins and stuff firmly, moulding and shaping the face. You will now notice a complete lack of chin; this is added in the following way. Gather around the outside edge of the chin pattern piece, pull on the gathering thread slightly and stuff; pull the gathers tightly and secure the thread. This chin piece is then ladder stitched on to the head just below the nose tip in the chin position. Ensure before you stitch the chin piece in place that the pile line of the chin fabric matches the pile line of the head fabric. The chin at this stage will appear rather strong and masculine and not completely part of the head; this will be rectified by needle-modelling later.

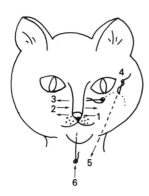

Fig 7 I Love Little Pussy: Needle-modelling

Nose Needle-model the cat's nose by taking a series of stitches, using strong thread, from one side of the bridge of the nose to the opposite side, working from the tip of the nose upwards towards the forehead for approximately 4.5cm (1¾in). As you progress, pull on the stitching and this will raise the bridge of the nose. When satisfied that a well-shaped cat nose has been created, fasten off. Clip the fur pile on the nose which will also aid shaping. It may help positioning the features to pin an ear pattern piece into place on the head first.

Cheeks Take the stitching from the top of the cheek and place it through the stuffed face and well down into the neck, then pull; this will brace the toy skin against the filling and puff out the cheek. Treat the other side of the face in the same way. If the cheeks do not look quite right, this can be rectified after the head has been stitched to the body by taking a few stitches well down the neck and up to the lower half of the cheek; secure the thread then take needle and thread through to the top of the cheek where the needle-modelling was started, and pull on the thread to puff the cheek outwards. Beware that you do not form two balls instead of cheeks.

Chin Needle-model the previously applied chin, from underneath upwards into the face to shape it. It is really a case of trial and error, although it is surprising how quickly a student becomes adept at needle-modelling; the forming of a face is very exciting and satisfying. Next add the felt nose tip, neatly overstitching into place around the outside edge.

Eyes and Ears It is not easy to sew an eye directly on to a shaped, needle-modelled face, especially when recessed. It is easier to assemble the eye on to a felt backing, stuffing lightly before finally closing and fastening off. Neatly cut around the outside edge of the eye, leaving a narrow piece of the backing showing. Place a pin through the completed eye so that it can be pinned on to the head and, if necessary, moved around until the correct expression is obtained. Do not stitch to the head at this stage.

With the right sides facing, pin and stitch one fur-fabric ear piece and one felt lining together, leaving the bottom straight edge open. Turn to the right side; overstitch the bottom edges together, pull on the thread to form a gentle curve, then secure the thread. Prepare the other ear in the same way. Pin the ears into place. So often one is confronted with a toy cat with the ears straight across the top of the head shape. Cats' ears have their inner edge curved forward at an angle and the longer outside edges further back.

Now is the time to complete the cat's

expression. All toys, even if made from the same pattern, form themselves into their own characters. It may be due to a variation in the stuffing, the needle-modelling or the construction, so a toy designer should never stipulate the exact position of the features on this type of toy. The main problem which arises with any toy is the eye placing; keep the eyes fairly low on the face. Once satisfied with the position of the features, ladder stitch the ears in place, and over-stitch the eyes to secure to the head. If, however, the expression eludes you, lay the toy aside until the next day; you will possibly then see immediately what is wrong.

Mouth Shape the mouth using three strands of pink embroidery cotton. Take a long stitch from under the nose tip a to b, in at b and out at c, back to b, in to d, back out and in to b. Curve slightly at c and d to give a smiling effect. If a sad expression is required, lower at corners c and d to a droop. The chin on the cat will assist in the mouth placing. Add whiskers either side of the nose and above each eye.

Body Pin together and then backstitch seams a to b on both inner leg pieces. Insert these between the back legs on the body pieces with the right sides facing. Back-

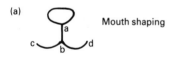

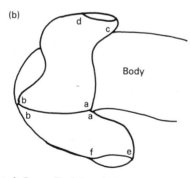

Fig 8 I Love Little Pussy: Back leg placing

26

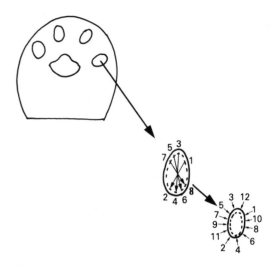

Fig 9 I Love Little Pussy: Pad application. The pad application is simplified if the stitches are worked in rotation; see numbering to indicate the moves

stitch seams c to a together then d to b together on one leg, then seams a to e together and b to f on the other leg. Back-stitch all around the outer body, leaving an opening for turning where indicated on the pattern. Insert the white felt pads in the two back legs, pin into place then backstitch. Turn the body to the right side, removing all pins. Stuff the body and top leg firmly, but leave the underleg lightly stuffed to enable the top leg to lie flat. Close the opening with ladder stitching. Add the front pads to the front legs where indicated on the pattern, using ladder stitching, and add felt paw markings using a neat overstitching (see Fig 9). Ladder stitch the prepared head on to the body where indicated on the pattern.

Tail Cut a piece of white acrylic shaggy-pile fur-fabric 6.4 x 28cm (2½ x 11in). Fold in half lengthways with the right sides facing and pin then backstitch together, closing one end with gathering. Remove pins then turn to the right side and stuff very lightly; the long pile will add sufficient bulk to the tail size. Ladder stitch to the body where indicated. After carefully grooming the cat to ensure the pile lies in the correct way, add a ribbon to the neck and tie in a bow.

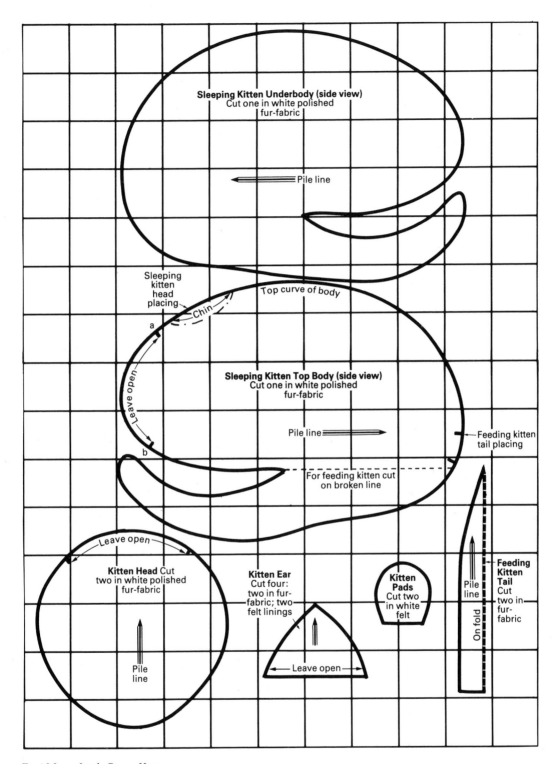

Sleeping Kitten Underbody (side view)
Cut one in white polished
fur-fabric

⇐ Pile line

Sleeping
kitten
head
placing

Top curve of body

Chin

a

Leave open

b

Sleeping Kitten Top Body (side view)
Cut one in white polished
fur-fabric

Pile line ⇒

Feeding kitten
tail placing

For feeding kitten cut
on broken line

Leave open

Kitten Head Cut
two in white polished
fur-fabric

Kitten Ear
Cut four:
two in fur-
fabric; two
felt linings

Kitten Pads
Cut two
in white
felt

Pile
line

On fold

Feeding Kitten Tail
Cut
two in
fur-
fabric

Pile
line

Leave open

Fig 10 Love Little Pussy: Kittens

This cat can be attached, by stitching around the base outline, to a lined cushion cover and used as a nightdress or pyjama case. One seam of the cushion cover can be left open and Velcro added to a neatly turned hem.

Kittens

These are designd to have the 'blind' look of very young kittens. Quantities are given for one kitten.

A piece of white polished fur-fabric 40.6 x 28cm (16 x 11in)

Oddments of felt for the eyes, nose and paw markings

White felt for the foot pads; sleeping kitten 6.4 x 3.8cm (2½ x 1½in), feeding kitten 12.7 x 7.6cm (5 x 3in)

Pink or white felt for the ear linings, 7.6 x 11.5cm (3 x 4½in)

White terylene toy filling

Horsehair for the whiskers

Sleeping Kitten Cut out all pattern pieces. Place together the two head pieces with the right sides facing, pin and backstitch around the outside edge, leaving open where indicated on the pattern. Remove the pins and turn to the right side. Stuff firmly. Close the opening with ladder stitching. Lay aside.

With the right sides facing, place the two body pieces together. Backstitch around the outside edge, leaving open where indicated for stuffing. Turn to the right side. Stuff firmly ensuring that the filling reaches the tail tip. Ladder stitch to close the opening. Needle-model to shape the two front legs where indicated on the pattern. Neatly stitch a pad under each front leg just in from the outside edge. Work a running stitch along the inner curve on the tail from tail base to tail tip, pull gently to curve the tail and fasten off.

Ladder stitch the head to the stuffed body where indicated, facing sideways (see photograph). Make ears and whiskers as for the Mother Cat. Ladder stitch to the head. Needle-model the face following the Mother Cat instructions, and apply the nose. Using Fig 10 as a guide, apply whiskers.

For the legs, press a to b then needle-model to form the front legs; apply a pad to the underneath of each leg.

Feeding Kitten This is made in the same way as the sleeping kitten, with the following adjustments.

The body is made minus the tail – see dotted line on the pattern. The body therefore appears to be more elongated. The tail is made separately, then ladder stitched on to the body. The head is placed facing towards the front of the body.

This kitten has four pads: two placed on the front legs after needle-modelling has been completed and two placed 6.4 (2½in) from the tail, facing slightly outwards with a 3.8cm (1½in) space between the back edge of each paw.

NOTE: If a complete cat family is required, make the Father Cat in the same way as the Mother Cat, but leave the chin protruding and reduce the eyes slightly to produce a more slanting eye expression; highlights can be added to the pupils if required. Work four straight stitches from the top of each foot down to the felt pads in-between the paw markings, and pull up slightly to produce claw shaping. Add a blue neck ribbon and tie in a bow. See photograph.

Mary Had a Little Lamb

Mary had a little lamb,
Its fleece was white as snow,
And everywhere that Mary went,
The lamb was sure to go.

* * *

Toy type: Doll made from ladies' nylon stockings or tights, and lamb (colour picture page 18)
Size of toy: Height 45.7cm (18in)

Nylon-stocking dolls are more difficult to make than sock dolls, as socks have a much firmer texture. However, discarded stockings or tights are usually readily available and inexpensive. Avoid using any part of the nylon which may be damaged. Mary's lamb is made from lamb pattern No 1 in Little Bo Peep.

Nylon stockings in a suitable skin-tone colour
Two pieces of white sock material 10.3 x 11.5cm (4 x 4½in) for the socks
A piece of felt to tone with the dress material 17.8 x 12.7cm (7 x 5in) for the shoes
Two small buttons for the shoes
Two light-brown buttons for the eyes, approximately 0.7cm (¼in) in diameter; substitute felt eyes if the doll is for a very young child
One hank of ginger-coloured angel hair
1m (39½in) narrow ribbon to tone with the dress material for the hair ribbons
Brown-mixture cotton print for dress, quantity as for Little Miss Muffet page 105
2m (79in) narrow cream lace trimming for the dress
An oddment of narrow ribbon for the neck bow to tone with the dress
Cream-coloured cotton-type material 48.2 x 50.8cm (19 x 20in) for the petticoat and pantees
Cream-coloured lace trimming for petticoat, 2½m (98¾in)

A piece of 3.8cm (1½in) wide lace trimming 25.4cm (10in) for the front trimming on the petticoat
Two snap fasteners
Elastic for the pantees, 55.9cm (22in)
Toy filling

Lengths to cut from the stocking prior to sewing: body and head combined, 19.2cm (7½in); arms cut one piece 15.3cm (6in) and cut in half lengthways twice; legs cut one piece 25.4cm (10in) and cut in half lengthways twice.
Head and Body Turn in and gather one end of the piece. Stuff to form the head to a depth of 11.5cm (4½in) measured from the top of the head to the neck. The measurement around the head is approximately 25.4cm (10in). Gather around the neck, but do not pull up too tightly, and stuff the neck well. Stuff the body to a length of 16.6cm (6½in); the measurement around the waist is approximately 25.4cm (10in). Fold in the open ends at the base of the body as per the instructions for the sock doll (see page 37). Fasten off.
Arms Take one arm piece and with the right sides facing, stitch the long edges together, this seam to be under the arm, and curve one end for the hand. Cut off any excess material at the hand end. Turn to the right side. Stuff firmly, shaping well. The measurement around the arm at the elbow is approximately 11.5cm (4½in); the finished length of the arm is approximately 17.8cm (7in). Fold in the top raw edges and over-stitch together, pulling up slightly, and attach to one side of the body 2.5cm (1in) down from the neck gathering. Make the

other arm in the same way and attach to the opposite side of the body.

Legs Take one leg piece. With the right sides facing, stitch the long edges together, this seam to be at the back of the leg. Stitch a curve in one end for the foot. Cut off any excess material. Turn to the right side and stuff firmly. The width of the leg at the knee is approximately 10.3cm (4in); the finished length of the leg is approximately 20.9cm (8¼in). Turn in the top raw edges and attach to the base of the body at one side. Make the second leg in the same way and attach to the opposite side of the body base.

Hair Divide the hank of angel hair in half. Lay one half aside. Take the other piece and lay it from the forehead of the doll, pinning to hold, down the back of the head to the neck and pin to hold at the neck. Stitch across in both pinned places to secure, and remove the pins. Take the second half of the angel hair and fold at the centre. Place a small elastic band to hold it together at the fold, leaving a 2.5cm (1in) loop of hair. Place this loop in the centre of the head and stitch to hold. Take the hair down either side of the head, fan it out to meet the back hair and cover the head, and fasten at the neck by stitching. Take the two side hair pieces to the back of the head, lay these with the previously applied hair and tie all together with some of the ribbon. Tie a ribbon bow around the top knot over the elastic band and leave tails of the ribbon hanging. Do not trim the hair at this stage.

Needle-modelling Using the photograph as a guide, needle-model a small nose measuring approximately 1.3cm (½in) long, then add two tiny nostrils. Work a slightly curved smiling mouth, measuring approximately 1.3cm (½in), using a single strand of embroidery cotton in a beige tone. Stitch the two buttons in place, pulling the thread through the head from one eye to another to recess the buttons into the head slightly. Fasten off. Trim the fringe if necessary and cut the ends of the hair at the back. If the fringe and side hair pieces are rather unruly, the underneath pieces can be glued to frame

the face, taking care to use the adhesive sparingly and leaving the top layers free.

Work a dimple either side at the elbow on each arm. For the wrist on each arm, gather approximately 6.4cm (2½in) from the tip of the hand. Stab stitch to form the fingers on each hand and add four dimples across the top of the hands at the base of the fingers. Add a dimple either side of each leg at the knees approximately 9cm (3½in) from the top of each leg. Gather across the front of each leg for the ankles 3.8cm (1½in) from the tip of each foot for a distance of 3.8cm (1½in). Stab stitch to form the toes on each foot.

Socks Take one of the sock pieces. With the right sides facing, fold in half lengthways. Stitch the seams together, continuing the stitching to one short end, and stitch in a curve for the foot. Fasten off. Turn to the right side and place on one of the doll's feet. Treat the second piece in the same way and place on the doll.

Shoes Cut out four pieces in the pattern and place together in pairs. Take one pair and backstitch or machine stitch together where indicated. Turn to the right side. Stitch a small button to the outside strap. Cut a slit in the other strap as a button-hole. Place on the doll's foot. Treat the other shoe in the same way. It may be necessary to run a loose gathering around the top edge of the shoes as the feet may not be stuffed to the size of the original model.

Dress Make as instructions for Little Miss Muffet, trimming with the narrow cream-coloured lace around the skirt edge and sleeves, and gathered lace around the neck of the dress. A tiny bow toning with the dress material is stitched to the centre of the neck line. Due to the elasticity of the stocking or tights' material for the doll's body, the size of the doll may vary from the original. The dress is a very basic design so if any alteration in size is necessary, it should be very easy to do.

Pantees Cut two pattern pieces in cream-coloured material. Stitch the front and back seams and neaten. Stitch crutch seams and

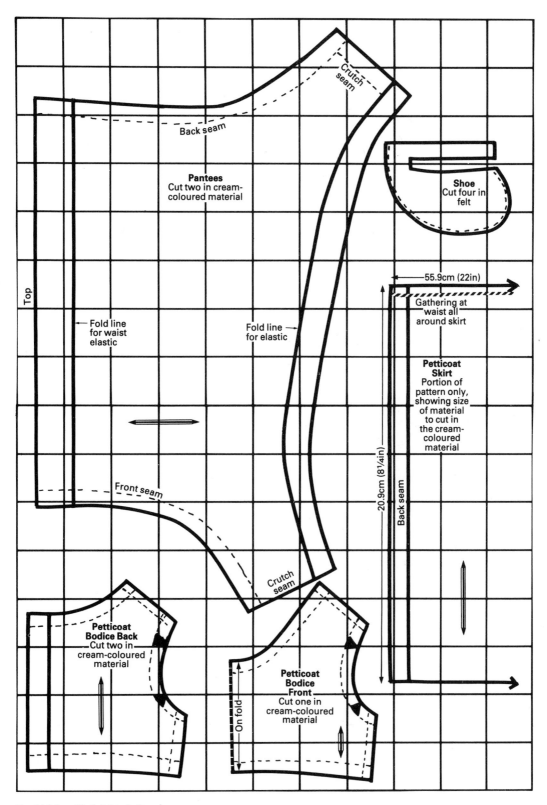

Fig 11 Mary Had A Little Lamb

neaten. Fold the top of the pantees to the fold line then over again to make a double hem, leaving a small gap to thread the elastic through. Do the same for the leg elastic but clip the lower edge first. Cut a piece of elastic to the doll's waist size plus 1.3cm (½in). Thread through and stitch to fasten. Cut two pieces of elastic to the doll's leg size plus 1.3cm (½in). Thread through each leg and stitch to fasten.

Petticoat Cut out the pattern pieces comprising one bodice front, two bodice backs and one skirt. With the right sides facing, join bodice front and backs together at the shoulder seams. Stitch under 0.7cm (¼in) on the armhole and neck edges. Stitch the side seams together.

Turn up a hem on one long edge of the skirt as on the armhole and neck. Gather the opposite long edge between X–X and join the skirt to the bodice, adjusting the gathers evenly. Join the back of the skirt edges together for 7.6cm (3in) up from the hem. Turn a 1.3cm (½in) seam on either side of the bodice, right up to the top and stitch. Turn to the right side and finish with two snap fasteners.

Trim around the hem of the skirt with narrow lace stitched behind the hem so that the scalloped edge shows below the hem edge. Stitch a second row of lace around the skirt just above the stitching line of the hem, on the top of the skirt. Stitch a wider piece of trimming from the centre of the neck at the front, right down the petticoat to the top row of lace. Trim around the arms and the neck with the narrow lace.

Place the lamb under the doll's left arm and stitch the tips of the left hand to the dress skirt to hold it in place.

There Was a Monkey

There was a monkey climbed a tree,
When he fell down, then down fell he.

* * *

Toy type: Fur-fabric and felt monkey (colour picture page 36)
Size of toy: Height (sitting down) 21.5cm (8½in)

Beige-coloured short-pile fur-fabric 48.2 x x 40.6cm (19 x 16in) for body, head, arms and legs
Beige-coloured felt 30.5 x 26.7cm (12 x 10½in) for face, ears, hands and feet
Sixteen pipe cleaners
One pair brown 12mm safety-lock eyes
Copydex adhesive
Brown stranded embroidery cotton for the features
Toy filling

Cut out the body, head, arms and legs in the beige fur-fabric and the face, ears, hands and feet in the felt.

Body and Head With the right sides facing, place the side body pieces together and pin then backstitch from A–C on the back seam. Join the front body piece to the side body pieces matching A–B on both sides. Insert the base, matching B–C on both sides and leaving a stuffing opening where indicated. Turn to the right side and stuff firmly, taking care to retain the shape of the toy skin. Close the opening using ladder stitching.

Place the side head pieces right sides together, and join edges F–G using backstitching. Do not turn to the right side.

Face Join H–I on the face to H–I on the chin piece using backstitching. Dart the face

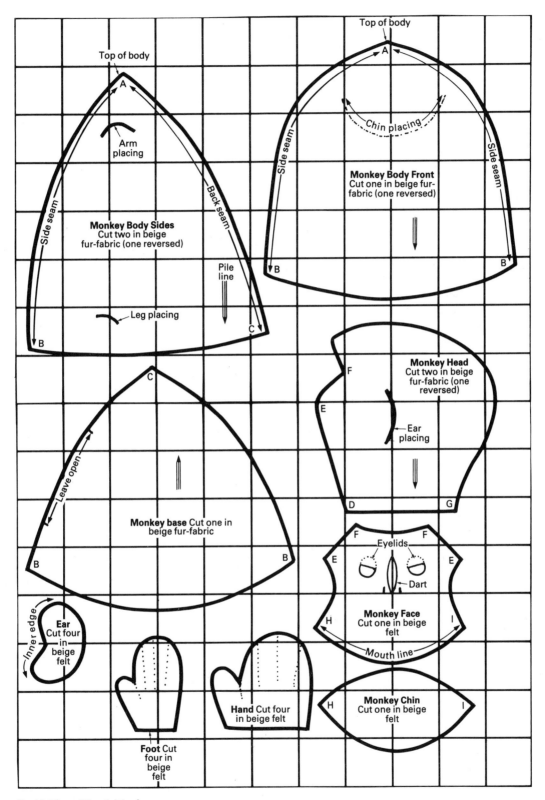

Fig 12 There Was A Monkey

where indicated. Cut the eyelid slits where shown. Insert the face and chin piece combination, with the right sides facing, into the previously stitched side head pieces, matching F–E on the face to F–E on the head piece. Pin then backstitch in place. Cut two pieces of the beige felt each to measure 2.5cm (1in) square; apply Vilene or fabric stiffener to one side. Insert a safety-lock eye into each piece. Apply some adhesive to the backs of the eyelids. Press an eye forward into each eyelid (from the wrong side of the face) and the eye slit, taking care not to smear the adhesive on to the rest of the eyes. Using Copydex adhesive, glue the stiffened 2.5cm (1in) squares of felt on the eyes to the inside back of the face mask. Allow to dry completely.

Turn the head to the right side and firmly stuff. Ladder stitch to the top of the front body piece at a slight angle to add appeal to the toy; if necessary, just prior to closing add more toy filling to balance the head well. Although the eyes are glued to the eyelids and also to the back of the face, if this toy is for a very young child it would be wise to omit the manufactured eyes and substitute felt or embroidered eyes.

Ears Glue the ear pieces together in pairs using Copydex adhesive, leaving the inner edges of each ear free from the adhesive. When dry, ladder stitch an ear on either side of the head where indicated, slightly curving to shape.

Arms and Hands Cut two pieces of the fur-fabric to measure 5.7 x 15.3cm (2¼ x 6in). Take one piece and fold it in half lengthways with the right sides facing. Backstitch to join the long edges. Turn to the right side. Make the second arm in the same way.

Place hands together in pairs. Take one pair and backstitch around the outside edge, leaving the bottom straight edges open. Turn to the opposite side. Insert four 2cm (¾in) pieces of pipe cleaner for the fingers, and stab stitch each one in place. Stuff the thumb and the rest of the hand with toy filling. Gather the wrist slightly and insert into one end of the arm (the pile on the arm should face towards the hand). Turn in the end of the arm and ladder stitch to the wrist. Treat the second hand in the same way.

Insert three pipe cleaners into one arm and carefully stuff around them. Turn in the top open end of the arm and ladder stitch to the body. Treat the second arm in the same way.

Legs and Feet Stab stitch feet together in pairs, inserting pieces of pipe cleaner cut to the full length of each foot, for the toes. Stab stitch the pipe cleaners in place. The legs and feet are constructed in the same way as the arms and hands, but the leg pieces measure 7.6 x 12.7cm (3 x 5in) and four pipe cleaners are inserted into each leg prior to stuffing. The pipe cleaners can be omitted if the toy is for a very young child and, after stuffing, the inner seam on each arm and leg can have a line of running stitches worked, gently pulled, then fastened, to produce a curve in each limb.

Facial Markings Work two single chain stitches in dark brown stranded cotton for the nose, either side of the face darting. The mouth is worked following the stitching line where the chin piece was joined to the face; work a running stitch using two strands of stranded embroidery cotton, then work overstitching over these stitches. Curve the arms, hands, legs and feet to the front of the body, if necessary adding some ladder stitching from the top of each leg for about 2.5cm (1in) to hold it in position on the body.

(from top) Humpty Dumpty, There Was a Little Girl, and Jack and Jill

Wee Willie Winkie

Wee Willie Winkie runs through the town,
Upstairs and downstairs in his night-gown,
Rapping at the window, crying through the lock,
Are the children all in bed, for now it's eight o'clock?

* * *

Toy type: Sock doll and small teddy bear
  (colour picture page 18)
Size of toy: Doll height 45.7cm (18in),
  Teddy Bear height 17.8cm (7in)

Sock toys require very careful modelling
from within the toy skin to attain good
shaping. Due to the elasticity of most sock
materials it is very easy at the stuffing stage
to produce a pair of limbs that differ in size.
Once a good initial shape is obtained, dimples or needle-modelling can be added
where required to produce a good appearance to the toy.

One lady's white over-knee sock in plain or
  narrow rib, approximate length from toe
  to top of sock 68.5cm (27in) (the remaining sock of the pair can be used for
  another project)
A ball of 4 ply knitting yarn for the hair;
  oddments can be used, the longest length
  required is 14cm (5½in)
Stranded embroidery cotton for the features,
  white plus a colour to tone with the hair
  colouring
Toy filling
Cotton-type striped material, 80cm (31½in)
  of 90cm (35½in) width, for nightshirt
  and cap
One small polystyrene ball for the tassel
  base, 2.5cm (1in) in diameter
Wool or one skein of Anchor stranded
  embroidery cotton to match nightshirt
  for the tassel covering
Felt to tone with the nightshirt for the

slippers, 17.8 x 10.3cm (7 x 4in)
Two white lampshade trimming bobbles
Two small snap fasteners or pieces of Velcro
Oddments of rolled elastic for wrist frilling

Using Fig 13, cut the sock into the component parts.
Head and Body Stuff the toe part of the foot
of the sock (a) – this will be the head – until

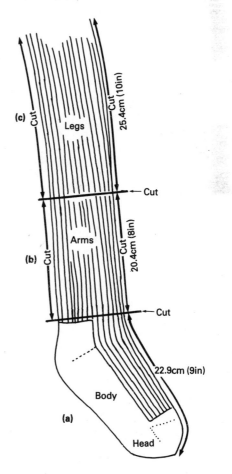

Fig 13 Wee Willie Winkie: Showing cutting lines

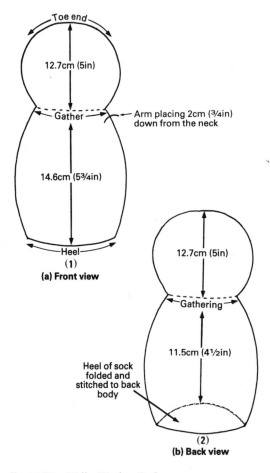

Fig 14 Wee Willie Winkie: Body construction

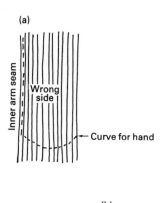

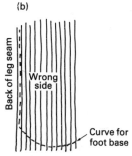

Fig 15 Wee Willie Winkie: (a) The stitching curve to form the top of the hand; (b) The curve to produce the foot base

the distance from the top of the head down the front face curve to the neck measures 12.7cm (5in) (see Fig 14 (a)). Gather around the neck just below the 12.7cm (5in) measurement and pull up gradually, adding more toy filling. The neck gathering should not be too tightly pulled up as this would produce a weak neck and floppy head. Stuff the body until firm and well shaped to a depth of 14.6cm (5¾in). Turn in the open heel raw edge and tuck in the leg raw edge and stitch together (see Fig 14 (b)).

Arms Take one piece and stitch the long edges together on the wrong side. Stitch the edges together on one short edge, curving the stitching to shape (see Fig 15 (a)). Turn to the right side. Fold in the top raw edges until the arm measures 17.8cm (7in). Stuff

firmly, shaping carefully; the arm at the elbow measures approximately 13.4cm (5¼in) round. Overstitch to close and attach the arm to the body 2cm (¾in) down from the neck. Add dimples to the elbows 6.4cm (2½in) from where the arm is attached to the body. Gather to form a wrist 5cm (2in) from the curved end of the

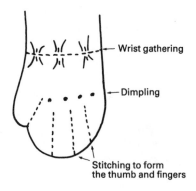

Fig 16 Wee Willie Winkie: Finger, thumb and wrist shaping

arm; pull up to shape. Fasten off. Shape the hand – see Fig 16. Treat the second arm and hand in the same way.

Legs Make the legs in the same way as the arms, using shaping line Fig 15 (b), and stuff firmly. Add dimpling either side of the knees 10.3cm (4in) up from the ankle shaping. Turn up the bottom of each leg for the feet shaping, for 2.5cm (1in), and stitch from the top of each foot to each leg; this produces a dart as for the feet on the Lavender's Blue doll.

Hair Cut strands of the yarn 14cm (5½in) long. Take six strands and stitch together at the centre. Fold in half to form a tuft and stitch in a circle around the head, the diameter of the top centre circle to measure 5.7cm (2¼in). Stitch more tufts to fill the inner circle at the top of the head and continue until a good covering is obtained; the last few pieces are not folded in half, but are laid across the centre of the head with the stitching forming a parting division. This doll has more appeal if the hair is left hanging at various lengths.

Features Using the feature pattern, lightly draw in the features with a soft lead pencil. Work the eyes in satin stitch using three strands of the embroidery cotton. The freckles are French knots using two strands of the embroidery cotton. The mouth is worked in chain stitch, also using two strands only.

Nightshirt With the right sides facing, stitch the centre front seams together to the X, neaten both edges and press open. Turn to the right side. Press the two long edges of

the front opening to make a strip 2.5cm (1in) wide. Turn under a small seam at one end. With the neck edge of the nightshirt towards you, stitch the front opening to the left-hand side with the raw edge at the neck. Turn up a small hem on the bottom of both sleeves and stitch. Stretch and stitch elastic to the line to make a frill. Stitch the sleeves to the back and the front of the nightshirt, matching the notches. Neaten. Turn under a single hem on the bottom of the nightshirt and stitch, if possible using a zig-zag stitch as this gives a nice finish. Gather round the neck edge to fit the bias strip. Stitch the bias strip to bind the neck. Sew two snap fasteners or small pieces of Velcro to the front opening to close.

Nightcap Place the two pieces together with the right sides facing, and stitch together leaving the bottom straight edges open. Neaten. Slip stitch the hem into place easing the side seams. Turn to the right side.

Tassel Remove the paper number band on the Anchor stranded embroidery cotton. Lay the skein out flat with the strands parallel to one another. Tie a piece of cotton around the centre of the skein, pull up tightly and knot, leaving a long end with which to sew the tassel on to the nightcap. Lay the polystyrene ball on the centre knot, fan out the strands either side and pull up until the ball is covered with the embroidery cotton. Gather the strands into a bunch at the top of the ball, tie tightly together and knot. Trim the top of the strands to form a tassel and fluff out with a needle. The tassel is then stitched to the top point of the night-

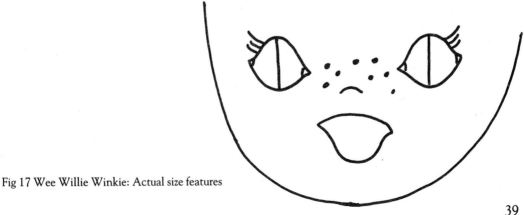

Fig 17 Wee Willie Winkie: Actual size features

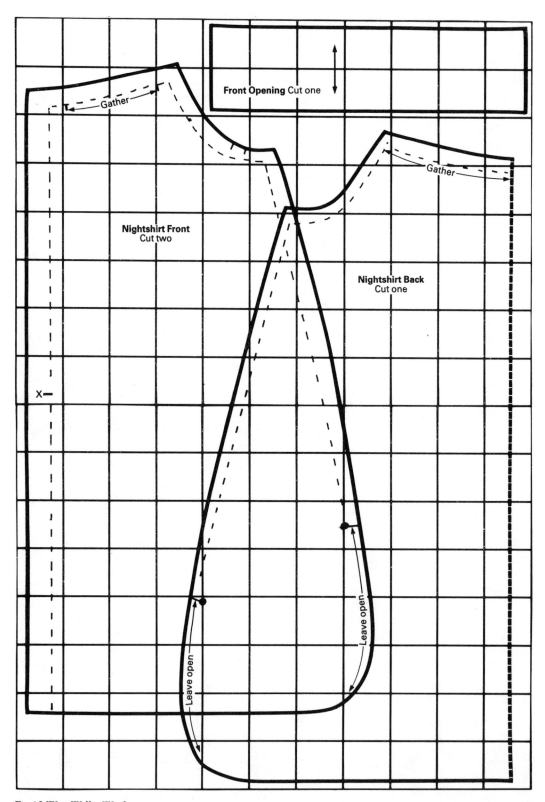

Front Opening Cut one

Nightshirt Front
Cut two

Nightshirt Back
Cut one

Gather

Gather

X—

Leave open

Leave open

Fig 18 Wee Willie Winkie

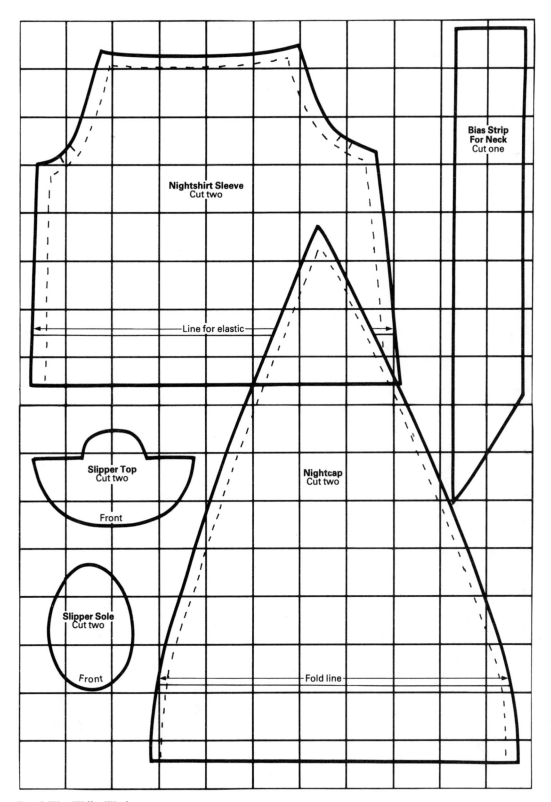

Bias Strip
For Neck
Cut one

Nightshirt Sleeve
Cut two

Line for elastic

Slipper Top
Cut two

Front

Nightcap
Cut two

Slipper Sole
Cut two

Front

Fold line

Fig 19 Wee Willie Winkie

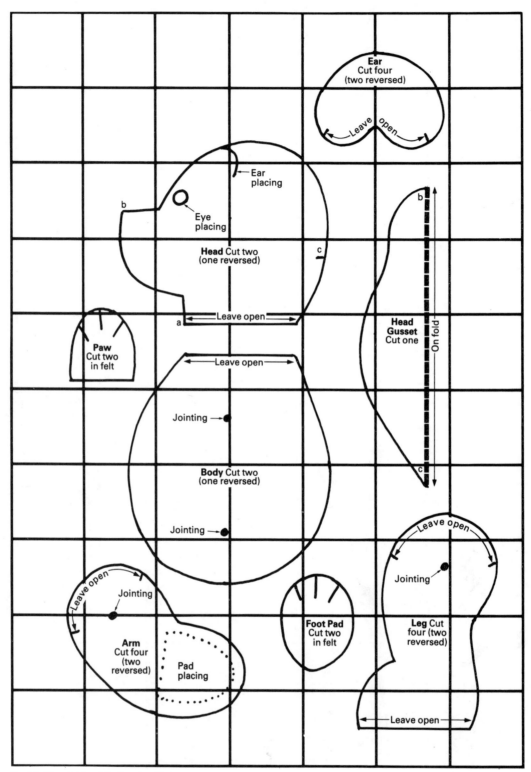

Fig 20 Wee Willie Winkie: Teddy Bear

cap. A tassel can, if preferred, be made in the more conventional way.

Slippers Cut out the pattern pieces. Take one top piece and one sole and overstitch together where indicated. Stitch a bobble to the centre front. Repeat for other slipper. Place on the doll and stitch to hold.

Teddy Bear

A piece of fawn-coloured courtelle fleece for the body, head, arms, legs and ears, 20.4 x 35.5cm (8 x 14in)

Dark-brown felt for the pads, paws, nose and eyes, 5 x 7.6cm (2 x 3in)

Four snap fasteners approximately 1.3cm (½in) in diameter for jointing the arms and legs

½m (19¾in) of narrow ribbon to tone with Wee Willie's nightshirt and nightcap

Toy filling

Cut out the head, body, ears and limbs in courtelle fleece. Cut the paws, pads, nose and eyes in dark-brown felt.

Head Place the two main head pieces together right sides facing and join seams A–B using backstitch. Insert the head gusset matching b to b. Stitch one side of the gusset first and fasten off then go back to b and stitch the other side of the gusset to the side head. Turn to the right side. Stuff firmly, gather the neck edge, inserting more filling if necessary to make a firm neck base, and fasten off.

Body With the right sides facing, pin then backstitch around the outside edges, leaving the top straight edge open. Turn to the right side and firmly stuff. Gather the opening and treat as the head neck base, producing a firm top. Ladder stitch the head to the top of the body.

Arms Place together in pairs with the right sides facing. Take one pair and backstitch around the outside edge, leaving open where indicated. Fasten off. Turn to the right side and stuff. Ladder stitch to close the opening. Ladder stitch a paw piece in place. Add the claw markings using three strands of embroidery cotton. Treat the

other arm in the same way. Lay to one side.

Legs Place together in pairs with the right sides facing. Pin then backstitch around the outside edges, leaving open where indicated. Insert a foot pad into the base of the foot. Turn to the right side and stuff firmly. Ladder stitch the top opening to close. Add the claw markings. Treat the other leg in the same way. Lay to one side.

Ears Place together in pairs with the right sides facing and pin then backstitch around the outside edges, leaving open where indicated; turn to the right side. Loosely overstitch the opening to close and pull up slightly to shape. Fasten off. Treat the other ear in the same way. Ladder stitch in place on the head. Stitch the snap fasteners in place on both sides of the body and on the inner side of the limbs where indicated on the pattern, then snap the limbs into place; this will form hinging to move the limbs.

Features Ladder stitch the nose in place, add mouth markings using straight stitches.

Cut two 0.7cm (¼in) diameter circles in brown felt for the eyes. Stitch these in place, keeping them well down on the nose – this will produce a younger and more appealing expression. Add highlights just above the centre of the eyes using three strands of light-beige stranded embroidery cotton. Place the piece of narrow ribbon around the bear's neck and tie in a bow at the front; cut off any excess ribbon. The bear is held under Wee Willie Winkie's left arm; his hand is secured to his nightshirt by two small squares of Velcro.

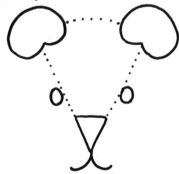

Fig 21 Wee Willie Winkie Teddy Bear: Feature placing

KNITTED STRIP TOYS

Humpty Dumpty

Humpty Dumpty sat on a wall,
Humpty Dumpty had a great fall,
All the king's horses and all the king's men,
Couldn't put Humpty together again.

* * *

Toy type: Knitted-strip toy (colour picture page 35)
Size of toy: Height 43.7cm (17in)

The toys in this section are very simple as they consist of strips of knitting which are easily constructed into attractive toys. The knitting must be even and of a firm tension. Whilst this is an excellent means of using up yarns remaining from other projects, great care should be taken to choose colours which complement one another. It is essential to the appearance of the knitted toys that matching yarns are used to stitch the pieces together. The toy filling should be lightweight: terylene is very suitable as it is springy to handle and fills the knitted skin easily and with very little weight. To produce a really good toy, attention should be given to the surface of the toy continually during the stuffing process.

One ball of double-knitting yarn in flesh colour
One ball of double-knitting yarn in pale blue
Oddments of double-knitting yarn in dark blue for the shoes, white for the sock stripes and light brown for the hair
One pair of 3¼mm (No 10) knitting needles
Oddments of white, medium-brown, black and deep-pink felts for the features
White felt for the collar, 40.6 x 5cm (16 x 2in)
White felt for the cuffs, 11.5 x 6.4cm (4½ x 2½in)
Terylene toy filling
1m (39½in) narrow dark-blue ribbon for the shoe laces
1m (39½in) deep-pink 2.5cm (1in) wide ribbon for the neck bow

NOTE: The word yarn covers the various knitting types available. The original toy was made in a double-knitting yarn consisting of 50 per cent pure wool and 50 per cent acrylic. It is uneconomical to purchase the smallest amounts required, so with the knitted-strip toys I usually purchase 40gm or 50gm balls.

This toy is worked entirely in garter stitch.

44

Body and Head Cast on 35 sts in the pale-blue yarn, knit for 10.3cm (4in), change to the flesh-coloured yarn and knit for 30.5cm (12in), change to the blue yarn and knit for 10.3cm (4in). Cast off.

Legs Cast on 20 sts in the pale-blue yarn, work 30 rows, change to white yarn and work 4 rows, change to pale-blue yarn and work 4 rows, change to white yarn and work 4 rows. Cast off. Make the other leg piece in the same way.

Arms Cast on 18 sts in the pale-blue yarn, work 30 rows, change to the flesh yarn and work 16 rows. Cast off. Make the second arm piece in the same way.

Shoes Cast on 10 sts in the dark-blue yarn, knit for 10.3cm (4in). Cast off. Make the second shoe in the same way.

To Make Up Body and Head With the right sides facing, fold the body and head piece in half, lining up the two colours respectively, and pin to hold. Backstitch across the top corners of the flesh-coloured head to curve; remove pins. With the matching yarn colours, overstitch or backstitch the side seams together to join, leaving the bottom edges open. Turn to the right side. Carefully stuff, forming an elongated shape. Gather the open end, pull up and fasten off. The original model measured, when stuffed, approximately 34.3cm (13½in) from the top of the head down the front to between the leg placing and 41.9cm (16½in) around the stuffed body at the centre. These measurements will vary according to the tension and amount of toy filling used.

To Make Up Arms Take one knitted piece and fold in half lengthways with the right sides facing. Join the long seams together. Gather the flesh-coloured hand end, pull up and fasten off. Turn to the right side. Stuff. Close the arm opening with gathering. Fasten off. Treat the second arm in the same way. Ladder stitch an arm to either side of the body, with the top of the arm in line with the pale-blue knitting of the body and the seaming placed under the arm.

To Make Up Legs and Shoes Take one knitted piece. Fold in half lengthways with the right sides facing and join the long seams together. Gather one end to close. Turn to the right side. Stuff the leg. Gather the opposite end to close. Treat the second leg in the same way.

Take one knitted shoe piece and, with the right sides facing, fold in half across the shortest measurement. Join both of the side seams together, leaving the short end open. Turn to the right side. Stuff. Gather the open end to close. Make the second shoe in the same way.

Holding a shoe with the gathering at the back farthest away from you, take one of the legs with its seam at the back and the white

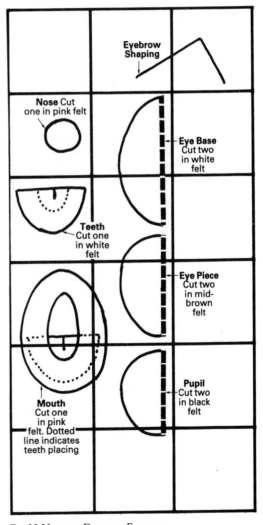

Fig 22 Humpty Dumpty: Features

stripes nearest the shoe to simulate the socks, and ladder stitch the leg to the top of the shoe. This leaves the shoe protruding at the front of the leg by approximately 4.5cm (1¾in). Apply the second shoe in the same way.

Ladder stitch a leg on either side at the base of the body, leaving a gap of approximately 2.5cm (1in) at the centre front. Cut the piece of narrow dark-blue ribbon in half for the two shoe laces. Take one piece and thread it through the top surface of the shoe, forming three flat pieces of the ribbon across the front, each measuring 2.5cm (1in), and working up the shoe to the top edge at the ankle base. Tie the ends into a bow. Treat the other shoe in the same way.

Features Cut out the pattern pieces in felt. Remove the centre oval for the mouth and insert the teeth felt piece behind as indicated on the pattern by the dotted lines, using the photograph as a guide to correct placing. Apply the eye combination: start with the largest white pieces, then the brown pieces and lastly the pupils, using a small running stitch. The mouth and nose are applied using small overstitching. Before closing the nose, add a small amount of toy filling. Work the eyebrows in the light-brown wool, using straight stitches, to the size given on the graph.

Hair Leaving a bald top to the head measuring approximately 12.7cm (5in) across the head from side to side and 7.6cm (3in) from the front to the back of the head, work the hair by forming loops measuring 5cm (2in) and stitching them close together. If you stitch with the right hand and hold the yarn with the first finger of the left hand to the length of the loop required, this will prevent the yarn tangling as you work; it also removes the need to check the measurements constantly and the result will be an evenly applied circle of loops.

Collar Take the piece of white felt measuring 40.6 x 5cm (16 x 2in). Wrap it around the top of the blue knitting with the short ends at the centre front of the body and the felt lying on the face. Stitch the lower long edge to the body all around and fasten off. Fold the top unstitched edge of the collar down over the shoulders and at the back of the head. Tie a large bow in the deep pink ribbon, stitch to the top of the body at the centre front and tuck under the felt collar points.

Cuffs Cut two pieces in the white felt, each measuring 11.5 x 3.3cm (4½ x 1¼in). Take one piece and place it around one arm at the wrist on the pale blue line of knitting, with the other long edge of the felt lying over the hand and the short ends of the felt at the outside of the arm. Pin to hold. Backstitch in place. Fasten off. Remove the pins. Fold the cuff up the arm. Treat the second cuff in the same way.

Jack and Jill

Jack and Jill went up the hill,
To fetch a pail of water,
Jack fell down and broke his crown,
And Jill came tumbling after.

* * *

Toy type: Knitted-strip toy rabbits (colour picture page 35)
Size of toy: Height 35.5cm (14in)

These toys demonstrate how versatile a basic strip toy can be. Dressed in very simple clothes they become an attractive extension to the concept of a knitted-strip toy.

A pair of 3¼mm (No 10) knitting needles
One 40gm ball of white double-knitting yarn for each rabbit
Red felt for Jack's cap and dungarees, 28 x 28cm (11 x 11in)
White felt for Jack's collar, 21.5 x 3.8cm (8½ x 1½in)
Oddments of Jill's dress material for Jack's neck bow and pocket handkerchief
Scraps of black felt for Jack's buttons and dark-blue felt for the eyes
Black stranded embroidery cotton for the features
White stranded embroidery cotton for eye highlights
Toy filling
Jill's dress fabric (red and white), 101.6 x 16cm (40 x 6¼in)
Matching fabric for Jill's pantees, 40.6 x 10.3cm (16 x 4in)
White felt for Jill's collar, 25.4 x 5cm (10 x 2in)
2m (79in) 0.7cm (¼in) wide red ribbon
Red felt for Jill's shoes, 14 x 12.7cm (5½ x 5in)
A piece of Vilene Funtex in grey for bucket, 15.3 x 10.3cm (6 x 4in)
A piece of Vilene Funtex in dark blue, 15.3 x 7.6cm (6 x 3in)
One pipe cleaner

Scraps of white Velcro to secure the bucket handle to the rabbits' paws

NOTE: If Funtex is not available use ordinary felt, and iron on Vilene or fabric stiffener prior to making the bucket.

Knitted in garter stitch. Each rabbit requires two bodies and two arms.
Body Starting with the legs. Cast on 10 sts. Knit for 7.6cm (3in) (32 rows). Break the yarn and leave these stitches on the end of the needle. Cast on another 10 sts and knit for 7.6cm (3in) (32 rows). Now knit across both legs (20 sts). Knit on these 20 sts for 15.3cm (6in) (64 rows); this will be the body. Do not cast off but knit on the first 10 sts only for 7.6cm (3in) (32 rows); this will be an ear. Cast off. Go back to the 10 sts left on the needle and knit to match for the other ear. Cast off. Make another piece the same for the second half.
Arms Cast on 16 sts. Knit for 7cm (2¾in) (28 rows). Cast off. Make a second arm piece.
Construction Place the two combined body pieces together and overstitch around the outside edges, leaving a stuffing opening on one side of the body. Backstitch to curve the tops of the ears. Turn to the right side. Take the two outside edges of an ear at the base, fold inwards to the centre to form the ear shaping and overstitch to hold. Treat the other ear in the same way. Carefully stuff and shape the body and legs, and overstitch to close the side opening. Measure down approximately 9cm (3½in) from the centre top of head, and gather along this line to form the neck. Using ladder stitching, dart

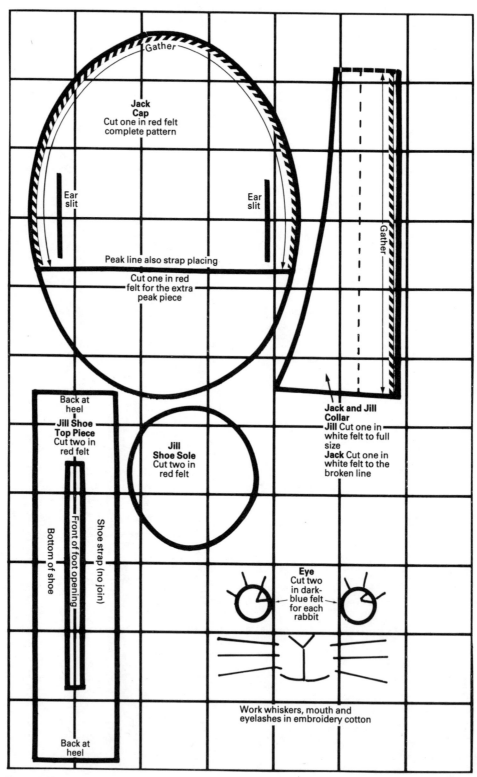

Jack Cap
Cut one in red felt
complete pattern

Gather

Ear slit

Ear slit

Gather

Peak line also strap placing

Cut one in red felt for the extra peak piece

Jack and Jill Collar
Jill Cut one in white felt to full size
Jack Cut one in white felt to the broken line

Back at heel

Jill Shoe Top Piece
Cut two in red felt

Jill Shoe Sole
Cut two in red felt

Bottom of shoe

Front of foot opening

Shoe strap (no join)

Eye
Cut two in dark-blue felt for each rabbit

Work whiskers, mouth and eyelashes in embroidery cotton

Back at heel

Fig 23 Jack And Jill

the leg at the front to form the feet approximately 4.5cm (1¾in) from the base on the Jill rabbit; the Jack rabbit has no foot darting.

Take one of the arm pieces and fold in half with the line of garter stitch going around the arm; overstitch the long edges to join. Gather one end, pull up and fasten off. Turn to the right side. Stuff, then ladder stitch to the body approximately 2cm (¾in) down from the neck. Fasten off. Treat the other arm in the same way. Apply the features and add white highlights to the eyes – the same for both rabbits.

Dungarees Cut two leg pieces in red felt to measure 12.7 x 14cm (5 x 5½in). Take one leg piece and cut one 12.7cm (5in) edge using pinking shears. Fold in half lengthways and overstitch from the serrated edge for approximately 9cm (3½in). Fasten off. Treat the second leg piece in the same way. Place the leg pieces togther with the front edges matching and overstitch a front seam to join. Cut the bib piece in red felt 7.6 x 5.7cm (3 x 2¼in). Cut one long edge with pinking shears. Lay the plain long edge to the centre of the joined front seam on the dungarees, with the serrated edge lying over the leg pieces. Join the bib edge to the dungaree top edge using backstitch. Fasten off. Place the dungarees on the rabbit.

Make a white bobble for the tail, diameter approximately 5cm (2in), and apply to the base of the body at the centre back. Cut two straps in red felt, each measuring 15.3 x 1.3cm (6 x ½in). Take one strap and join to the back of the dungarees at the open top edge. Join the second strap to the opposite top edge of the opening. Cross the straps over each other, take one over each shoulder and stitch to the front of the bib either side at the top. Cut a 5 x 3.8cm (2 x 1½in) piece of the red felt for the pocket. Stitch to the left leg of the dungarees using the photograph as a guide to correct placing. Cut two 1.3cm (½in) diameter circles in black felt for the buttons and stitch in place on the straps at the front. Place the white felt collar around the rabbit's neck and stitch together

at the top edge points. Fasten off. Tie a small bow in material matching Jill's dress, and stitch to the collar. Cut a 3.8cm (1½in) square of the same material, fold it into a triangle and place in the pocket of the dungarees as a handkerchief.

Cap Cut one full pattern piece and one extra peak piece where indicated, in the red felt. Lay the extra peak piece under the cap piece and stab stitch together. Gather around the remaining edge of the crown and pull up. Fasten off. Cut ear slits either side of the cap. Cut a strip of the felt to measure 11.5 x 0.7cm (4½ x ¼in). Place the cap on the rabbit's head. Lay the felt strip across the brim in front of the ears, turn the ends under the brim either side and stitch to secure. Fasten off.

Dress Turn a hem on one long edge of the material. With the right sides facing, join the two short ends. Turn to the right side. Fold in a narrow hem on the other long edge and gather; pull up slightly and with the seam at the back, cut a slit either side for the armholes. Do not pull up or fasten off the neck gathering. Hem around the armholes, place on the rabbit then pull up the gathering and fasten off. Cut the collar in white felt and place around the neck; it may be necessary to gather the collar slightly to obtain a neat fit. Attach the collar to the front of the dress, leaving a 4.5cm (1¾in) gap between the collar edges. Tie a small bow in the ribbon and, leaving two long ribbon tails, stitch to the dress in the gap between the collar edges. Tie a second bow and, leaving tails hanging, stitch to the top of the head between the ears.

Pantees Hem one long edge of the material. Hem the two short edges separately. Fold in a hem on the remaining long edge, place around the body and gather to fit the waist. Join together at the top for approximately 0.7cm (¼in) only and also from the bottom edge for 0.7cm (¼in); place these joins at the back of the rabbit. Join the bottom hemmed long edge at the centre between the legs for approximately 0.7cm (¼in). Gather each leg opening separately and pull up to fit. Fasten off. Make a bobble for the tail, diameter approximately 5cm (2in), and stitch in place.

Shoes Cut out the pattern pieces in red felt. Take one top piece and join at the back using overstitch. Fasten off. Insert the sole and overstitch around the outside edge to join to the top. Gather a length of the ribbon on one edge and pull up to form a rosette. Attach to the outside of the shoe on the strap. Treat the second shoe in the same way. Place the shoes on the rabbit and stitch to secure.

Bucket In grey Funtex cut a piece to measure 14 x 7cm (5½ x 2¾in). Fold in half and glue the shorter edges together, overlapping slightly. Apply adhesive to one circle edge of the tube and lay this circle on to a piece of dark-blue Funtex. When the adhesive is dry, cut around to remove the excess Funtex. Cut a piece of grey Funtex sufficiently wide and long enough to cover the pipe cleaner. Apply with adhesive. When dry, bend into an oval and glue to the inside of the bucket to a depth of 2cm (¾in) on

either side to form the handle.

Trim the top of the bucket with a piece of dark-blue Funtex measuring approximately 15.3 x 1.3cm (6 x ½in); glue into place. Cut two small pieces of Velcro, each to measure 0.7 x 1.3cm (¼ x ½in). Take the two pieces of Velcro apart and glue the two hooked halves to either side of the bucket on the handle 2.5cm (1in) up from the top edge; stitch the second, softer halves of each Velcro piece on to the rabbits' paws – on Jill's left paw and Jack's right paw – over the gathering on the arms and in line with the Velcro pieces on the bucket. Fixing the softer pieces on the rabbits will mean that the toys remain soft to the touch when played with separately; the hooked Velcro halves would feel rather sharp to the child.

NOTE: The Jack and Jill size will vary according to the degree of stuffing; it may be necessary to adjust the size of the collar on both rabbits, also Jill's shoes. The adjustment in both cases should be made at the back seam.

One, Two, Three, Four, Five

One, two, three, four, five,
Once I caught a fish alive,
Six, seven, eight, nine, ten,
Then I let it go again.

* * *

Toy type: Knitted-strip teddy bears (colour picture page 36)
Size of toy: Height approximately 40.6cm (16in)

This toy further demonstrates the range of the simple strip toy. It can be developed into a game for a group of children to play with. Each child requires a teddy bear, and the bears should be dressed in different coloured dungarees. The purpose of the game is that the children each fish with their bear, and then add the total of the numbers of the fish caught; the bear with the highest total is the winner. The duckling on the pond forms an obstacle to make the task of catching the fish more difficult. The quantities given are for each bear.

One pair 3¼mm (No 10) knitting needles
One 40gm ball of double-knitting yarn in medium brown

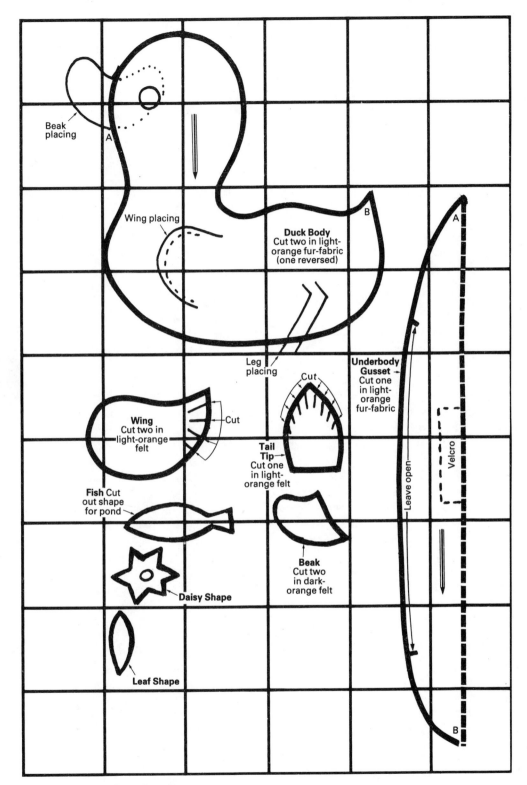

Fig 24 One, Two, Three, Four, Five

One 25gm ball of double-knitting yarn for dungarees

One pair of 14mm safety-lock eyes; if for a very young child substitute felt or embroidered eyes

Scraps of black double-knitting yarn for the features

Toy filling

Knitted in garter stitch throughout.

Body, Head and Arms

Make as for the There Was a Little Girl doll (page 56) with the following exceptions. Prior to stuffing, stitch across each corner for the ears, on the right side. Apply the safety-lock eyes first, adding felt or extra support to the knitted skin behind the eye placing. Replace the bows at the doll's wrist by gathering a wrist on the bear. The ankle bows are replaced by ladder stitching a dart 4.5cm (1¾in) up from the base of each leg (after the bear is stuffed).

Muzzle Cast on 30 sts and knit 8 rows. Cast off. Join the short ends of the knitted strip by overstitching. Gather one long edge. Pull up and fasten off. Turn to the opposite side. Run a gathering thread on the remaining long edge. Pull up slightly and stuff, then pull up again until almost closed. Place a holding stitch but do not detach the sewing yarn. Ladder stitch to the face approximately 2cm (¾in) up from the neck. Work the nose and mouth on the muzzle in black yarn, using the photograph as a guide to correct placing.

Dungarees Cast on 24 sts. Knit for 20.4cm (8in). Knit another piece in the same way. For the bib, cast on 12 sts and knit 16 rows. Make the straps by knitting the first 3 sts, then cast off 6 sts, and on the remaining 3 sts work 46 rows. Cast off. Rejoin the wool to the remaining 3 sts and complete as for the first strap.

Construct as for the felt dungarees on Jack Rabbit (page 49) with the following slight alterations. These dungarees are overstitched then turned to the opposite side, not top overstitched as on the felt dungarees. As the bear has no tail, the back seams are joined and the straps are crossed at the back and attached either side of the back seam on the inside of the dungarees, just below the top edge.

Pond

One 20.4cm (8in) round silver-covered cake board, 1.3cm (½in) or more deep

One 25.4cm (10in) thin round cake board

One 20.4cm (8in) diameter circle of blue felt

A piece of 73.7 x 12.7cm (29 x 5in) polished or long-pile green fur-fabric

Oddments of white, green and lemon felt for the flowers

Various coloured pieces of Vilene, Funtex or Furmofelt for the fish; if these materials are not available apply iron-on Vilene to ordinary felt

Orange short-pile fur-fabric for the duckling, 22.9 x 16.6cm (9 x 6½in)

Orange felt for the wings and tail, 5 x 6.4cm (2 x 2½in)

Scraps of bright-orange felt for the beak and black felt for the eyes

A piece of Velcro, 2.5cm (1in) long

One pipe cleaner

Toy filling

Pieces of 0.7cm (¼in) dowel rod for the fishing rods, each rod to measure 21.5cm (8½in)

Pieces of strong fine thread for the fishing lines, 40.6cm (16in) for each rod

Small magnets, one for each rod

Small fine metal rings to attach to the fish, one per fish

Oddments of sequins to decorate the fish

All-purpose adhesive

Black felt-tipped pen

Cut seven of the given fish shape out of the blue-felt circle, the fish to be at different angles to one another. Apply adhesive to one side of the felt. Lay the felt on to the silver side of the 20.4cm (8in) round cake board. Press well with the hand until

Three Little Kittens with the Fiddle De Dee mobile

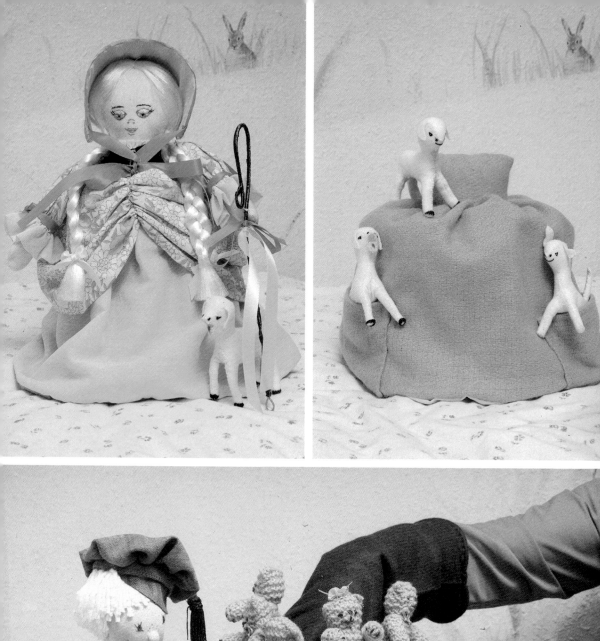

smooth. Allow to dry. The cut-out fish shapes are now silver fish as the cake-board covering shows through. Take the 73.7 x 12.7cm (29 x 5in) piece of green fur-fabric and, using strong thread, gather the top edge, with the pile line facing downwards, to fit the 20.4cm (8in) cake board. Fasten off. Apply adhesive around the outside edge of the cake-board circle and attach the gathered edge of the fur-fabric, with the right side facing inwards, by gluing it to the outside edge of the cake board with the gathered edges level with the base of the circle. Allow to dry. Trim off any excess material around the gathered edge. Fold the remaining long edge of the fur-fabric over to the outside. Turn the cake board upside down and insert toy filling between the fur-fabric and the board edge. Stuff unevenly to add interest to the shape of the pond; avoid the appearance of a roll of fur-fabric. Take the 25.4cm (10in) thin round cake board. Apply adhesive to the wrong side of the board, ie the side not silver covered; lay the pond and fur-fabric edge on to this board and press to bond together. It will be necessary to press the cut edge of the fur-fabric to the board edge, leaving the fur-fabric pile free so that it will cover the board edge.

Daisy For each daisy, cut out one white flower, one yellow centre and two green leaves. Glue a yellow centre to a white flower. Glue the base of a leaf at either side of the flower at the back. Part the pile of the fur-fabric that is around the pond and glue a flower and leaf combination to the backing of the fur-fabric. Scatter and apply the flowers around the fur-fabric and when dry, dot the centres of the flowers using the black felt pen.

Fish Cut out the fish shapes as given. Attach a metal ring to each one. Decorate the fish with sequins or draw in the fins using felt- or fibre-tipped pens. Attach a piece of thread

measuring 40.6cm (16in) around the top of a dowelling rod cut to measure 21.5cm (8½in). Glue to secure in place. Tie a small magnet to the end of the thread. Place the fish in the pond.

Duckling Cut out the pattern pieces. Place the two side body pieces right sides facing and pin together, inserting the beak pieces where indicated on the head. Backstitch

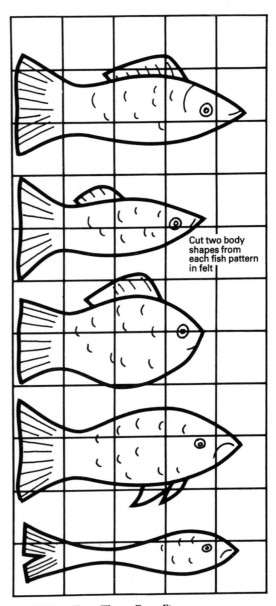

Cut two body shapes from each fish pattern in felt

Fig 25 One, Two, Three, Four, Five

Little Bo Peep with her lambs under her skirt; *(and below)* A Dillar, A Dollar with the Tickling Rhyme bears and I Had A Little Hen

55

together from A to B across the top of the body. Insert the underbody gusset matching A and B. Backstitch together leaving an opening where indicated. Turn to the right side. Stuff firmly. Close the opening using ladder stitching. Add a wing at either side where indicated and stitch into place. Stitch the tail piece in place at B. Cut two small circles in black felt for the eyes. Stitch in place on either side of the head. Glue the beak pieces together. Cut two pieces of the pipe cleaner to measure 3.3cm (1¼in).

Cover with orange felt using overstitching. Bend each pipe cleaner as shown, and stitch to the body on either side as indicated on the pattern. Take the two layers of the 2.5cm (1in) long piece of Velcro apart. Glue the sharper hooked piece to the pond and stitch the softer half to the base of the duckling's body. When the glued half is dry, place the Velcro pieces together to secure the duckling in place on the pond.

The child holds the fishing rod to the arm of a bear and they fish together.

There Was a Little Girl

There was a little girl,
And she had a little curl,
Right in the middle of her forehead.

✳ ✳ ✳

Toy type: Knitted-strip toy with a manufactured doll mask (colour picture page 35)
Size of toy: Height 40.6cm (16in)

A pair of 3¼mm (No 10) knitting needles
One 50gm ball of double-knitting in white
One 40gm ball of double-knitting in pale blue
1m (39½in) of narrow blue ribbon
Toy filling
A small lock of hair or wool for the curl: blonde if the doll mask has blue eyes, brown if it has brown eyes
A doll mask, back of head measurement from top of head to the base 10.3cm (4in)
White felt for the skating boots, 25.4 x 15.3cm (10 x 6in)
Grey felt for the blades, 15.3 x 6.4cm (6 x 2½in)
A piece of very narrow blue ribbon measuring 30.5cm (12in) to hang the boots on
Two black brocatelle beads
Black thread for laces
Clear all-purpose adhesive

The toy is knitted in garter stitch throughout.
Legs Using the white yarn, cast on 10 sts. Knit for 15.3cm (6in) (64 rows), break the wool and leave the stitches on the needle. Cast on another 10 sts and knit to match.
Body and Head Knit across both sets of 10 sts and continue on these 20 sts for 33cm (13in) (136 rows). Then on first 10 sts only, knit for 15.3cm (6in) and cast off. Go back to the 10 sts left on the needle, knit 15.3cm (6in) and cast off.
Arms Cast on 18 sts. Knit 10.3cm (4in) (44 rows). Cast off. Make the second arm in the same way.
Strip for around Face Mask Using the pale-blue yarn, cast on 4 sts and knit for 20.4cm (8in) or 22.9cm (9in), length to be sufficient to fit around the doll mask being used. Cast off.
Skirt Using the pale-blue yarn, cast on 90 sts. Knit for 5cm (2in) (16 rows). Next row knit 2 tog all across to decrease. On the 45 sts now on the needle, knit 2.5cm (1in) (9

rows) more and cast off.

Scarf In the pale-blue yarn, cast on 10 sts and knit for 40.6cm (16in). Cast off.

To Make Up Body and Head Fold in half right sides facing, matching the leg pieces. Overstitch around the outside edge, leaving a centre stuffing opening at one side of the body. At the top fold of the body backstitch to curve at the corners; this will be the top of the head shaping. Turn to the right side. Stuff evenly and firmly. Close the opening. Gather approximately 10.3cm (4in) from the top fold on the body to form the neck. Pull up slightly and fasten off. Place the doll mask into position just above the neck gathering and stitch around the outside edge to join to the stuffed body; just prior to closing, insert toy filling to support the doll mask, close and fasten off. Take the blue knitted strip and join the short ends, using overstitching. Place on to the doll mask to cover the stitched mask edge. Turn back the strip and overstitch to the knitted head at the mask edge. Take the small lock of hair for the curl and stitch to the seam at the centre of the forehead, then bring the strip forward on to the mask and over the join of the lock of hair. If the strip around the mask does not fit perfectly, then carefully apply one or two drops of adhesive around the doll mask and press the strip to secure.

To Make Up Arms Take one arm piece and fold in half lengthways. Overstitch the long edges together. Gather one end, pull up and fasten off. Turn to the right side and stuff. Ladder stitch to the body 2cm (¾in) down from the neck edge on one side. Make and apply the second arm in the same way on the opposite side of the body. To form the wrists, place a piece of narrow blue ribbon around each arm approximately 3.8cm (1½in) from the arm gathering and tie in a bow. Thread a piece of the narrow ribbon at the front of each leg at the ankles, approxi-

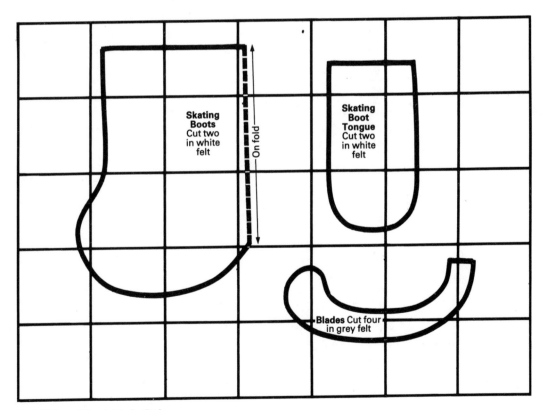

Fig 26 There Was A Little Girl

mately 5cm (2in) up from the foot base. Tie in a small bow on each leg.

To Make Up Skirt and Scarf With right sides facing, place the short seams together and overstitch to join. Turn to the right side. Place on the doll with the seam at the back and stitch around the top edge to secure it to the waist. Using white yarn and chain stitch, work around the skirt just above the lower cast-on edge. Work a second row of chain stitch just above the first row, leaving two rows of the blue skirt showing through in-between.

Using white yarn, work four tassels at each end of the scarf. Each loop is made by overstitching loops together on the scarf edge, then holding the loops together and wrapping the wool round at the base and fastening off. The loops are then cut. Trim the tufts of the four tassels to a uniform length. Work two rows of chain stitch either end, leaving a space between as on the skirt. Place the scarf around the doll's neck and stitch to secure at the left shoulder.

Skating Boots Take one main pattern piece and fold in half where indicated; overstitch around the outside edges to join, leaving the top straight edge and front straight edges open. Place a boot tongue inside the boot and stitch the curved edge to secure at the centre front of the boot, with the straight edge of the tongue level with the top edge of the boot. Take two of the felt blade pieces

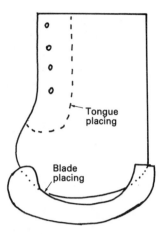

Fig 27 There Was A Little Girl: Boot construction

and apply adhesive to the inside of each. Put the blade pieces on to the base of the boot and press firmly together (see diagram for correct placing). Using a length of strong thread, lace the front edges of the boot together, adding a black brocatelle bead to each end, then knot to hold each bead in place. Treat the second boot in the same way. Stitch one end of the narrow blue ribbon to the inside of a boot approximately 1.3cm (½in) down from the top edge. Attach the second boot in the same way to the opposite end of the ribbon. Place the centre of the ribbon twice around the right shoulder of the doll to hold the boots in place.

The Tickling Rhyme

Round and round the garden,
Like a teddy bear,
One step, two step,
Tickle you under there!

∗ ∗ ∗

Toy type: Felt glove with knitted miniature teddy-bear family (colour picture page 54)
Size of toy: Glove length 45.7cm (18in) Bear sizes 9 and 11.5cm (3½ and 4½in)

The bear family is constructed from knitted strips, then attached to a felt glove to enable them to 'walk' around the palm of the child's hands. These toys have been designed with simplicity as the main criterion. You could make the bears separately and dress the Mother in mob cap and apron and the small bears in dungarees or pinafore skirts.

A pair of 3¼mm (No 10) knitting needles
One 20gm ball of beige-coloured knitting yarn, or oddments
1m (39½in) 0.7cm (¼in) wide green ribbon
1m (39½in) very narrow green ribbon
½m (19¾in) very narrow ribbon in each of the following colours: yellow, blue and red
Yellow felt for the Mother Bear's skirt, 12.1 x 9cm (4¾ x 3½in)
Red felt for the Father Bear's waistcoat, 15.3 x 6.4cm (6 x 2½in)
Oddments of dark-brown felt for the Father Bear's pads
Dark-brown felt for the glove, 48.2 x 45.7cm (19 x 18in)
Two pipe cleaners
Five pieces of 2.5cm (1in) wide Velcro, each measuring 12.7cm (5in)
Stranded embroidery cotton in dark brown and white
Five thimbles, assorted sizes
Toy filling

The bears are worked in garter stitch throughout.

Father Bear

Leg Cast on 5 sts. Knit 14 rows (3.8cm/ 1½in). Break the wool and leave the sts on the needle. Cast on another 5 sts. Knit to match the other leg.
Body Knit across all 10 sts for 50 rows (12.7cm/5in). Then on the first 5 sts knit 14 rows and cast off. Return to the other 5 sts and knit 14 rows. Cast off.
Arms Cast on 9 sts. Knit 14 rows. Cast off. Make the second arm piece in the same way.

Mother Bear and Small Bears

Legs Cast on 4 sts. Knit 10 rows. Break the wool and leave the sts on the needle. Cast on another 4 sts. Knit 10 rows.
Body Knit across all sts for 50 rows. Then on the first 4 sts work 10 rows and cast off. Return to the 4 sts and knit 10 rows. Cast off.
Arms Cast on 7 sts. Knit 10 rows. Cast off. Make the second arm piece in the same way. Make four bears from this pattern.

To Make Up Small Bears

Fold body and legs in half as shown in Fig 28. Overstitch around the outside edges to join, leaving sufficient space at one side of the top fold of the head to allow turning. Turn through. Stuff the legs firmly using small quantities of toy filling at a time; stuff combined body and legs and partially stuff the head. Approximately 3.8cm (1½in) down from the top of the head, tie a piece of wool tightly round to form the neck. Form a small ball of toy filling, place inside the head

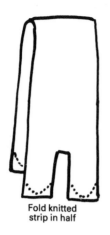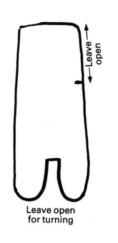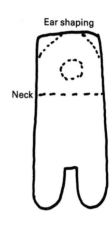

Fold knitted strip in half

Leave open for turning

Ear shaping

Neck

Fig 28 The Tickling Rhyme: Bear body

and push out to form the nose point. Fully stuff the head and close the opening with neat overstitching. Backstitch across each top corner to form the ears. Gather a circle of approximately 1.3cm (½in) diameter around the nose point; pull up to form the snout. Fasten off.

Fold one arm piece in half lengthways, ie with the knitted rows going around the arm piece. Overstitch the long sides together and also one short end. Turn and stuff firmly. Ladder stitch to the side of the body just below the neck. Treat the second arm in the same way.

Using three strands of brown embroidery silk, work the mouth, nose and eyes with straight stitches. Highlights can be added to the eyes using two strands of white embroidery cotton if desired. Work three claws on the inside of each paw and four claws on the front of each foot (see Fig 29). Turn each foot upwards slightly by ladder stitching the top of each foot to a leg and pulling on the stitching to turn the foot. Make three bears in this way, one with a narrow neck ribbon and bow in yellow, one with a green ribbon and the third with a blue ribbon.

To Make Up Mother Bear

This bear is constructed using the pattern for the small bears, but her feet remain pointed. Cut the skirt pattern in yellow felt

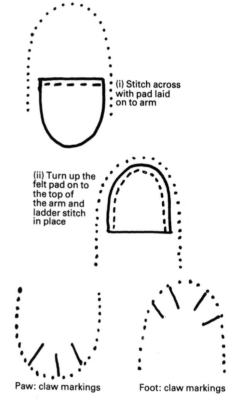

(i) Stitch across with pad laid on to arm

(ii) Turn up the felt pad on to the top of the arm and ladder stitch in place

Paw: claw markings   Foot: claw markings

Fig 29 The Tickling Rhyme
(opposite)
Fig 30 The Tickling Rhyme: Adjust the length of the fingers to fit the manipulator's hand. The middle two fingers are narrower at the base than the others for a firm grip to hold the glove in place and enable easy manipulation of the other fingers. The thumbs should also be a firm grip

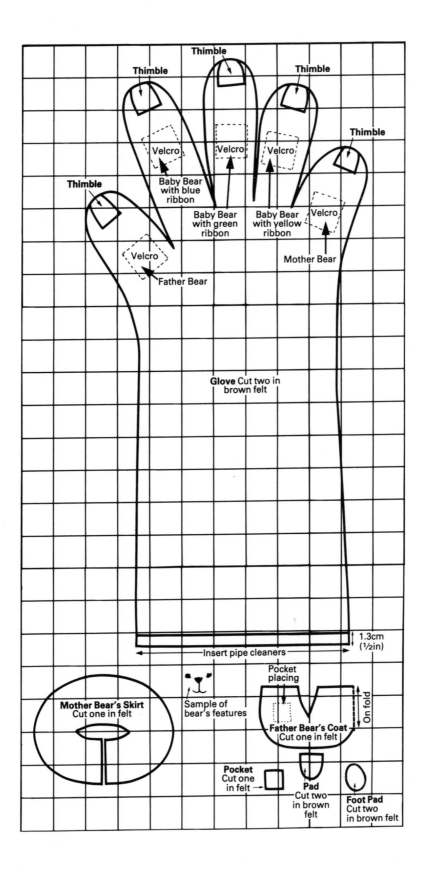

Thimble

Thimble

Thimble

Velcro

Velcro

Velcro

Baby Bear with blue ribbon

Baby Bear with green ribbon

Baby Bear with yellow ribbon

Thimble

Velcro

Mother Bear

Thimble

Velcro

Father Bear

Glove Cut two in brown felt

1.3cm (½in)

← Insert pipe cleaners →

Mother Bear's Skirt
Cut one in felt

Sample of bear's features

Pocket placing

On fold

Father Bear's Coat
Cut one in felt

Pocket
Cut one in felt →

Pad
Cut two in brown felt

Foot Pad
Cut two in brown felt

and place around the waist, overlapping slightly at the back and stitching to secure. A piece of narrow green ribbon is placed around the waist and the ends crossed over each other at the back, leaving small tails. Stitch to secure at the back, leaving the ends of the ribbon hanging. Gather a strip of matching green ribbon to form a rosette and stitch to the top of the bear's head. Using a piece of very narrow ribbon in the same colour green, tie a tiny bow and stitch to the centre of the rosette.

Father Bear

Make from the larger pattern. Construct as the other bears. Turn up the feet as for the smaller bears. Apply the foot and paw pads using Fig 29. Place a very narrow piece of red ribbon around his neck and tie in a small bow at the centre front. Cut the waistcoat pattern in red felt. Join the shoulders using backstitch. Turn to other side. Stab stitch pocket in place on left front of waistcoat.

Glove

It may be necessary to adjust the length of the fingers to fit the manipulator's hand. The middle two fingers are narrower at the base than the others for a firm grip to hold the glove in place and allow easy manipula-tion and flexibility of the other fingers. Take the five 2.5cm (1in) pieces of Velcro apart and stitch the hooked halves to the glove – see pattern for correct placing. Place the glove pieces together and overstitch around the outside edges to join, leaving the bottom straight edges open; as you stitch, hold the edges being sewn together between the thumb and first finger of the left hand (reverse if left-handed) and pull the sewing thread to the felt edges but do not pull too tightly or you will form ridges. The glove must have a clear outline.

Choose a thimble to fit the thumb and each finger of the manipulator. Turn the glove inside out. Apply some all-purpose adhesive to the flat base of each thimble and place a thimble on the centre top of each finger and the thumb of the glove. When dry, turn in a narrow hem on the top straight edge of the glove, insert the pipe cleaners and close. Turn the glove to the right side.

Stitch the five softer halves of the Velcro pieces to the backs of the bears. Place the Father Bear on the thumb Velcro piece, then the three small bears on the next three fingers and the Mother Bear on the small finger. They can be moved from finger to finger or played with separately.

Three Little Kittens

The three little kittens,
They found their mittens,
And they began to cry,
Oh! Mother dear,
See here, see here,
Our mittens we have found.

Toy type: Knitted-strip cat and kittens (colour picture page 53)
Size of toy: Mother Cat height 30.5cm (12in), two kittens height 20.4cm (8in), one kitten height 17.8cm (7in)

Many patterns have been produced in books and magazines to depict the above rhyme, often using the pretty image of attractively dressed cats. The designs here are based on real cats who often have their white feet called 'mittens'.

One pair 3¼mm (No 10) knitting needles
The Mother Cat and three kittens took just over three 40gm balls of black double knitting yarn (50 per cent pure wool and 50 per cent acrylic); if no oddments of the yarn are available then it will be necessary to purchase two 40gm balls and one 50gm ball
A small ball of white double-knitting yarn for the mittens
½m (19¾in) narrow pale-pink, pale-blue and pale-green ribbons for the kittens' bows
1m (39½in) of 2.5cm (1in) wide lemon ribbon for the Mother Cat's bow
Oddments of pale-pink felt for the noses, lemon and blue felt for the eyes, red felt for the Mother Cat's tongue
Terylene toy filling, a dark colour if possible

All the cats are worked in garter stitch.

Mother Cat
Body and Head Using the black yarn, cast on 35 sts. Knit for 50.8cm (20in). Cast off.
Tail Cast on 18 sts. Knit for 28cm (11in). Cast off.
Paws In the white yarn cast on 8 sts. Knit 10 rows. Cast off. Make another paw in the same way.

Kittens
For each kitten make the following.
Body and Head Cast on 20 sts. Knit for 35.5cm (14in) ie 142 rows. Cast off.
Tail Cast on 10 sts. Knit for 15.3cm (6in), ie 60 rows. Cast off.
Paws Cast on 6 sts. Knit 8 rows. Cast off. Make another paw in the same way.

To Make Up Mother Cat
With the right sides facing, fold the body and head piece in half. Join both side seams. Turn to the right side.

Lightly stuff the top corner points at each side of the head to make ears. Work running stitches across one corner – the depth from the ear tip to the ear base centre is approximately 3.8cm (1½in) – pull up slightly to curve and fasten with an overstitch. Pull the inner edge of the ear forward to curve, place a holding stitch but do not fasten off. Take the needle and yarn through the head to the inner curve of the opposite ear corner and treat in the same way. Fasten off.

Stuff the body, adding extra filling either side at the front for the legs and shaping the back of the cat. Stab stitch to form the legs; the space between the legs at the front of the body measures 5cm (2in). The approximate length of each leg from where the shaping starts to the base is 10.3cm (4in); the roundness of each leg measures 7.6cm (3in). Firmly stuff the legs from the base and close

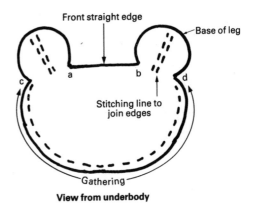

View from underbody

Fig 31 Three Little Kittens and Mother Cat: Base of body construction. Gather the base of the body c–d, pull up and work a holding stitch; place in a line to a–b and overstitch together to join

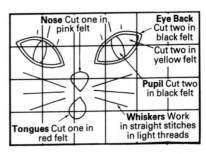

Fig 32 Three Little Kittens: Mother Cat's features

63

the openings. Complete the body stuffing, gathering the back half-circle at the base to the open straight seam between the legs, and overstitch to join. Gather around the body to form the neck approximately 14cm (5½in) from the top of the head. Do not pull up the gathering too tightly.

Place one mitten piece on each leg with the straight edge level with the leg base. Overstitch the mitten pieces in place, leaving the top edge on each mitten free.

With the right sides facing, fold the tail piece in half lengthways. Join the long edges together. Gather and close one short end. Turn to the right side. Stuff. Ladder stitch to the base of the body at the centre back.

Cut out the features in felt. Stitch the yellow-felt eye pieces to the black-felt eye backs, stuffing slightly prior to closing. Add the eye pupils then overstitch the eyes and nose into place, using the photograph to aid correct placing. Attach the tongue by the point to just below the nose. Work the whiskers either side of the mouth and above each eye, using white cotton and straight stitches. Place the lemon ribbon around the cat's neck and tie in a large bow at the centre front; trim to remove any excess ribbon.

Kittens

It would be rather boring for the recipient if the three kittens were identical. Variation is introduced by altering the size and position of the eyes, and giving each kitten a different mouth. The tail positions are all different. The kittens' bodies, eyes and tails are constructed as for the Mother Cat, stuffing two bodies to a height of 20.4cm (8in) and the third body to a height of 17.8cm (7in).

Kitten (a) has blue eyes, a pink nose and a straight mouth. The tail is curved up the kitten's side and stitched at the top to hold in place. Add a blue ribbon around the neck and tie in a bow.

Kitten (b) has blue eyes, a pink nose and tongue. The tail is curved round the front of the body over the paws and stitched to hold. Place a pink ribbon around the neck and tie in a bow.

Kitten (c) has yellow eyes, a pink nose and embroidered smiling mouth. The tail is held erect behind the body and stitched to hold in place. Tie a green-ribbon bow around the neck.

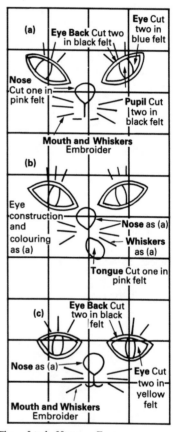

Fig 33 Three Little Kittens: Features

NOVELTY TOYS

A Dillar, A Dollar

A dillar, a dollar,
A ten o'clock scholar,
What makes you come so soon?
You used to come at ten o'clock,
But now you come at noon.

✳ ✳ ✳

Toy type: Mop stick puppet (colour picture page 54)
Size of toy: Height 30.5cm (12in)

This toy has a lightly needle-modelled face and demonstrates how an attractive article can be made out of a very simple object.
It is based on the early marotte or folly head doll, a carved stick with a head at one end.

One dish mop with cotton-strand ends
A 22.9cm (9in) square of 1.3cm (½in) polyester wadding (batting)
Flesh-coloured jersey or knitted cotton 22.9 x 30.5cm (9 x 12in) for the head and hands
Cotton or linen material, brown-stripe mixture, 53.3 x 66cm (21 x 26in) for the tunic and cap
Cream-coloured calico for the collar, 20.4 x 20.4cm (8 x 8in)
Tan felt 10.3 x 15.3cm (4 x 6in) for the school bag
Coloured Vilene 10.3 x 5cm (4 x 2in) for the book cover

Pieces of notepaper cut to the same size for the book leaves
Black Vilene for the slate, 9 x 10.3cm (3½ x 4in)
Two pieces of tan-coloured Vilene 9 x 10.3cm (3½ x 4in) for the slate back and frame (or Furmofelt or felt backed with Vilene)
½m (19¾in) narrow brown ribbon for the neck tie
A brown tassel for the cap
Black and brown fibre-tipped pens
Copydex adhesive
Toy filling
Oddments of short pile fur-fabric and matching felt for the mouse
One pair of small goggle eyes, or scraps of felt
White cotton for the mouse's whiskers

Head Lift up all the cotton strands at the end of the mop handle and tie loosely together to keep them out of the way whilst forming the head; this will be the puppet's hair eventually. Bind the mop handle from under the

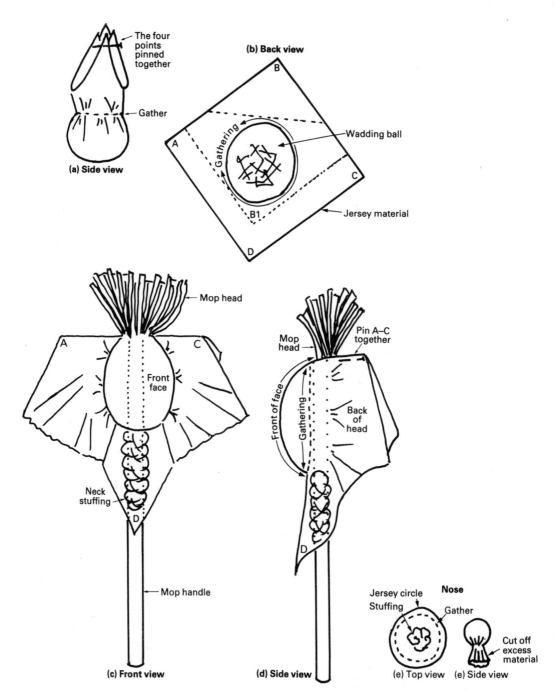

(a) Side view

The four points pinned together

Gather

(b) Back view

B

A

Gathering

Wadding ball

Jersey material

B1

C

D

(c) Front view

A

C

Mop head

Front face

Neck stuffing

D

Mop handle

(d) Side view

Mop head

Pin A–C together

Front of face

Gathering

Back of head

D

Nose

Jersey circle

Stuffing

Gather

Cut off excess material

(e) Top view   **(e) Side view**

Fig 34 A Dillar, A Dollar: (a) Side view: the wadding package encased in the 22.9cm (9in) square piece of jersey. Gather just above the wadding with the points of the square pinned together at the top. (b) Back view: showing the wadding ball encased in the jersey material. Leave point D as the neck piece. Fold point B down to B1 as dotted line. (c) Front view: the point of jersey material at D will cover the neck stuffing. Turn point D under prior to stitching the neck piece at the back of the neck. (d) Side view: Place the back of the wadding ball parallel to the mop handle and just under the mop head. Take ends A and C to the back of the handle, pin together to hold. (e) Nose: top view showing the ball of the toy filling placed in the centre of the jersey material circle which is gathered round the outside edge. Stitch to hold and cut off any excess material, see side view

mop head down to a depth of 10.3cm (4in), using toy filling and wrapping round with cotton to hold in place. Form a ball of toy filling slightly smaller than the size of a tennis ball. Lay this in the centre of the 22.9cm (9in) square of polyester wadding (batting). Fold the wadding to encase the toy filling ball and stitch to hold, making sure that all the stitching is to the back and a smooth front remains for the face.

Cut a 22.9cm (9in) square in the flesh-coloured jersey material and lay the wadding package in the centre with the smooth side downwards. Place all the points of the jersey material together and pin to hold, see Fig 34 (a). Run a gathering thread around the jersey material close to the wadding shape and pull up to gather; this will form the round shape for the head. Fasten off. Fold the top point B down to B1 at the back as shown in Fig 34 (b). Place the head on to the mop handle close to the mop head with point D facing down the handle, then take points A and C to the back of the handle and pin to hold together at the top (see Fig 34 (c) and (d)). Turn under point D and stretch the fabric to fit round the toy filling on the handle to form the neck; pin then stitch at the back of the neck, neatly turning in the raw edges. At the back of the head, trim off points A and C and any excess material, leaving sufficient material to turn in. Pull the ends tightly to place the head firmly to the handle, turn in the raw edges and neatly overstitch together.

Untie the mop head strands and bring

Fig 35 A Dillar, A Dollar Stick Puppet: Actual size features

them down around the face for the hair, trimming if necessary. Gather a 2cm (¾in) circle in the jersey material for the nose (see Fig 34 (e)). Stuff firmly into a ball, pull up the gathering and add a holding stitch. Trim off any excess material and ladder stitch to the face using Fig 35 as a guide to the correct placing. Add a dimple either side at the cheeks. Using the black fibre pen, mark in the eyes. With the brown pen draw in the freckles above the nose. A single strand straight stitch is sufficient to indicate the mouth, using flesh-coloured embroidery cotton.

Hands Cut four in the flesh-coloured jersey material. Place together in pairs. Backstitch around the outside edges, leaving the bottom straight edges open. Turn to the right side. Lightly stuff. Using overstitch close the openings. Top stab stitch to indicate the fingers. Lay to one side.

Tunic Cut a piece of the striped material to measure 50.8 x 25.4cm (20 x 10in). Turn a narrow hem on one long edge. With the right sides facing, join the 25.4cm (10in) edges. Turn to the right side. Turn in the top raw edge, and gather to fit the neck of the doll, making sure the seam is at the back. Fasten off.

Sleeves Cut two pieces each measuring 15.3 x 17.8cm (6 x 7in) in the striped material. Take one piece and with the right sides facing, fold the 17.8cm (7in) measurement in half. Join the 15.3cm (6in) edges together and turn to the right side. Turn in one end for the wrist and gather up to the width of a hand. Place a holding stitch, then insert the prepared hand into the sleeve end and stitch the gathering to the hand at the wrist. Turn in the top of the sleeve and gather to the same width as the wrist; place a holding stitch and stitch to the tunic 2cm (¾in) from the top gathering on the tunic. Treat the other arm and hand in the same way.

Collar Cut two pattern pieces in calico and turn in a narrow single hem on each (see inner dotted line on the pattern piece) and glue in place using Copydex or a similar

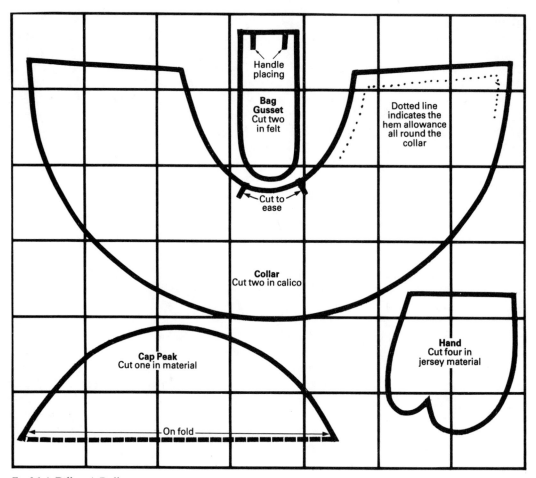

Fig 36 A Dillar, A Dollar

latex-based adhesive. Lay to one side to dry slightly. When the hems are secure but whilst still damp, lightly glue all the surface on one collar piece, then lay the collar pieces together and press with the hands to bond. If the calico used is rather coarse and the collar edges appear too bulky, then quickly – whilst the adhesive is still wet – open out the hems on one collar piece and cut away, and use this piece as it is, as an under lining with no hems. When the collar is dry, place around the puppet's neck and glue at the front by laying the corner of one top point just over on to the opposite top corner. Tie a bow in the ribbon and stitch this in place over the collar join as a neck tie; cut away excess ribbon.

Cap Cut one peak piece in the striped material, fold in half and glue together making sure the edges are well joined. Whilst still damp, form the peak into an oval. Leave to dry then trim the edges to neaten if necessary.

For the cap band, cut a piece measuring 22.9 x 5cm (9 x 2in) in the striped material. With the right sides facing, fold in half and join the long edges and one short edge. Turn to the right side, turn in the open end and press flat. Place one short edge just over the opposite short edge and stitch to join in a circle. Lay to one side.

Cut a 22.9cm (9in) diameter circle in the striped material for the crown. Gather around the outside edge and pull up to fit the cap band. Insert the gathered edges of the crown into the cap band and slip stitch in place. Fasten off. Stitch the peak to the centre front of the cap band.

In the striped material, cut a piece to measure 10.3 x 5cm (4 x 2in) for the tassel strap. With the right sides facing, fold in half lengthways and join the long edges and one short edge together. Turn to the right side. Turn in the open end and neatly over-stitch and press flat. Attach the tassel to one end. Stitch the other end to the centre of the cap with the end of the strap lying parallel to the side of the toy.

Slate Place the 9 x 10.3cm ($3\frac{1}{2}$ x 4in) piece of black Vilene on top of a piece of the tan-coloured Vilene cut to the same size. Cut out a centre piece measuring 7 x 8.3cm ($2\frac{3}{4}$ x $3\frac{1}{4}$in) from the second piece of tan-coloured Vilene to form the slate frame. Using white poster paint or emulsion paint or similar, write A B C and 4 + 4 = 8 on the slate. When dry, tuck under the puppet's right arm and stitch the tip of the right hand to the side of the tunic to hold in place.

School Bag Cut a piece of the tan-coloured felt to measure 6.4 x 12.7cm ($2\frac{1}{2}$ x 5in). Fold in half. Cut two tan felt gusset pieces and stab stitch in place either side. Cut a tan felt piece for the strap to measure 15.3 x 1.3cm (6 x $\frac{1}{2}$in) and stitch each short end to a gusset piece.

Book Fold the piece of coloured Vilene measuring 10.3 x 5cm (4 x 2in) in half. Cut several pieces of notepaper to the same size. Place a piece of strong thread round the spine of the cover and pages, and knot to secure. Using the brown fibre pen, add lines to form decoration down the outside of the book cover and print Tom Brown's School-days as the title. Place in the school bag and attach by the strap to the puppet's left hand.

Mouse Cut out the pattern pieces. Place the body pieces right sides together and back-stitch around the outside edges A to B. Insert the base with the right side facing

inside and match A–A and B–B. Backstitch around the outside edge, leaving open where indicated. Turn to the right side. Stuff firmly and ladder stitch to close the opening. Stitch the tail at B on the body. Slightly gather the straight edge of one ear piece, place a holding stitch and ladder stitch to the body where indicated. Treat the second ear in the same way.

If the toy is for a young child, apply tiny felt circles for the eyes. If using small goggle eyes, glue firmly into place where indicated; it assists adhesion if the pile is clipped where the eyes are to be applied so that the eye backs are then glued to the toy skin. Finally, using white cotton, apply whiskers on either side of the head where indicated.

Place the mouse either in the school bag, or tucked under the collar on the puppet's shoulder.

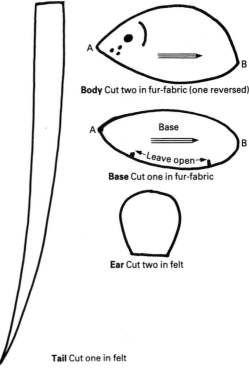

Body Cut two in fur-fabric (one reversed)

Base Cut one in fur-fabric

Ear Cut two in felt

Tail Cut one in felt

Fig 37 A Dillar, A Dollar: Actual size patterns for mouse

Birthdays

Monday's child is fair of face,
Tuesday's child is full of grace,
Wednesday's child is full of woe,
Thursday's child has far to go,
Friday's child is loving and giving,
Saturday's child works hard for a living,
But the child that is born on the Sabbath day,
Is bonny and blithe and good and gay.

* * *

Toy type: Dolls made from feather dusters (colour picture opposite)
Size of toy: Height of dolls not including the handles 25.4cm (10in)

These dolls developed as a result of seeing a container full of feather dusters in a hardware shop. The range of attractive colours certainly gave them potential, and the resulting dolls are very versatile in play, because of their long handles. They are simple in construction, require a modest amount of material, and are all basically the same; the variation being in colouring, trimmings and accessories. It is essential for the overall effect to tone fabrics and ribbons to the colouring of the feathers. Any particular material requirements are listed under each day; the basic materials are all based on Monday's child. The materials have been broken down into separate units to enable the reader to use materials they may already have. Whilst the colouring of each original model is given, the reader's choice may be decided by the colouring of the feather dusters available. If the reader wishes to economise, then it is possible to construct the feather dusters by using dowelling rod and binding coloured feathers to one end with electrical tape; Friday's child was constructed in this way as a sample of this method.

Monday's Child Fig 39 (a)
One turquoise feather duster

Turquoise patterned cotton material 91.5 x 15.3cm (36 x 6in) for the skirt
Matching cotton material 12.7 x 6.4cm (5 x 2½in) for the bodice
Matching cotton material for the sleeves, 30.5 x 12.7cm (12 x 5in)
Matching cotton material for the hat, 17.8 x 12.7cm (7 x 5in)
A 3.8cm (1½in) diameter circle of pink fur-fabric for the powder puff
A piece of felt 7.6 x 5cm (3 x 2in) for the mirror
One broderie-anglaise daisy for the mirror trimming
1¼m (49¼in) of 0.7cm (¼in) wide turquoise ribbon
A hank of yellow stranded embroidery cotton for the hair. If using an alternative, make sure the material is not too thick – it should be scaled to the size of the doll
A small amount of toy filling
A 10.3cm (4in) circumference (3.8cm (1½in) diameter) impacted cotton ball in white, cut in half. One ball will make two dolls' heads
A small bead for the nose
All-purpose adhesive
Black fibre-tipped pen
Red fibre-tipped pen
An oddment of card for the hat base

Birthdays, the feather-duster dolls (Monday's child etc)

A 2cm (¾in) diameter circle of silver baking foil for the mirror
Flesh-coloured cotton-jersey material, sufficient to cover the half of the cotton ball
Sufficient corset lace to cover a pipe cleaner
One pipe cleaner

Bodice Place the bodice piece right sides facing and join the short edges using backstitch. Turn to the right side. Fasten off. Place on to the handle and down over the shaped part which contains the tops of the feathers. Turn in a narrow hem at the bottom edge, pull up and fasten off. Turn in a narrow hem at the top edge and gather. Pull up slightly; insert some toy filling to shape the body. Pull up the gathering and fasten off.

Skirt Turn a narrow hem on one long edge of the skirt piece. With the right sides facing, join the two short edges together. Turn to the right side. Fold in the top edge and gather slightly, then place over the handle and down level to the bottom edge of the bodice. Pull up the gathering to fit and fasten to hold; the seams at the back of bodice and skirt should be placed in the same position. Slip stitch the top of the skirt to join to the bodice.

Sleeves Fold the sleeve piece in half lengthways, right sides facing. Join the long edges together using backstitch. Turn to the right side. Lay aside.

Arms Take a pipe cleaner and insert this into a piece of corset lace, cut to the same length. Apply clear all-purpose adhesive to the open ends of the corset lace and press flat. When dry, shape either end to form the hands. Fold in the ends of the previously stitched sleeve piece, until it measures 22.9cm (9in) in length. Gather to frill approximately 2.5cm (1in) in from each end and pull up to fit each wrist. Fasten off. Place the centre of the sleeve and arm combination to the centre of the bodice at the

back and stitch to hold in place. Fold the arms to the front of the doll.

Head Take one half of the impacted cotton ball and glue a tiny bead just above the centre of the curved side, for the nose. Cut a circle of the cotton-jersey material just large enough to cover the face by gathering around the outside edge, pulling it over the curved face and fastening off at the back. The jersey material must be well stretched over the face and nose to produce a firm, smooth surface. Apply adhesive down the centre back of the head in line with the handle. Glue to the handle and press down so that the chin of the face rests on the top of the bodice. When the head is dry and secure, take half of the skein of stranded embroidery cotton for the hair and glue it around the top and sides of the head at the front of the handle. Take the remaining half of the stranded cotton and glue it to the back of the handle behind the head, and arrange it so that the cotton covers the back of the head. Cut the looped ends of the cotton and leave it hanging freely. Draw in the features using the fibre pens.

Hat Cover the card hat brim with the patterned material to match the dress, gluing in place. Cut a piece of the same material to measure 17.8 x 6.4cm (7 x 2½in) for the crown. With the right sides facing, fold in half and join the short edges using backstitch. Turn to the right side. Turn a hem and gather one long edge, then pull up, leaving a circle to the diameter of the handle. Turn a hem and gather the top edge, pull up and leave the same diameter circle as the previous gathering. Cut a 25.4cm (10in) length of narrow ribbon. Place evenly across the centre of the crown lengthways. Glue to the brim. Glue the base of the crown to the brim centrally. Make a hole in the centre of the covered card brim to line up with the holes in the crown and put the hat on to the handle and down on to the doll's head. Tie the ribbon into a bow under the chin.

Powder puff Cut a 3.8cm (1½in) diameter circle of pale-pink fur-fabric. Gather around

Cock A Doodle Doo with Chook, Chook, Chook, the felt hen and chicks

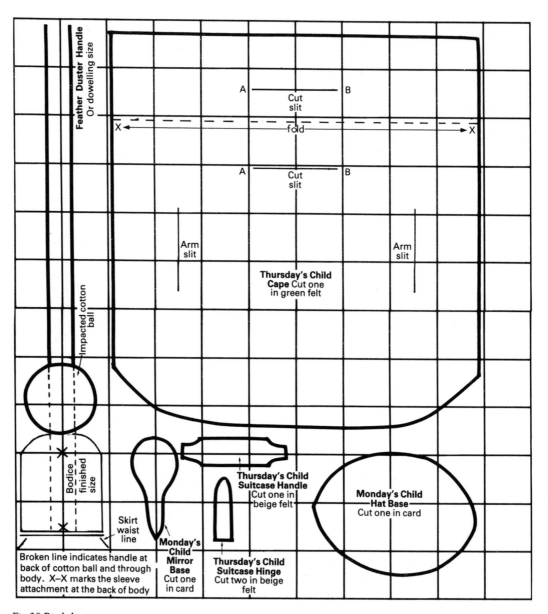

Feather Duster Handle
Or dowelling size

A ——————— B
Cut
slit

X ←————————— fold —————————→ X

A ——————— B
Cut
slit

Arm
slit

Arm
slit

Thursday's Child
Cape Cut one
in green felt

Impacted cotton
ball

Bodice
finished size

Thursday's Child
Suitcase Handle
Cut one in
beige felt

Monday's Child
Hat Base
Cut one in card

Skirt
waist
line

Monday's
Child
Mirror
Base
Cut one
in card

Thursday's Child
Suitcase Hinge
Cut two in beige
felt

Broken line indicates handle at
back of cotton ball and through
body. X–X marks the sleeve
attachment at the back of body

Fig 38 Birthdays

the outside edge, pull up slightly and stuff with toy filling. Pull up the gathering and fasten off. Glue to the doll's right hand.

Mirror Cover one side of the card shape with turquoise felt and glue into place. Apply a broderie-anglaise daisy as decoration. Cut a circle of silver baking foil and glue to the other side. Cover the handle on this side with turquoise felt. Glue the handle of the mirror to the doll's left hand. Glue one end of the remaining turquoise ribbon to the base of the feather-duster handle, placing the end just inside the top of the hat crown. Bind the ribbon around the handle in a spiral pattern, spacing it well, and glue to secure at the top. Cut off the remaining ribbon and tie in a bow. Attach this at the top of the handle to cover the glued end. The ribbon bow should be in line with the front of the doll.

Tuesday's Child Fig 39 (b)

One mauve feather duster

The material quantities for the head, arms, hair and ribbons are the same as for Monday's child, using mauve-toned materials and ribbons. The dress is made in mauve nylon. The skirt material measures 101.6 x 25.4cm (40 x 10in). The sleeves and bodice are the same as for Monday's child.

17.8cm (7in) narrow lace for the neck decoration

7.6cm (3in) mauve broderie-anglaise trimming for the crown

Tuesday's child is made in the same way as Monday's child with the following exceptions. The skirt front is gathered from the centre of the hem up to the waist, and the gathering is then pulled up and fastened off at the waist. The narrow lace is gathered on one long edge and pulled up to fit the doll's neck and fastened off at the back.

The piece of broderie-anglaise trimming for the crown is stitched into a circle and placed over the handle of the feather duster down on to the doll's head and glued into place. The front half of the hair is left hanging and the back of the hair is folded upwards to form a chignon to cover the back of the head completely.

Wednesday's Child Fig 39 (c)

One pale-blue feather duster

The patterned cotton material is black with a blue-and-pink design. The ribbons are pale pink. The hair is black. The material quantities are the same as for Monday's child except that 2m (79in) of the narrow ribbon is required

Three tiny seed pearls for the tears

A 7.6cm (3in) square of fine white material for the handkershief

As for Monday's child. Glue two seed pearls under one eye and down the cheek, and one seed pearl under the other eye, as tears. Cut around the outside edge of the handkerchief piece using pinking shears. Fold and glue it to the doll's right hand. The doll's hair is left

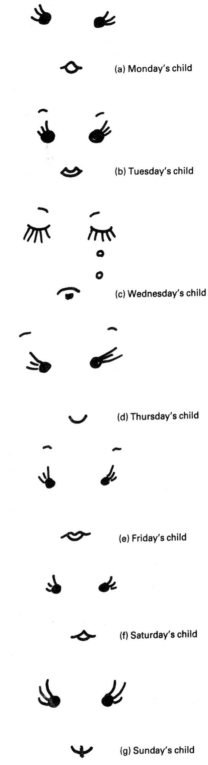

(a) Monday's child

(b) Tuesday's child

(c) Wednesday's child

(d) Thursday's child

(e) Friday's child

(f) Saturday's child

(g) Sunday's child

Fig 39 Birthdays: Actual size features

hanging in loops, with a small bow glued to the top of the head. A length of the ribbon is placed around the dolls waist and tied in a bow at the back with ribbon tails left hanging.

Thursday's Child Fig 39 (d)

One green feather duster

The patterned material is toning. The hair is light brown. The dress, head and hair are as for Monday's child. The ribbon is green

Green felt 21.5 x 21.5cm (8½ x 8½in) for the cape

A piece of pipe cleaner 12.7cm (5in) long for the umbrella

Brown felt to cover the pipe cleaner

A 17.8cm (7in) diameter circle of soft material, and sufficient narrow lace to stitch to the diameter of the circle

A piece of material matching the dress 14 x 5cm (5½ x 2in) for the dorothy bag

A 2.5cm (1in) diameter circle of green felt for the base

One small empty matchbox and sufficient oddments of beige-coloured felt to cover it for the suitcase

Oddments of black felt for the suitcase hinges and handle

Make as for Monday's child. Cut the cape pattern in the green felt. Fold the line X–X and line up both A–B slits. Place the handle of the duster through A–B and take the cape down to line up with the top of the doll's head. Place the doll's arms through the arm slits and stitch the cape fronts together at the centre front to hold in place. Join the open ends of the hood together at the back, from the base, for 5cm (2in), then stitch across the back of the hood to join. This forms a stitched 'T' shape.

Place the material for the dorothy bag right sides facing and join the short edges. Turn to the right side. Turn a hem and gather one long edge then pull up. Fasten off. Gather the opposite edge likewise. Stitch the circle of green felt over one lot of gathering, as the bag base. Make a small

loop of the narrow green ribbon, stitch it to the top of the bag and attach to the doll's right hand.

For the umbrella, cover the 12.7cm (5in) length of pipe cleaner with the brown felt and overstitch in place. Stitch the narrow lace around the edge of the 17.8cm (7in) diameter circle of soft material and pull up; do not fasten off. Cut a small hole in the centre of the material circle and place the material on to the covered pipe cleaner, letting one end protrude at the base by 1.3cm (½in). Pull up the lace gathering to fit the pipe cleaner. Fasten off. Stitch around the cut hole at the base to fit the pipe cleaner. Fasten off. Fold the top of the pipe cleaner as a handle and lay to one side.

Cover the matchbox with felt, gluing in place, for the suitcase. Add two narrow strips of black felt as the hinges and glue into place. Cut a strip of black felt as the handle, and stitch at each end to secure across the top of the case. Place on the doll's left arm. Place the umbrella in the doll's left hand and hold in place by working a few small stitches.

Friday's Child Fig 39 (e)

One pink feather duster

Material amounts are as for Monday's child. The dress is in pink satin. The hair is blonde. The ribbons are pink and cream, 1m (39½in) of each

1m (39½in) narrow cream-coloured lace for the dress trimming

A small gift-wrapped box for the birthday present

Make as for Monday's child, but before making the skirt, turn a narrow hem and trim one long edge with the narrow lace. The bodice is trimmed down the centre front with two rows of narrow lace. The dress has a cream ribbon sash tied in a bow at the back. The hair is left with loops and has a pink hair ribbon tied in a bow and glued to the top of the head. The birthday present is glued under the sleeve of the left arm.

Saturday's Child Fig 39 (f)

One orange feather duster

Material amounts are as for Monday's child. The dress is in orange checked material. The hair is dark brown. The handle ribbon and apron ties are in orange

1½m (59¼in) narrow orange coloured lace for the dress trimming

Oddment of narrow brown ribbon for the neck bow

Square of yellow felt 6.4 x 6.4cm (2½ x 2½in) for the duster

A piece of pipe cleaner 6.4cm (2½in) long for the small feather duster

A few soft white feathers

Brown embroidery cotton or similar as binding

1m (39½in) pre-gathered broderie-anglaise trimming 10.3cm (4in) wide for the apron and mob cap

Make as Monday's child, applying lace to the hem of the skirt. Cut a 22.9cm (9in) strip of the narrow lace and gather on one long edge. Place around the doll's neck and stitch to secure at the back. Tie the piece of brown ribbon into a tiny bow and stitch to the front of the dress at the neck.

Cut a piece of the broderie-anglaise trimming to measure 38.1cm (15in) for the apron. Hem both short ends. Attach ribbon ties to either side at the top. Place around the doll's waist and tie in a bow at the back.

Cut a piece of the broderie anglaise to measure 43.7 x 7.6cm (17 x 3in) for the mob cap. With the right sides facing, join the short ends. Turn to the right side. Fold in the top raw edge for 0.7cm (¼in) and gather. Place over the handle and down to within 5cm (2in) of the doll's head. Pull up and fasten off. Gather around the opposite patterned edge approximately 1.3cm (½in) from the edge. Pull up to fit the top of the doll's head and fasten off. Fold yellow felt duster and place in doll's left hand.

Bind the feathers to the pipe cleaner, then bind the entire length of the pipe cleaner using stranded cotton or similar. Stitch to the doll's right hand.

The Child That Is Born On The Sabbath Day Fig 39 (g)

One yellow feather duster

Materials are as for Monday's child. This doll is dressed in pale-yellow terylene material. The ribbons are yellow. The hair is dark brown

1¼m(49¼in) of 5.7cm(2¼in) wide white lace for the dress trimming, hat and veil

½m (19¾in) very narrow yellow ribbon

As for Monday's child. The skirt of the dress has two bands of the lace, at the front, applied after it has been attached to the bodice. The bands of lace, each measuring approximately 5.7 x 17.8cm (2¼ x 7in), are stitched to the hem at the front of the skirt with a 6.4cm (2½in) gap in-between. Then the top of each band of lace is folded over, and gathered then stitched to the waist with the edges of lace touching. A bow in the narrow ribbon, with long tails, is stitched to the centre front of the waist.

Cut a 55.9cm (22in) length of the lace. Fold in half, the 5.7cm (2¼in) measurement, and cut a slit in the fold to the size of the handle. Place on the handle and down to the top of the doll's head. Gather across the front of the head 0.7cm (¼in) in from the outside edge, leaving approximately 14cm (5½in) ungathered on either side as the veil. Pull up the gathering to fit the doll's head. Fasten off. Gather the opposite side of the lace at the back in the same way and pull up tightly or until the 14cm (5½in) veil ends hangs well together. Fasten off. Tie two small bows in the ribbon leaving 5cm (2in) tails, and stitch a bow to either end of the gathering at the front.

Cut the remaining lace to 2.5cm (1in) wide, gather the raw edge and pull up to form a rosette; stitch the short ends to join. Gather a strip of the ribbon and pull up to fit the centre of the lace rosette; stitch in place. Cut a 20.4cm (8in) strip of the very narrow ribbon. Fold in half then form small loops at the centre; stitch to hold in place. Stitch to the centre of the rosette. Stitch the rosettes to the doll's left hand.

Cock A Doodle Doo!

Cock a doodle doo!
My dame has lost her shoe,
My master's lost his fiddling stick,
And knows not what to do.

* * *

Toy type: Wired felt cockerel with embroidery (colour picture page 72)
Size of toy: Height 55.9cm (22in); length 30.5cm (12in)

For this cockerel design it was decided to use very basic embroidery stitches as a contrast to the matt felt surface, to add highlights and also to add support to the construction of the toy. It also provides added interest for a child. Another important design criterion after playability is a good 'feel' to the toy. The shaping of the body had to be suitable to fit under a young person's arm comfortably. The underbody gusset was therefore kept clear of feathers, other than embroidered ones, so that the main handling areas are uncluttered.

This cockerel is an excellent subject for using oddments of felts, so the material quantities given have been broken down into the smallest units.

Body, Wings, Tops of Legs and Tail Feathers (No 6): Dark-brown felt 68.5 x 58.4cm (27 x 23in)
Feathers:
No 1 Bright-yellow felt 10.3 x 19.2cm (4 x 7½in)
No 2 Bright-yellow felt 5 x 14cm (2 x 5½in)
No 3 Red felt 12.7 x 28cm (5 x 11in)
No 4 Mustard-coloured felt 9 x 22.9cm (3½ x 9in)
No 5 7.6 x 17.8cm (3 x 7in) each of tan, medium-brown, beige and dark-brown felt
No 7 Light-beige felt 15.3 x 25.4cm (6 x 10in)
No 8 Two in light-green felt, each measuring 15.3 x 9cm (6 x 3½in)

No 8 Two in tan-coloured felt 15.3 x 9cm (6 x 3½in)
No 9 Two in dark-beige felt, each measuring 10.3 x 5cm (4 x 2in)
Comb, Wattle and Tongue: Red felt 17.8 x 17.8cm (7 x 7in)
Claws and Leg Bases: White felt 10.3 x 10.3cm (4 x 4in)
Claw Collars: Scraps of beige-coloured felt
One pair of 10mm green or brown saftey-lock eyes
Various coloured Anchor stranded embroidery threads to tone with the colouring of the felts
Oddments of fawn or dark-yellow 4 ply knitting yarn for binding the legs
A roll of electrical tape: sufficient to bind all the wiring
One roll of 1.3cm (½in) wide white tape for binding the wires; lampshade tape is suitable or cut-up strips of sheeting
A roll or wire for the internal armature shape and the legs, to the approximate gauge of a No 12 or 13 knitting needle
The wiring has to be strong enough to support the toy without being too strong for the felt skin (wire is available in small rolls from ironmongers and DIY stores)
Toy filling
Copydex or similar latex-based adhesive

Cut out all the pattern pieces in felt.
Body Insert the safety-lock eyes into the head, placing them through an eye piece each side where indicated in Fig 41. Place the two body pieces together, pin to hold, then stab stitch around the outside top edges leaving A–B open. Stuff the head firmly making sure that the eye shanks are kept level into the head and not pushed at

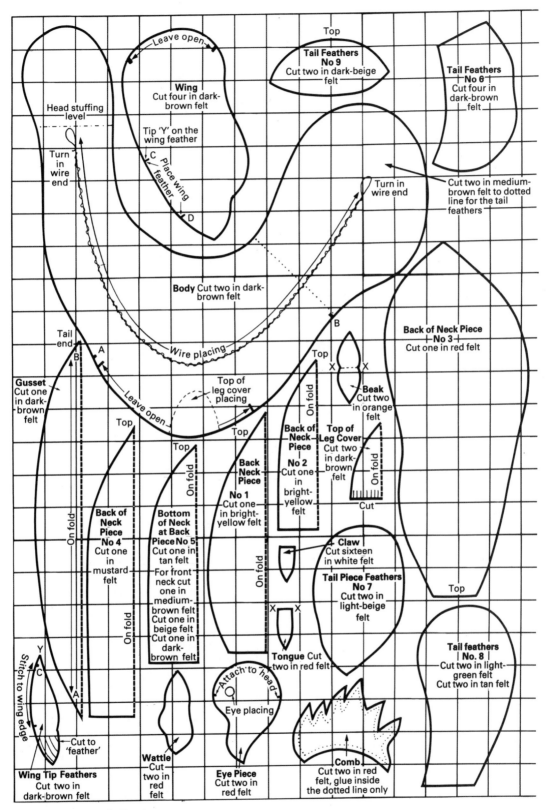

Fig 40 Cock A Doodle Doo!

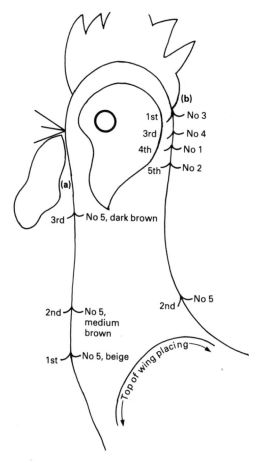

Within the figure:

(b)

1st — No 3
3rd — No 4
4th — No 1
5th — No 2

(a)

3rd — No 5, dark brown

2nd — No 5, medium brown

2nd — No 5

1st — No 5, beige

Top of wing placing

Fig 41 Cock A Doodle Doo! This diagram shows the features and feather placing. The numbers refer to the pattern pieces; the correct application order is also given. (a) Front of neck feathers: to secure the front neck feathers to the body, blanket stitch for 6.4cm (2½in) down either side from the top of piece No 2 and 9cm (3½in) either side from the top point of No 5 pieces. (b) Back of neck feathers: stitch pattern piece No 3 at the top point, to attach to the body, and lay down the back of the neck; continue the centre line of stitching for 12.7cm (5in). Apply pattern piece No 5 using blanket stitching either side of the top point for 2.5cm (1in). Attach the top points of feather pieces Nos 4, 1 and 2 to the body skin and then lay the pieces on top of one another in line down the back of the cockerel and backstitch down the centre of the feather pieces for 10.3cm (4in) to secure to the previous layers. Trim where necessary to shape. Work chain stitch highlighting on a few feathers using matching thread to the feather tones

an angle. Balance the head stuffing carefully by adding small quantities of the filling at a time and building up the bulk gradually. Stuff to a level of 7.6cm (3in) measured from the top of the head down the neck.

Cut two wires for the body armature, each measuring 48.2cm (19in), and twist together to join. Form in a curve to the body shape, making sure the ends of the wire are well turned in. Prepare as per the instructions on page 13. The neck is narrow so, when covering the wire, build up with the stuffing in this area of the wiring prior to binding with the tape; this will then almost fill the neck and only a small amount of filling will need to be inserted around the armature. As explained under the head and neck stuffing instructions, because of the small width between the eyes this area of the head is stuffed firmly without any wire support and therefore the armature starts at the throat level. Lay the prepared body wire to one side.

Legs and Feet The legs and feet are constructed as one unit with a central curve which is placed in the body. Cut four wires, each measuring 66cm (26in). Place a curve in the centre of the wires – the width at the centre of the curve should be approximately 7.6cm (3in). Bind the wires together with the adhesive tape, leaving 7.6cm (3in) free at either end. Bend three of the free 7.6cm (3in) wires upwards to the front of the shape for the front toes, and bend one wire for the back of the foot. Treat the opposite end of the wire in the same way for the other foot. Do not bend the end of these wires as one would normally do on an armature, but bind each of the toe wires very carefully, with the adhesive tape, paying particular attention to the wire ends. Complete the preparation of the wires as given in the techniques section but omitting to build up the toe wires with toy filling – simply bind with the tape on top of the adhesive tape (cutting the tape in half lengthways prior to covering will help to produce a slim line). To enable this toy to be played with, the legs are made thicker and not in true proportion to the body. Starting at the toes, bind each one carefully with the 4 ply yarn. Stitch to secure each end of the yarn to the tape; if necessary bind with the wool a second time to cover the base fully. Next bind the legs, again stitching at the start and finish. Bind a second time if necessary. The legs should be approximately 7.6cm (3in) thick, the toes approximately 3.8cm (1½in) thick.

Place the claw pieces together in pairs. Blanket stitch around the outside edges using small stitches, leaving the top straight edges open. Stuff each claw. Place a claw on to the end of each toe and overstitch to join to the tape and binding. Cut eight pieces of beige-coloured felt approximately 0.7cm (¼in) wide and long enough to fit around the toes; these are the 'collars' to be placed around the joins between the claws and the yarn binding. Working one toe at a time, lay a felt piece around the join between the claw and toe with the short ends joined underneath. Stitch the top line to the claw, then fold the 'collar' back up the toe and overstitch in place. Treat all the other claws in the same way.

You may notice on the foot and leg construction that because of stitching the yarn binding to the tape, the area at the base of the leg where the toes fan out is not very neat. This is rectified by cutting a circle of white felt just large enough to cover the area – the circle on the original model measured 2cm (¾in) in diameter. Make a small ball of toy filling large enough to fill the circle of felt, loosely gather around the outside edge of the felt and place a holding stitch. Lay this stuffed circle over the area which requires covering and neatly stitch into place. Treat the other leg in the same way.

Join the lower curve of the body wire to the top curve of leg wire construction by binding firmly with the soft tape and stitch firmly in place. To make easy working and because of the rather complex foot construction, these wires were made separately; normally an armature is constructed as one unit at the intitial stage when the uncovered wires are twisted together.

Inserting the Wire Armature Stuff the back of the neck, the top of the body and the top curve of the tail. Stand the armature upright and lower the cockerel on to it, adjusting the curve on the body wire where necessary to fit the body shape. Without disturbing the placing of the armature, insert the front of the body gusset as far as the front of the legs. Pin to hold, then stab stitch in place. Lay the cockerel on its side with the feet protruding over the edge of the working surface and firmly stuff around the body wiring, completely filling the front and top areas of the body and carefully moulding the toy filling to the felt toy skin. Ensure that the outside surface feels smooth with no unsightly lumps. Pay careful attention to the area where the end of the armature is inserted into the neck – a weakness could occur if insufficient toy filling is used.

Take the unattached piece of the body gusset between the legs and pin, then stab stitch one side of the gusset only to attach to the body. Use the opposite side as a stuffing opening and continue to build up the filling until the toy is firmly supported. Stab stitch to close the opening. Overstitch the gusset and body sides to secure to the legs. Using matching embroidery thread, blanket stitch around all the outside edges on the body. Using various toned brown and fawn embroidery threads, work strips of chain stitch on the front of the gusset and slightly darker tones of chain stitching on the back of the gusset (see Fig 42). Take one of the top leg covers, place at the side of the body centrally to the leg with the straight edge at the bottom, and blanket stitch in place. Cut a strip of the dark-brown felt to measure 2.5cm (1in) wide by the length around the leg. Cut to feather and stitch around the top of the leg to form extra leg feathers. Treat the other leg in the same way.

Wings Place together in pairs. Stab stitch around the outside edges leaving the top open. Lightly stuff. Stab stitch to close the opening. Pin the wing feathers in place, then blanket stitch all around the outside

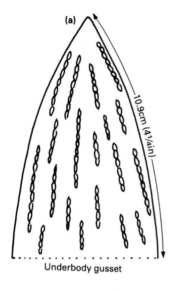

(a)

10.9cm (4¼in)

Underbody gusset

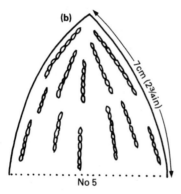

(b)

7cm (2¾in)

No 5

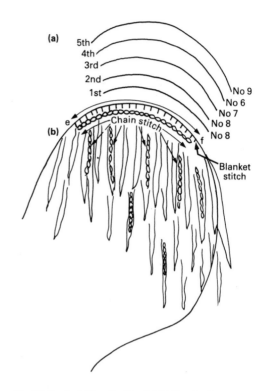

(a) 5th 4th 3rd 2nd 1st

No 9
No 6
No 7
No 8
No 8

e — Chain stitch — f

(b)

Blanket stitch

Fig 43 Cock A Doodle Doo! (a) The feather pattern pieces are placed in the order shown; duplicate coloured pieces both sides of the tail, layer on to layer, following the outline shape of the top of the tail. (b) The pieces are stitched e–f at the top of the tail in a curve to correspond with the tail shaping, using blanket stich to hold in place. Trim all the feathers at different levels to form layers and shaping

Fig 42 Cock A Doodle Doo! (a) Showing the direction lines of chain stitching on the underbody gusset. Worked at both ends of the gusset, using various brown and beige tones. Light colouring at the chest, darker tones at the bottom end. (b) Direction of the chain stitching at the top of pattern piece No 5. Worked in brown, beige and white tones. For both (a) and (b) vary the number of embroidery strands used. Work the very light tones in one strand only

edges using the blanket stitch to secure the wing to the body, and the feathers to the wing. Treat the other wing in the same way.
Comb Using Copydex or similar latex-based adhesive, glue the centre of the comb pieces together to the dotted line on the pattern, leaving all the outside areas of the comb free from adhesive. The reason for using the adhesive is that on live cockerels the comb flops over although it is firm in the centre, so making the soft toy cockerel in this way adds a touch of authenticity. Blanket stitch around the outside shaped edges of the comb using matching thread; use the blanket stitch to secure the curved base of the comb at either side to the top of the head. The blanket stitching must be small and neat. Blanket stitch around the top curve of each eye piece to attach to the head, then continue to blanket stitch leaving the base pieces hanging free.
Beak, Tongue and Wattle Place the two beak pieces together. Glue then blanket stitch around the outside edges to join. Treat the tongue pieces in the same way. Fold the beak in half across the centre and stitch the tongue in place matching X–X on each. Ladder stitch the beak to the head. Stitch the two wattle pieces together at the top

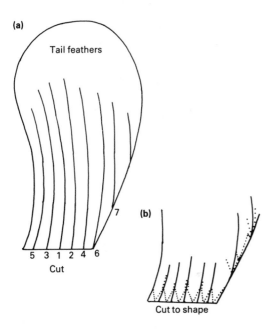

(a)

Tail feathers

7 (b)

5 3 1 2 4 6

Cut

Cut to shape

Fig 44 Cock A Doodle Doo! Feather shaping (a) To cut each neck, tail, wing or leg feather, first cut into the centre of each piece No 1, then cut No 2 etc; this produces a good line. (b) Then cut the top of each strand into a point or half point; cut at different lengths to avoid conformity

points and ladder stitch to the head just below the beak placing.

Feathers Using Figs 41 and 43, place the feathers into position at the chest, back of head and neck and on the tail. Pin into place first, before stitching to secure, as this will enable them to be moved around to obtain the correct balance to the toy. Felts vary in thickness; a thin felt may look a little sparse, in which case cut out extra feathers from the patterns and add these. The various feather pieces require cutting into individual strands to simulate feathers – see Figs 44, 45, 46, 47 which show the correct cutting angles. The chain stitching is added where necessary to add highlights; vary the number of strands used as this will add visual depth to the toy. Finally, add blanket stitching to the top curve of the chest feathers and also along the top edge of the tail feathers.

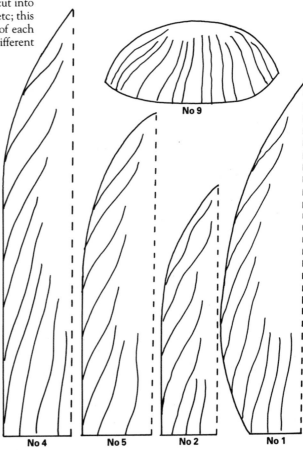

No 9

Fig 45 See overleaf

No 4   No 5   No 2   No 1

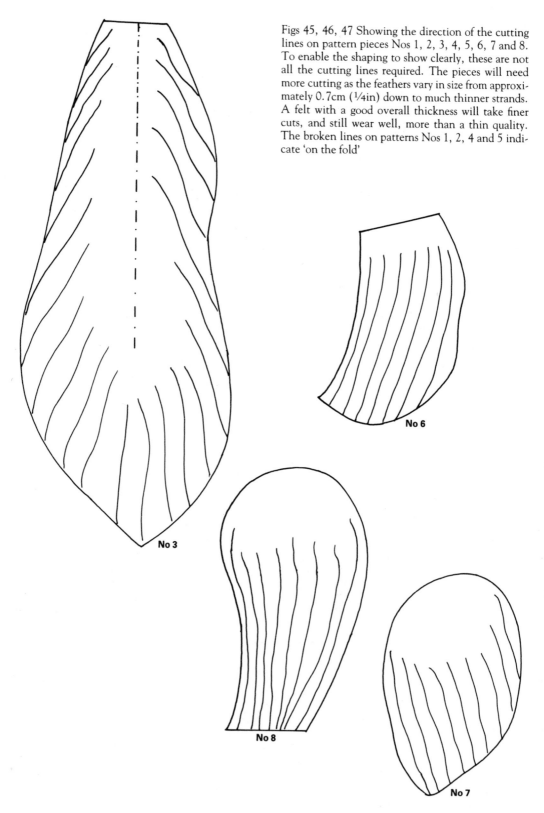

Figs 45, 46, 47 Showing the direction of the cutting lines on pattern pieces Nos 1, 2, 3, 4, 5, 6, 7 and 8. To enable the shaping to show clearly, these are not all the cutting lines required. The pieces will need more cutting as the feathers vary in size from approximately 0.7cm (¼in) down to much thinner strands. A felt with a good overall thickness will take finer cuts, and still wear well, more than a thin quality. The broken lines on patterns Nos 1, 2, 4 and 5 indicate 'on the fold'

No 6

No 3

No 8

No 7

I Had a Little Hen

I had a little hen,
The prettiest ever seen,
She washed me the dishes,
And kept the house clean.

* * *

Toy type: A decoratively trimmed basic-shaped hen (colour picture page 54)
Size of toy: Height 17.8cm (7in); length 15.3cm (6in)

This toy would make an attractive addition to a girl's bedroom, and it also makes an excellent container for an Easter egg. It permits the toymaker to be imaginative and is a useful way of using oddments from a box of trimmings, though quantities are given. The original model was made in a brown cotton material with a tiny flowered pattern in cream. The trimmings were brown ribbon, cream lace, brown felt and brown velvet. It is essential to tone all the trimmings to the body material used.

Small-print cotton material for the body, 43.7 x 35.5cm (17 x 14in)
A piece of smooth strong card for the body base lining, 10.3 x 5.7cm (4 x 2¼in)
Scrap of felt for the beak
Four pipe cleaners
Felt for wing decoration, 10.3 x 10.3cm (4 x 4in)
Velvet for wing decoration, two 7.6cm (3in) diameter circles
3½m (138¼in) of 1.3cm (½in) wide ribbon for wing, head, neck and tail decoration (preferably satin ribbon which shows up well against the matt surface of the body)
1¼m (49¼in) of 1.3cm (½in) wide lace for wing, comb and tail decoration
Optional extra trimmings: On the original model a small gold leaf-shaped sequin was added to either end of the wings as top decoration. The eyes were made from a round sequin with brown brocatelle beads glued to the outside edge and a gold brocatelle bead in the centre. Patterned buttons could be used for the eyes, size approximately 0.7cm (¼in) diameter circle
Toy filling

Cut out the pattern pieces for the body, wings and base. Cut the card base to the inner line on the pattern. Place the side body pieces together right sides facing, and if possible, machine stitch around the outside edges to join. Snip into any curves to ease, then turn to the right side. Lay the card base in the centre of the base material and gather around the outside edge. Pull up tightly and fasten off. Stuff the body evenly and firmly. Turn in the base edge and stitch, using very small stitches. Insert the covered base into the base of the body, and pin to hold. Overstitch neatly to join the base to the body; before finally closing, insert more toy filling, carefully filling all areas. Close and fasten off.

Beak and Head Fold the cone in half and overstitch the straight edges to join. Stitch to the head where indicated.

Neatly stitch the 1.3cm (½in) wide satin ribbon as shown in Fig 49, on both sides of the head. Gather a 22.9cm (9in) length of the ribbon on one edge only and pull up to form a rosette; place a holding stitch and stitch to the head for the eye surround. Make a second rosette in the same way for the other eye, and apply. Stitch a small decorative button to the centre of each rosette for the eyes.

Comb Gather a 38.1cm (15in) length of the ribbon on one edge, then fold in half; the comb should now measure approximately 6.4cm (2½in). Stitch to the top of the head

85

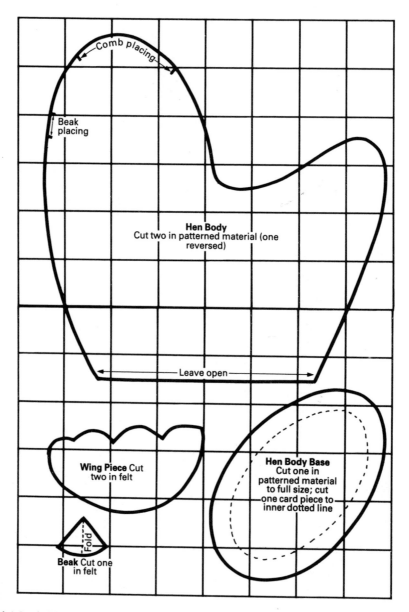

Comb placing

Beak
placing

Hen Body
Cut two in patterned material (one
reversed)

Leave open

Wing Piece Cut
two in felt

Hen Body Base
Cut one in
patterned material
to full size; cut
one card piece to
inner dotted line

Fold

Beak Cut one
in felt

Fig 48 I Had A Little Hen

where indicated. Gather a 35.5cm (14in) length of the lace and pull up to the length required to encase the base of the ribbon comb. Stitch to secure.

Tail Cut a 50.8cm (20in) length of the ribbon, fold in half and pin a central loop of 3.8cm (1½in); pin to secure then stitch to hold either side of the base of the loop. Fold second loops either side of the first to a size of 2cm (¾in) and place these to leave 1.3cm (½in) of the top loop showing. Stitch at either side of these loops to secure. Form two more loops in the same way leaving 1.3cm (½in) of the second loops showing. Stitch to the tail, leaving the ribbon ends hanging on to the body. Tie a bow to measure, finished size, 6.4cm (2½in) and place this at the back of the tail where indicated. Gather a 28cm (11in) piece of the lace, pull up and fit around the base of the

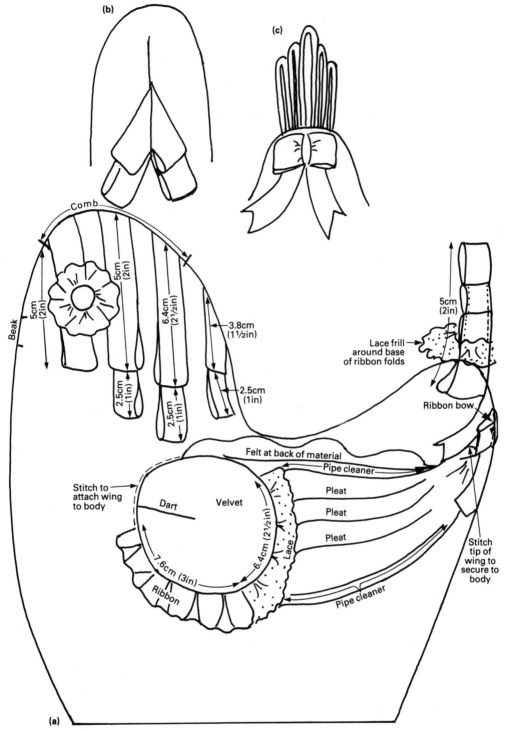

Fig 49 I Had A Little Hen (not to scale): (a) Diagram showing placing of decoration on to the body; (b) Back of head at base showing the folding of the neck ribbon; (c) Back view of the tail showing the ribbon folds and ribbon bow placing. The lace frill has been omitted in this diagram to enable the ribbons to be clearly defined

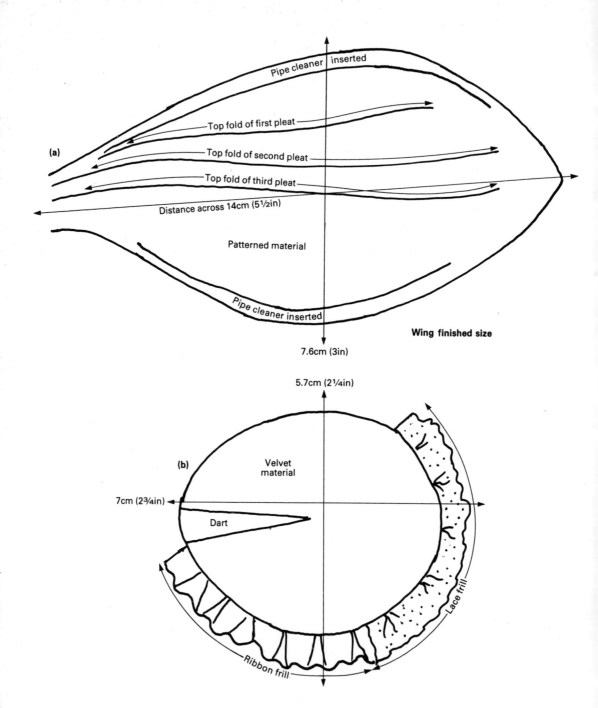

(a)

Pipe cleaner inserted

Top fold of first pleat

Top fold of second pleat

Top fold of third pleat

Distance across 14cm (5½in)

Patterned material

Pipe cleaner inserted

Wing finished size

7.6cm (3in)

5.7cm (2¼in)

(b)

Velvet material

7cm (2¾in)

Dart

Lace frill

Ribbon frill

Fig 50 I Had A Little Hen: Wing diagrams

Pussycat, Pussycat string puppet; *(and below)* Cocks Crow and Hickety Pickety My Fair Hen, glove puppets

tail ribbon loops; fasten off.

Wings Cut two 15.3 (6in) diameter circles in the patterned material. Take one piece and turn a narrow hem around the outside edge, inserting a pipe cleaner, cut to 15.3cm (6in), on one side, and a second pipe cleaner cut to the same size on the other; when the wing piece is folded, the pipe cleaners will form the top and bottom edges of the wings. Pleat across the wing as shown on Fig 50 (a), pin to hold, then slip stitch to hold in place without pressing the pleats too flat.

Cut two 7.6cm (3in) diameter circles in toning velvet. Take one piece and dart as shown. Gather around the outside edge, pull up slightly and lightly stuff. The velvet piece should fit the front of the wing, see Fig 49. Fasten off. Gather a 25.4cm (10in) length of the lace and pull up to fit the inner curve of the velvet piece (see Fig 50 (b)), fasten off and stitch to the velvet piece. Gather a 25.4cm (10in) length of the ribbon, pull up and stitch to the lower edge

of the velvet piece. Stitch the felt wing pattern piece behind the wing at the top, leaving the top shaped edge showing. Make a second wing in the same way and apply to the body, making sure you reverse the pieces for the opposite side of the body. Finally, add any extra trimmings, for example sequins, to complement those already applied. Be careful at this stage not to over-trim which could make the hen look very cluttered. A lace apron can also look pretty, depending on the intended use.

Apron Gather and pull up a 40.6cm (16in) length of 5.7cm (2¼in) wide coffee-coloured lace until it measures 9cm (3½in). Fasten off. Turn in a narrow hem at each end. Cut in half ¼m (10in) of very narrow brown ribbon. Make a loop at one end of a ribbon piece and stitch to one side of the apron at the top gathered edge, then treat the opposite tie in the same way. Place on the front of the hen, take a ribbon tie under each wing on either side and tie off on the back in a bow.

Little Bo-Peep

Little Bo-Peep has lost her sheep,
And doesn't know where to find them,
Leave them alone, and they'll come home,
Bringing their tails behind them.

✳ ✳ ✳

Toy type: Stump doll and lambs (colour picture page 54)
Size of toy: Doll height (top of head to hem on dress) 40.6cm (16in)

Stump dolls have no legs, which makes a good design for this toy as Bo-Peep has a skirt with pockets underneath in which are placed her lost lambs. Turn her upside down

and the skirt reverses over her head and the lambs are found.

Bo-Peep
Calico for the body and arms, 30.5 x 38.1cm (12 x 15in)
Plain lemon-coloured lightweight material for the skirt, blouse, hat lining and sleeve frills, 76.2 x 55.9cm (30 x 22in)
Lemon-and-green patterned cotton-type material for the overskirt, sleeves and hat, 76.2 x 53.3cm (30 x 21in)

Little Miss Muffet and her Spider, string puppets

Piece of interlining 22.9 x 10.3cm (9 x 4in)

Light-green fine wool or mixture fabric for the underskirt and pockets, to simulate green grass

Black felt for bodice, 20.4 x 5cm (8 x 2in)

1m (39½in) of 1.3cm (½in) wide lemon ribbon for the plaits and the crook

2m (79in) of 1.3cm (½in) green ribbon for the hat ties, wrist ribbons and crook

1m (39½in) very narrow green ribbon for the edge of the hat

One hank of light-coloured angel hair

Embroidery cotton for the features in black, white, fawn, beige and green

Toy filling

Small hank of Turabast (synthetic raffia) or garden raffia for binding the crook

Wire for the crook 45.7cm (18in) long, strong but flexible

Head and Body Cut out the pattern pieces. With the right sides facing, pin then backstitch or machine stitch around the outside edge a 0.7cm (¼in) seam, leaving the bottom straight edge open. Turn to right side. Stuff firmly and ladder stitch closed.

Arms Place together in pairs, pin then backstitch or machine stitch around the outside edges, leaving the top straight edges open. Turn to the right side. Stuff firmly and close the opening using ladder stitch.

Blouse In the plain lemon material, cut a piece to measure 38.1 x 15.3cm (15 x 6in). With the right sides facing, fold in half and join the 15.3cm (6in) edges. Turn to the right side. Fold in a narrow hem at the top and gather slightly. Place on the doll's body with the 15.3cm (6in) seam at the centre back, pull up the gathering to fit the neck and fasten off. Fold in a narrow hem at the bottom and pull up the gathers to cover the base of the body. Fasten off. In the light-green woollen material, cut a piece to measure 25.4 x 7.6cm (10 x 3in). With the right sides facing, fold in half and stitch the 7.6cm (3in) edges together. Fasten off. Place the 7.6cm (3in) seam centrally on the material and backstitch one long edge together. Fasten off. Turn to the right side.

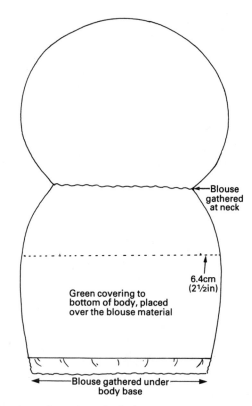

Blouse gathered at neck

6.4cm (2½in)

Green covering to bottom of body, placed over the blouse material

Blouse gathered under body base

Fig 51 Little Bo-Peep: Body diagram

Place this pocket-shaped piece on the bottom of the body with the seam at the back. Turn in the top raw edge for approximately 1.3cm (½in) and stitch to the blouse and body around this top edge using slip stitch.

Underskirt and Top Skirt Cut one piece of the green material to measure 76.2 x 30.5cm (30 x 12in). Cut one piece in the lemon material to the same measurements.

Cut two pieces of the green material, each measuring 28 x 12.7cm (11 x 5in). Turn a hem on one long edge of each piece, also hem the short edges. Stitch one pocket piece to each end of the green underskirt piece on the right side, lining up the side seams and bottom hems. Stitch down the centre of each pocket piece to make a total of four pockets. Place the green underskirt and the lemon top skirt right sides facing; pin then backstitch together, leaving the top straight edges open. Turn to the right sides. Fold in a hem at the top of each piece

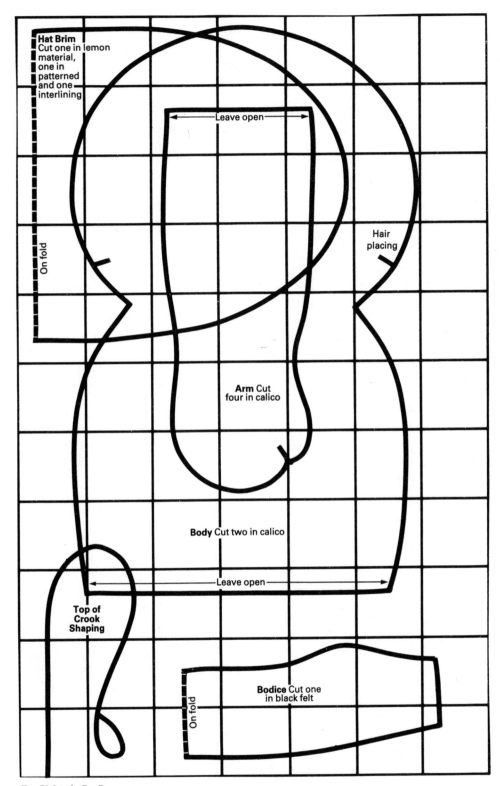

Hat Brim Cut one in lemon material, one in patterned and one interlining

On fold

Leave open

Hair placing

Arm Cut four in calico

Body Cut two in calico

Leave open

Top of Crook Shaping

Bodice Cut one in black felt

On fold

Fig 52 Little Bo-Peep

then gather to fit the doll's waist, approximately 25.4cm (10in), securing the green skirt to the top of the green material-covered body base and the yellow skirt to the blouse. Joining these skirt pieces to their respective materials on the body separately enables the skirts to be turned easily from one side to the other.

Patterned Overskirt In the patterned material cut a piece to measure 76.2 x 25.4cm (30 x 10in). Hem one long edge. With the right sides facing, fold in half and join the 25.4cm (10in) edges together. Turn to the right side. With the seam at the centre front of the body, turn in a hem at the top edge and gather to fit the body. Stitch around body and blouse to join; fasten off. Gather front-centre seam, pull up firmly; fasten off.

Bodice Cut the bodice pattern in black felt and place around the body at the top just above the overskirt gethering. Turn in a hem at the front two short edges and, using stranded embroidery thread, lace the bodice together, tying the ends in a small bow at the centre waist.

Arms and Sleeves In the patterned material, cut two pieces to measure 20.4 x 12.7cm (8 x 5in). Take a piece for each sleeve and turn a hem on one long side. With the right sides facing, fold in half and join the 12.7cm (5in) edges together. Turn to the right side. Take one of the sleeves and with the seam under the arm and the hemmed long edge at the top, place the sleeve on to an arm. Turn in a hem at the raw edge of the sleeve and gather to fit the wrist. Fasten off. Gather the top hemmed edge and stitch to the black-felt bodice and through the blouse to the body approximately 1.3cm (½in) down from the neck. The arm hangs loosely in the sleeve and is not attached to the body to enable it to swing easily when the doll is reversed. Repeat for other sleeve and arm.

Cut two pieces in the lemon material, each measuring 33 x 7.6cm (13 x 3in), one for each sleeve frill. Take one piece and with the right sides facing, fold in half lengthways. Join the two side edges each end. Turn to the right side. Fold in the top

raw long edges and gather to fit the wrist with the short ends at the outside of the arm. Fasten off. Stitch to secure to the gathered wrist edge of the patterned sleeve. Treat the other frill in the same way on the opposite arm. Tie a piece of the green ribbon around each wrist to cover the gathering and tie each piece in a small bow.

Hair Place the hank of angel hair evenly across the top of the head from side to side. Stitch to the head as a centre parting, and at either side where indicated on the pattern. Plait the hair and secure at the ends with small elastic bands. Cover the bands with the narrow lemon ribbon and tie small bows.

Features Lightly draw the features in pencil on the face, using Fig 53. All the features are embroidered using single strands of stranded embroidery cotton. Embroider the eyebrows in black short stitches. The outline of the eyes is in fawn-coloured chain stitch. The eyes are green circles worked in chain stitch, the pupils black French knots. The eyelids are white and worked in chain stitch. The nose and mouth are in beige tiny straight stitches, the nostrils are two French knots. The eyelashes are in black straight stitches.

Hat To make the brim, cut one pattern piece in the plain lemon material, one piece in the patterned material, and one piece in Vilene or similar interlining approximately 0.7cm (¼in) smaller all round than the pattern. Cover the interlining with the lemon material using Copydex or similar latex-based adhesive, gluing around the edges only and folding the material edges over the interlining. Cover the other side of

Fig 53 Little Bo-Peep: Actual size features

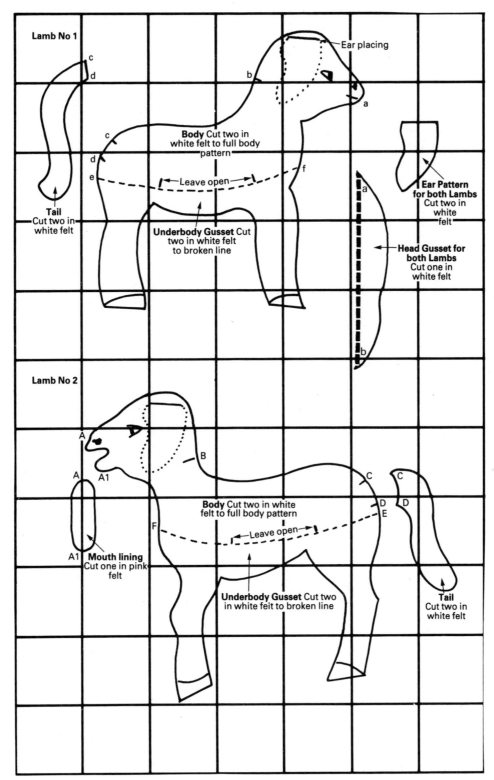

Fig 54 Little Bo-Peep: Lambs

the interlining with the patterned material, but folding the edge in and gluing to the interlining. When dry, glue the very narrow green ribbon around the edge of the brim to mask the joins.

To make the crown, cut a piece of the patterned material to measure 66 x 6.4cm (26 x 2½in). With the right sides facing, fold in half and join the short edges together. Turn to the right side, fold in a hem on one long edge and gather tightly. Fasten off. Gather the opposite long edge in the same way. Fasten off.

Cut a piece of the green ribbon to measure 101.6cm (40in). Lay across the hat brim on the patterned side (the longer measurement) and placed centrally. Glue at the centre of the brim for 10.3cm (4in). Take the gathered hat crown and glue the gathered circle on the crown on top of the ribbon at the centre of the brim to secure. Tie the ribbon ends into a bow and stitch the bow at the centre front of the body at the base of the felt bodice.

Crook Bend the piece of wire into the pattern shape, see Fig 51, taking care to turn the sharp ends in firmly. Bind with tape. Cover with the Turabast or garden raffia by binding tightly, taking care to secure the ends firmly. Stitch to secure to the left hand of the doll. Tie a green bow on the crook just below the hand position, and immediately underneath this, tie and knot a lemon ribbon leaving the tails hanging.

Lambs

Each lamb requires a piece of white felt measuring 28 x 20.4cm (11 x 8in)
A scrap of pink felt for mouth lining of Lamb No 2
Black Anchor stranded embroidery cotton
Terylene or lightweight toy filling

Cut out all the pattern pieces in white felt.
Lamb No 1 Place the two body pieces together. Overstitch from a at nose to f. Insert the head gusset matching a–b on the gusset to a–b on the body; pin then overstitch in place. Continue overstitching down the top

of the body to e. Place the two underbody gussets between the body pieces, matching e–f on the gusset to e–f on the body; pin together, leaving the base of each foot open and where indicated on the underbody gusset. Overstitch in place. Partially stuff the head and body. Gradually close the underbody opening using ladder stitching; as you close the opening, insert more toy filling making sure the body is firmly stuffed without adding too much strain on the stitching. Felt is composed of impacted fibres so the seams will split open if too much pressure is placed upon them.

Using minute quantities of filling, gradually stuff the legs, paying particular attention to the top of each leg before proceeding to the base of each leg. Felt varies considerably in texture, some qualities stretching more than others. When each leg is filled sufficiently, cut an oval of white felt to fit each leg base. Overstitch in place.

Overstitch the ears in place where indicated on the pattern. Overstitch both tail pieces together leaving the end c–d open. Using small quantities of toy filling, stuff the tail, then ladder stitch to the body at c–d.

Using two strands of stranded embroidery cotton, work straight stitches for the nose and eyes using the pattern as a guide to correct placing; work a slightly curved mouth. Work straight stitches as filling for the hooves, as shown on the pattern.

Lamb No 2 This is constructed in the same way as Lamb No 1 with the exception that this lamb has an open mouth with the pink mouth lining inserted, matching A–A1 on the body to A–A1 on the mouth lining; therefore when constructing the body, overstitch A1–F together, insert the head gusset A–B and then the mouth lining A–A1

Make any four lambs and place one in each pocket of the doll's underskirt. When the skirt is turned upside down over the doll's head the lambs appear; if left hanging as the doll's skirt, the lambs are hidden and lost as the nursery rhyme states.

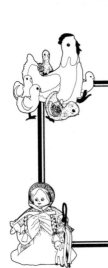

PUPPETS

Cocks Crow

Cocks crow in the morn to tell us to rise,
And he who lies late will never be wise,
For early to bed and early to rise,
Makes a man healthy, wealthy and wise.

* * *

Toy type: Glove puppet (colour picture page 89)
Size of toy: Height 30.5cm (12in)

White short-pile fur-fabric 60.9 x 24.1cm (24 x 9½in) for the puppet glove
White felt 34.3 x 29.9cm (13½ x 11¾in) for the neck, tail and wing feathers
Bright-red felt 7.6 x 9cm (3 x 3½in) for the comb, tongue and throttle
Yellow felt 3.8 x 4.5cm (1½ x 1¾in) for the beak
One pair of green 12mm safety-lock eyes
Toy filling

Cut out the pattern pieces and make the basic glove as for The Farmer's Wife, page 123. Construct the head and apply as for Hickety, Pickety, My Fine Hen, page 100, with the addition of a red-felt tongue glued to the inside of the beak on the centre fold.
Tail With the right sides facing, place the two fur-fabric tail pieces together and pin then backstitch around the outside edge, leaving the straight edge open. Turn to the right side. Lightly stuff and ladder stitch to

Fig 55 Cocks Crow and Hickety, Pickety: Feature placing

the centre back of the puppet glove with the bottom curved seam 5cm (2in) up from the straight edge on the glove. Cut two duplicate tail pieces in the white felt adding 7.6cm (3in) to the length of the pieces at the bottom. Stitch the two felt pieces together around the top curve and stitch to

97

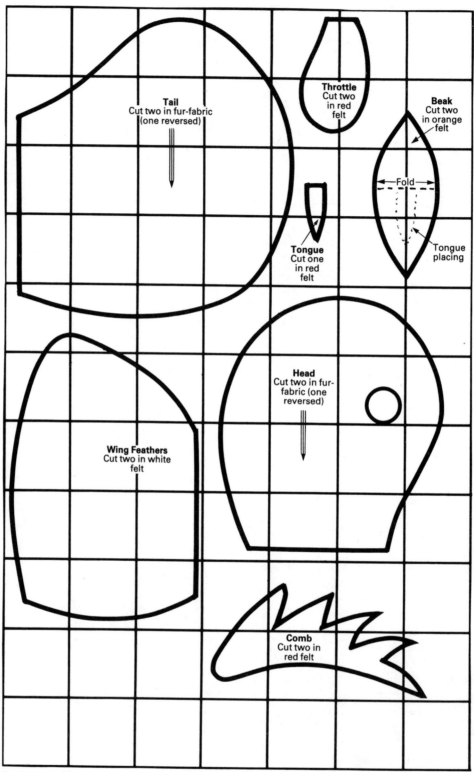

Fig 56 Cocks Crow

the matching curve on the fur-fabric tail piece. Cut into the felt in strands to within 3.8cm (1½in) of the top curve.

Feathers Cut two pieces of white felt measuring 11.5 x 19.2cm (4½ x 7½in) long for the neck. Shape and cut (see Fig 57). Place one on top of the other and stitch to the back of the head from where the comb ends, continuing down the centre back of the puppet glove.

Stitch the straight edge of a wing feather piece along the top seam of each puppet arm. Cut to feather.

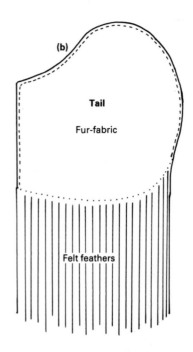

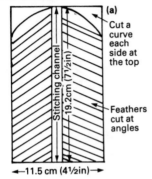

Fig 57 Cocks Crow Glove Puppet: (*left*) neck feathers in felt; (*above*) tail feathers in fur-fabric

Hickety, Pickety, My Fine Hen

Hickety, pickety, my fine hen,
She lays eggs for gentlemen,
Gentlemen come every day,
To see what my fine hen doth lay,
Sometimes nine and sometimes ten,
Hickety, pickety, my fine hen.

* * *

Toy type: Glove puppet with eggs and chicks (colour picture page 89)
Size of toy: Height 30.5cm (12in)

This hen puppet has ten felt eggs each containing a chick. The eggs are numbered to enable them to be used as a counting toy.

Ginger-brown short-pile fur-fabric 50.1 x 24.1cm (19¾ x 9½in) for the puppet glove
Ginger-brown felt 25.4 x 20.4cm (10 x 8in) for the neck, tail and wing feathers
Bright-red felt 7.6 x 9cm (3 x 3½in) for the comb and throttle
Yellow felt 3.8 x 4.5cm (1½ x 1¾in) for the beak
One pair of brown 10mm safety-lock eyes

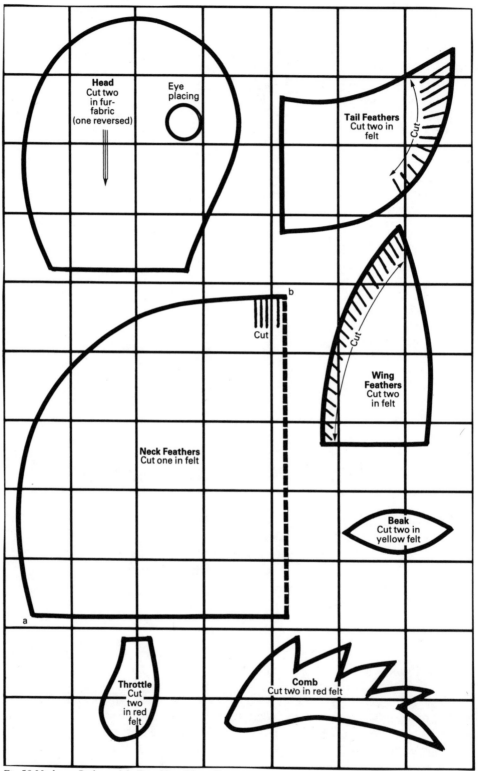

Fig 58 Hickety, Pickety, My Fine Hen Glove Puppet

Oddments of cream, brown or white felt for the eggs; each requires a piece 7.6 x 10.3cm (3 x 4in)

Brown stranded embroidery cotton

Oddments of yellow felt for the chicks; each requires a piece 5 x 10.3cm (2 x 4in)

Scraps of orange felt for the chicks' beaks and feet

A small basket with a handle, measuring approximately 6.4cm deep x 7.6cm top diameter (2½ x 3in)

A larger basket with small handles either side, depth 7.6 x 10.9cm top diameter (3 x 4¼in)

A small quantity of packing straw to line the baskets

Cut out all the pattern pieces. The glove is as for the The Farmer's Wife, page 123. Place the two glove pieces together with the right sides facing. Pin then stitch around the out-side edge, leaving the bottom straight edge open. Turn to the right side.

Head With the right sides facing, pin then stitch around the outside edge, leaving the bottom straight edge open. Turn to the right side and insert the safety-lock eyes. Stuff the head lightly and apply to the glove, stitching the neck edge to the glove; before finally closing, add more filling to produce a firm head, taking care not to obstruct the passage in the top of the glove.

Glue the two comb pieces together with Copydex or a similar adhesive, leaving the curved bottom edge free from the adhesive. When dry, ladder stitch to the top of the head along the adhesive-free edge.

Glue the two beak pieces together and fold the beak in half with the points level; whilst the adhesive is still damp curve the beak to shape.

Stitch the two throttle pieces together

Fig 59 Hickety, Pickety: Actual size chick and egg shell

along the straight edge and ladder stitch to the head underneath the beak.

Feathers Gather the top straight edge of the neck feathers and secure around the neck with the open seam at the back. Cut various size strands in the felt from the bottom edge to simulate feathers.

The short straight end piece on each of the wing feathers is stitched to the back of each puppet glove arm, leaving 5cm (2in) protruding. Cut where indicated.

Place the two tail pattern pieces together and cut where indicated, then glue the uncut areas together leaving the straight edges free from the adhesive. When dry, ladder stitch to the glove at the centre of the back at the base, with the point of the feathers facing to the top of the glove.

Eggs Place together in pairs. Overstitch to join curve A–B. Make ten. Work the numbers one to ten inclusive on one side of each shell using dark-brown stranded embroidery cotton and chain stitch.

Chicks Make ten chicks, each in the following way. Place body pieces together in pairs; overstitch around the outside edge, inserting toy filling prior to closing. Cut two wings for each bird and cut where indicated; overstitch to apply to the body at C–D on either side. Cut triangle shapes in orange felt for the feet and cut to shape; stitch to the body where indicated. Cut one beak in orange felt and stitch across the centre to the body at E. Cut tiny circles in black felt for the eyes and stitch in place.

Place the eggs and chicks into the baskets. The hen can be left as constructed or could have a white broderie-anglaise apron, made as for Little Miss Muffet with a slight adjustment in size.

Horsey, Horsey

Horsey, horsey don't you stop,
Just let your feet go clippety clop,
The tail goes swish, and the wheels go round,
Giddy-up we're homeward bound.

✳ ✳ ✳

Toy type: Horse and farmer boy glove puppets (colour picture page 107)

Size of toy: Horse height approximately 40.6cm (16in); farmer boy height approximately 40.6cm (16in)

Horse

Beige short-pile fur-fabric 60.9 x 48.2cm (24 x 19in) for the puppet glove, head and ears

Fawn felt 11.5 x 14cm (4½ x 5½in) for the ear lining and tail

Dark-brown felt 5 x 3.8cm (2 x 1½in) for the eyelashes

White felt 5 x 5cm (2 x 2in) for the eye bases

Two 2.5cm (1in) diameter circles of brown felt for the nostrils

Black felt 9 x 10.3cm (3½ x 4in) for the hooves

Blonde shaggy long-pile acrylic fur-fabric 14cm wide x 25.4cm long (5½ x 10in) for the mane, tail and hoof trimmings

One pair of brown 16mm safety-lock eyes

Toy filling

Cut out all the pattern pieces, and make the basic fur-fabric glove as for The Farmer's Wife, page 123.

Head Place the two head pieces together with the right sides facing. Pin, then stitch them together around the outside edge, leaving the straight edge at the neck open.

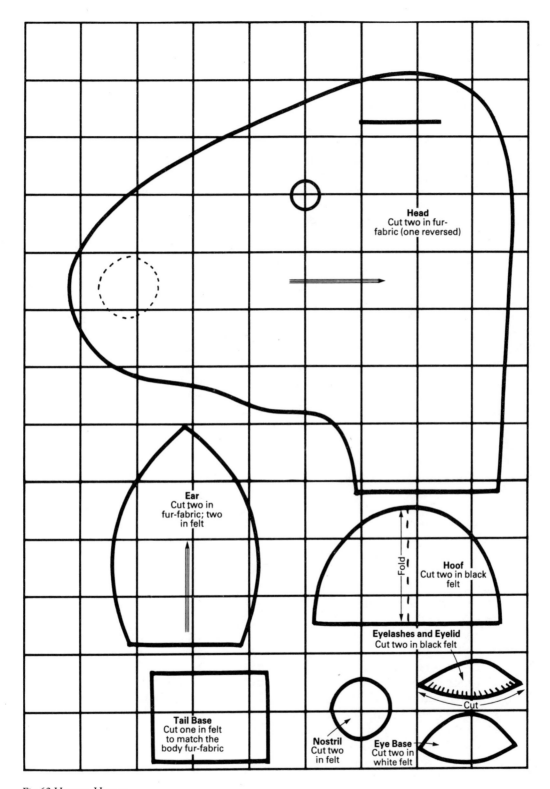

Head
Cut two in fur-
fabric (one reversed)

Ear
Cut two in
fur-fabric; two
in felt

Fold

Hoof
Cut two in black
felt

Eyelashes and Eyelid
Cut two in black felt

Cut

Tail Base
Cut one in felt
to match the
body fur-fabric

Nostril
Cut two
in felt

Eye Base
Cut two in
white felt

Fig 60 Horsey, Horsey

Turn to the right side. Insert the safety-lock eyes, with an eye base behind each one. Stuff the head firmly and apply to the glove. Stitch an eyelash piece immediately above each eye, stitching to the head at the top curve only. Stitch the nostrils to either side of the nose.

Place the ears together in pairs, consisting of one fur-fabric and one felt lining for each ear. With the right side of the fur-fabric inside, pin and then stitch together around the outside edge, leaving the bottom straight edge open. Turn to the right side. Overstitch along the bottom edge and pull up gently to form a curve; place a holding stitch and fold the ear in half. Ladder stitch to the head. Treat the other ear in the same way.

Mane Cut a piece of the shaggy-pile fur-fabric 6.4cm wide x 25.4cm long (2½ x 10in). Pin one narrow end 2.5cm (1in) in front of the ears and place between the ears with the pile line facing down the neck. Pin then ladder stitch down either side of the back seam.

Hooves Fold a hoof piece in half and over-stitch the edges together around the curve, leaving the bottom straight edge open. Stuff firmly and ladder stitch to the end of one of the puppet arms. Treat the other hoof in the same way. Cut two pieces of the shaggy-pile fur-fabric 10.3cm wide x 2.5cm long (4 x 1in), and with the pile line facing the end of each hoof, place one around each hoof where it is joined to the body. The joins in the shaggy fur-fabric pieces should be underneath each puppet arm in line with the under seam.

Tail Cut a piece of the shaggy fur-fabric to measure 7.6cm wide x 15.3cm long (3 x 6in). With the wrong sides facing, ladder stitch the edges together down the 15.3cm (6in) measurement on the right side. Take a 3.8 x 5.7cm (1½ x 2¼in) piece of fawn felt and roll it round the top of the tail piece, stitching the felt to hold it in a roll and also stitching it securely to the shaggy tail material. Ladder stitch to the base of the glove at the centre back.

Tom The Farmer's Boy

Flesh or beige-coloured felt 92.1 x 35.5cm (36¼ x 14in) for the puppet glove, head and legs

Oddments of felts for the features

Pink and light-brown embroidery cotton

Oddments of blonde-coloured long-pile acrylic fur-fabric for the hair

Brown felt for the hat; the crown 10.3 x 17.8cm (4 x 7in), the brim a 15.3cm (6in) diameter circle

A triangular piece of material for the scarf, 35.5cm (14in) along the top edge x 17.8cm (7in) to the centre-back point

Plain cotton material in dark brown 68.5 x 20.4cm (27 x 8in) for the smock

A piece of light-brown material 17.8 x 33cm (7 x 13in) for the trouser legs

Dark-brown felt 20.4 x 15.3cm (8 x 6in) for the boots

Thin cord or strong thread for the boot laces

A piece of natural-coloured hessian 22.9 x 12.7cm (9 x 5in) for the sack

Small quantity of dried grass or straw

Pink fibre-tipped pen

Toy filling

Cut out all the relevant pattern pieces – see Fig 74. The puppet glove, hat, trouser legs and boots are made as for the Farmer from The Farmer's in his Den, page 123.

Features and Hair Cut two eyes in dark-brown felt and glue into place. Draw the eyebrows in pink fibre-tipped pen. Work the mouth in a deeper pink tone to the skin felt, using one strand of embroidery cotton and stem stitch.

Gather a 2cm (¾in) circle of the body-colour felt for the nose, pull up slightly, stuff, pull up the gathering tightly and place a holding stitch. Ladder stitch to the face.

This puppet has a bald top to his head. The hair can be stitched or glued around the head. The features include a few French knots worked above the nose, using light-brown cotton or embroidery silk.

Scarf and Smock The triangular shaped material is neatly hemmed around the outside edge to make the scarf.

The smock is made as for the Farmer, but this puppet does not have a rotund stomach, so the smock is left hanging loose and three pin tucks are stitched on either side at the top front of the smock, with a space between the two groups of tucks of approximately 6.4cm (2½in).

Sack Fold the hessian in half. Stitch firmly down both sides twice, otherwise in use the hessian will fray. Turn to the right side. Add a small amount of clear all-purpose adhesive around the open top edge of the sack. When dry this will help to prevent fraying. Fill the sack with the dried grass or straw. Stitch the sack to the puppet's left hand. (If a variety of interchangeable accessories are being made for the puppets, then use Velcro to apply the sack to the hand so that it can, when required, be easily removed.)

Finally, when the puppet has been completed, push the hat-crown top seam inwards as for a trilby hat.

Little Miss Muffet

Little Miss Muffet,
Sat on a tuffet,
Eating her curds and whey.
There came a big spider,
Who sat down beside her,
And frightened Miss Muffet away.

Toy type: String-puppet doll and spider (colour picture page 90)
Size of toy: Height of doll 50.8cm (20in)

The Doll
The clothes of the original model were made in blue-and-white gingham material, trimmed with broderie anglaise threaded with blue ribbon. The pantaloons were made in the gingham material. The petticoat was made from white cotton material trimmed with wide blue-and-white pregathered broderie-anglaise material and broderie anglaise matching the dress trimming. The shoes were blue felt tied with blue ribbons. A puppet of this type and character requires a fresh, pristine appearance with a simple colour scheme.

½m (19¾in) of 100cm (39in) wide cream-coloured cotton poplin or calico for the doll's body

A 50gm ball of 4 ply yarn for the hair
½m (19¾in) of 100cm (39in) wide gingham for the dress
A piece of gingham or plain material 50.8 x 50.8cm (20 x 20in) for the pantaloons
A piece of white broderie-anglaise material 76.2 x 15.3cm (29 x 6in) for the apron
A piece of white cotton, terylene or similar material for the petticoat, 55.9 x 15.3cm (22 x 6in)
A 30.5cm (12in) piece of narrow ribbon for the shoe ties
1m (39½in) of 1.3cm (½in) wide ribbon to tone with the dress material for the hair ribbon
A 35.5cm (14in) piece of ribbon to match the ribbon in the broderie-anglaise trimming, for the apron ties
3½m (138¼in) of 2cm (¾in) wide broderie-anglaise trimming pre-threaded with ribbon to match the dress material for the dress and apron waist trimming

1½m (59¼in) of 2.5cm (1in) wide white broderie-anglaise trimming for the apron and shoulder straps

1¼m (49¼in) of 9cm (3½in) wide pre-gathered broderie-anglaise trimming for the petticoat

Felt to tone with the dress, 19.2 x 15.3cm (7½ x 6in), for the shoes

Brown, peach, white and pink felt odd-ments for the features

Brown, beige and white stranded embroid-ery cotton for the features

One small snap fastener

Four dressmaking weights

A pair of white baby socks, shoe size 0–2½ GB (16½–19 EUR)

A 55.9cm (22in) piece of flat narrow elastic for the pantaloons and petticoat

Toy filling

One small teaspoon

One small unbreakable bowl

Cut out all the pattern pieces (Fig 64).

Head Place the two head pieces together right sides facing and join the outside edges, leaving the bottom straight neck edge open. Clip where necessary to ease. Turn to the right side. Stuff to the broken line. Turn back the neck edge and work loose stitches across the base of the head on the inside from side to side; these will hold the filling in place, see Fig 64. Turn the neck edge down again to its correct position, turn in the bottom straight edge and overstitch to join.

Hair Cut the 50gm ball of yarn into lengths each measuring 63.5cm (25in). Stitch the lengths into a bunch at one end only, place at the top of the head slightly to the back and stitch to hold. Backstitch around the hair line where indicated on Fig 61 (a). Lift the hair lengths over the face and tie at the back of the head in a ponytail. Take several strands of the under back pieces and make them into a ringlet by twisting them together, then laying a finger across the centre of the twist, lifting up the end – still holding a tight twist – and folding the twisted piece in half. Remove the finger and

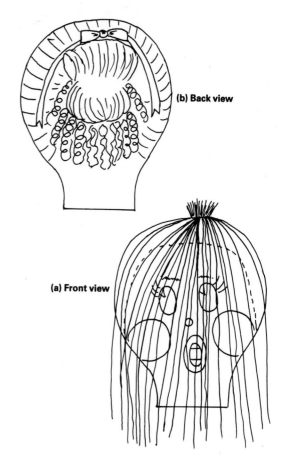

Fig 61 Little Miss Muffet: Hair style. (a) Front view showing hair tied at top of head then stitched to hold shape around the face; (b) Back view showing curls and double looped bun

let the yarn twist on to itself; stitch the raw ends to the head. Make bunches of ringlets of varying lengths (see Fig 61 (b)).

Fold the top layers into two half buns turning outwards from the centre – see Fig 61 (b) – turn in the ends and stitch to hold. Make eight separate ringlets and stitch four to either side of the head at the front, by inserting them under the layers of yarn on the head and stitching in place. Tie the metre of toning narrow ribbon into a small

The Farmer's In His Den: Farmer, Wife and Child; *(and below from left)* Horsey, Horsey with To Market, To Market, and Simple Simon; all glove puppets

Fig 62 Little Miss Muffet: Front view of hair style

bow, leaving the tails hanging, and stitch to the back of the head at the top of the bun.

Features Using Fig 62 as a guide, neatly stitch the features into place. The teeth are inserted and glued in place behind the mouth oval. The eyelashes, eyebrows and highlights are worked in stranded embroidery cotton, two strands only.

Body With the right sides facing, join the shoulder and side seams, leaving the neck and base of body open. Turn to the right side. Top stitch where indicated to form the waist. Evenly stuff the top of the body to the curve of waist stitiching. Turn in the top neck edge and overstitch to close. Treat the bottom of the body in the same way and close.

Arms and Hands Place the arm pieces together in pairs. Take one pair and, with the right sides facing, join the two side seams and one of the short ends together. Turn to the right side. Stuff the lower arm with the toy filling and top stitch across where indicated. Stuff the top of the arm. Turn the top raw edge in and gather. Pull up and fasten off. Make the second arm in the same way.

Place the hand pieces together in pairs. Take one pair and, with the right sides facing, join the outside edges together, leaving the straight edges open. Turn to the

Tom, Tom, The Piper's Son, an arm puppet

right side. Stuff firmly, inserting a dressmaker's weight into the palm of the hand, making sure it is completely surrounded by toy filling. Turn in the straight raw edges and overstitch to close. Top stab stitch to indicate the fingers. Make the second hand in the same way.

Legs Place the leg patterns together in pairs. Take one pair and, with the right sides facing, join around the outside edges, leaving the top straight edges open. Turn to the right side. Stuff the foot and lower part of the leg, inserting a dressmaker's weight into the base of the foot and completely encasing it with the toy filling. With the foot facing to the front, press the front and back seams together and stitch across for the knee, see Fig 63. Stuff the top of the leg. Turn in the top raw edges and overstitch to close. Treat the second leg in the same way.

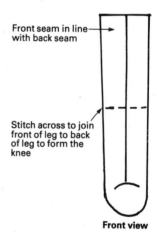

Front seam in line with back seam →

Stitch across to join front of leg to back of leg to form the knee

Front view

Fig 63 Little Miss Muffet: Leg stitching

Body Construction Ladder stitch the base of the neck to the top of the body where indicated.

The hands, arms and legs are attached using shank joints, which are threads stitched between the body, arms, hands and legs. Leaving a gap of about 1.3cm (½in); these threads are then bound with more thread as when applying a button to a garment; fasten off securely. Attach an arm either side of the body where indicated,

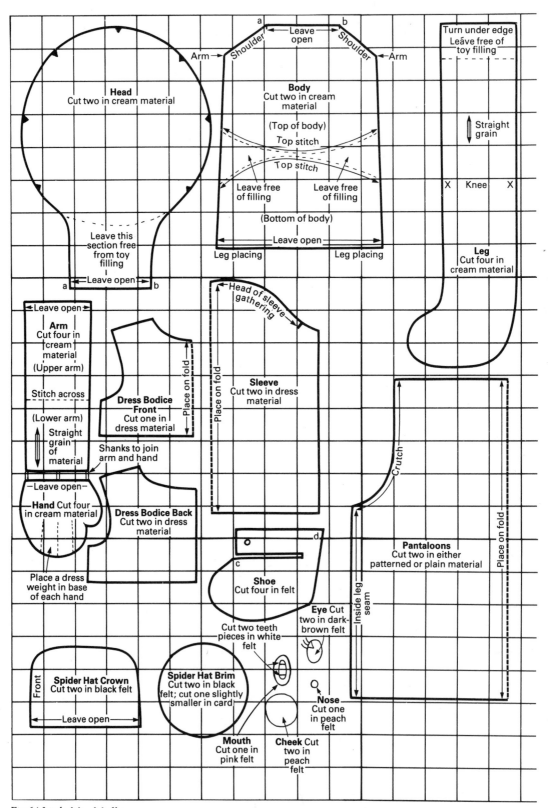

Fig 64 Little Miss Muffet

with one shank joint. Using three shank joints, evenly spaced apart, attach the hands to the arms, and a leg to either side of the base of the body, where indicated. If preferred the shank joints can be replaced by narrow tapes or cords. The main criterion is flexibility to allow the maximum of movement from the puppet.

Petticoat Take the strip of white cotton, terylene or similar material measuring 55.9 x 15.3cm (22 x 6in) and turn a narrow hem on one long edge. Turn a hem on the opposite long edge to form a casing for the elastic. Trim the lower hem with the 9cm (3½in) wide pre-gathered broderie-anglaise trimming. Trim with the pre-threaded ribbon broderie anglaise around the join of the wider broderie anglaise as top decoration. With the right sides facing, join the side seams. Turn to the right side. Thread a 28cm (11in) length of eleastic through the casing. Pull up slightly, if necessary, to fit the doll's waist loosely.

Pantaloons Turn a narrow hem on the bottom straight edge of each leg piece, and top trim with the pre-threaded ribbon broderie anglaise. Take one leg piece, fold it in half with the right sides facing and join the inside leg seams. Treat the second leg piece in the same way. Join the front seams together and then the back seams to form the crutch. Turn a hem on the top edge to form a casing for the elastic. Cut a 28cm (11in) length of the elastic and thread through the casing, pull up slightly, if necessary, to fit the doll's waist loosely. Turn to the right side.

Dress With the right sides facing, join the front and two back bodice pieces together at the shoulders and side seams.

Turn in a narrow hem on the short straight edge of each sleeve. Trim with the ribbon-threaded broderie anglaise on the right side. With the right sides facing, fold one sleeve piece in half and join the long straight edges. Gather the head of the sleeve where indicated and pin the sleeves into the armholes of the bodice, matching the underarm and sleeve seams. Pull up the gathering

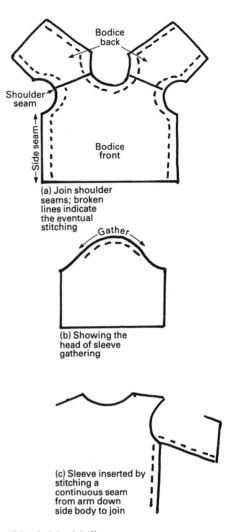

(a) Join shoulder seams; broken lines indicate the eventual stitching

(b) Showing the head of sleeve gathering

(c) Sleeve inserted by stitching a continuous seam from arm down side body to join

Fig 65 Little Miss Muffet

at the head of the sleeve to fit the armhole. Stitch the sleeve into place. Treat the second sleeve in the same way. Clip to ease at the curves. Turn in a narrow hem around the neck edge and top trim with the ribbon-threaded broderie-anglaise trimming.

Cut a strip of the gingham material to measure 99.1 x 22.9cm (39 x 9in) for the skirt. Turn a narrow hem on one long edge and trim with broderie anglaise on the right side to match the neck and sleeve trimming. With the right sides facing, join the short side seams. Gather the upper edge of the skirt and pull up to fit the bodice. With the seam at the centre back, join the gathered

111

skirt to the bodice. Turn the dress to the right side. Stitch a small snap fastener to the neck edges at the back to join.

Apron Take the strip of white broderie-anglaise material measuring 76.2 x 15.3cm (29 x 6in) and turn a narrow hem on the two short sides and one long edge. Trim with the 2.5cm (1in) wide broderie-anglaise trimming. Gather the raw top straight edge and pull up to the measure 22.9cm (9in). Trim at the waist with the ribbon-threaded broderie-anglaise trimming cut to measure 28cm (11in); this leaves a 2.5cm (1in) piece of trimming either side of the gathering as the waistband continuation. Turn in the ends neatly and add a ribbon tie measuring 17.8cm (7in) to each end of the waistband.

For each shoulder strap, cut a piece of matching ribbon-threaded broderie-anglaise trimming to measure 15.3cm (6in). Cut two pieces of the matching broderie-anglaise trimming – as used for the apron skirt trimming – to measure 20.4cm (8in). Take one strap and gather one piece of the trimming to measure 12.7cm (5in). Stitch the gathered piece, centrally, on to one side of the shoulder strap. Treat the second strap in the same way. Turn in each end of the straps neatly. Take one prepared shoulder strap and, with the frill facing the outside, join to the waistband 10.3cm (4in) in from one end. Join the other end of the shoulder strap to the waistband in the same way, approximately 4.5cm (1¾in) from the end. Apply the second shoulder strap on the opposite side in the same way. The central front distance on the waistband between the shoulder straps is 5cm (2in). Place the clothes on the puppet. Stitch a spoon in the right hand.

Socks Remove the toe piece from each sock, see Fig 66. Turn to the wrong side. Take one sock and backstitch to join the cut edges to the shape of the foot. Fasten off. Turn to the right side and place the sock on a foot. Treat the second sock in the same way.

Shoes Place pieces together in pairs. Take one pair and backstitch to join the outside edges c–d. Turn to the opposite side. Place on the doll's foot. Trim the strap length so

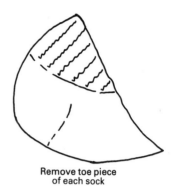

Remove toe piece
of each sock

Fig 66 Little Miss Muffet: Sock diagram

that the edges meet at the front of the leg. Make a hole in each strap where indicated. Cut the ribbon in half and thread one piece through each hole and tie in a bow to join the straps. Treat the second shoe in the same way.

The Spider
A 17.8cm (7in) diameter circle of black polished fur-fabric
A piece of black felt 34.3 x 14cm (13½ x 5½in) for the legs, base of body and the hat
A piece of white felt 0.7 x 30.5cm (¼ x 12in) for the hat band
Eight pipe cleaners
Black-and-white spotted ribbon or material for the bow tie, 2.5cm wide x 25.4cm long (1 x 10in)
A pair of 20mm goggle safety-lock eyes
Two oddments of card, one slightly smaller than the hat brim and the other slightly smaller than the base of the body circle
Toy filling

Body Gather the 17.8cm (7in) diameter circle of polished black fur-fabric and pull up slightly. Insert the safety-lock goggle eyes using the photograph as a guide to correct placing and taking into account that when the gathering is pulled up this will automatically lower the eye placing. Stuff firmly and pull up gathering. Cover the eight pipe cleaners with black felt, over-stitching around the outside edge; these will

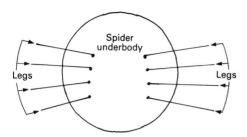

Fig 67 Little Miss Muffet: Placing of legs on spider underbody

be the legs. Cut two 7.6cm (3in) diameter circles in black felt and one slightly smaller in card for the lining.

Underbody Glue the card lining centrally on one of the felt circles. Place the ends of four of the pipe cleaner legs to one side of the card lining and the second four legs on the opposite side, as shown in Fig 67. Glue the second felt circle on to the top of the pipe cleaners. Allow to dry, then glue to the base of the fur-circle body over the gathering.

Bow Tie Tie a ribbon bow measuring 7.6cm (3in) and leave two short ends hanging at the centre. If using ordinary material, it will be necessary to fold the raw edges to the centre of the strip and stitch in place to hold, then fold a 7.6cm (3in) bow and stitch at the centre back to hold. Place the remaining material around the centre of the bow and stitch underneath. No raw edges should be visible. Stitch the bow tie to the front edge of the spider's body.

Hat To make the brim, glue the card circle to the centre of one felt circle. Glue the second felt circle on top. Overstitch around the outside edges to join the felt circles. To make the crown, place the two crown pieces together. Overstitch around the outside edges to join, leaving the bottom straight edges open.

Glue the base of the crown to the brim. Cut a piece of the 0.7cm (¼in) wide white felt to fit around the crown base and place around the crown for the hat band, the joins to one side. Form a 2.5cm (1in) wide bow in white felt and glue over the join in the hat band. Glue and stitch the front leg on the left hand side of the spider to the rim of the hat brim, balancing the hat on the leg and curling the end of the leg over the brim.

Puppet Control
Strong linen or nylon thread for the strings to tone with the proposed background; they should be as unobtrusive as possible
A needle to take the thread through the control holes
Seven flat buttons of approximately 1.3cm (½in) diameter, for securing the strings to the controls; if preferred coloured beads can be used, a different colour for each part of the puppet
Two 2.5cm (1in) diameter plastic or metal curtain rings
Two small screw eyes
One small round-headed screw size No 6
One medium-size cup hook
A piece of 20 x 10mm prepared soft wood for the control bar, measuring 47cm (18½in)
A piece of 25 x 5mm prepared soft wood for the extension bar, measuring 25.4cm (10in)
Copydex or similar adhesive

Using Fig 68 as a guide to sizes and correct placing, cut two pieces for the main control and one extension bar. Drill small holes for the strings where indicated. Glue the control together in the aeroplane shape as shown, and insert the screw eyes and cup hook as indicated. Cut the extension bar piece and drill small holes as shown.

The following general points on stringing a puppet can be related to Miss Muffet. The instructions for the addition of the spider are given at the end of the general stringing instructions.

Stringing a puppet requires two people: one to hold the control whilst the other does the stringing. The correct height from the ground is the one which the manipulator will feel is most comfortable when operating the puppet; this is usually just above waist level. There are two types of control used in string puppetry: the vertical and the horizontal. For this puppet a basic

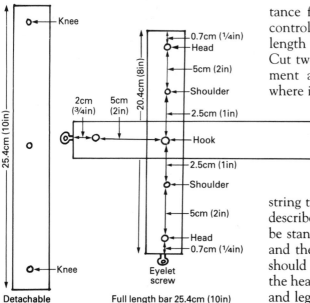

Fig 68 Little Miss Muffet: Puppet controls

Labels in figure:
Knee
0.7cm (¼in) — Head
5cm (2in)
Shoulder
2cm (¾in) 5cm (2in)
2.5cm (1in)
Hook
Back
20.4cm (8in)
25.4cm (10in)
2.5cm (1in)
Shoulder
5cm (2in)
1.3cm (½in)
Head
0.7cm (¼in)
Knee
Eyelet screw
Detachable extension bar
Full length bar 25.4cm (10in)
Cross bar 20.4cm (8in)

horizontal control is used. Fig 68 shows the placing of the various strings, ie at the shoulders, knees, head, hands and the back. The strings are attached to the holes in the control unit by passing each string through the correct hole in the control unit from the underneath, then through a button placed on the top of the control over the hole, and back down through the second hole in the button, back through the hole in the control unit, to the underneath of the control unit. Make a temporary tie by wrapping the string around the shank between the button and the control; this will enable the string to be adjusted to the correct level later. Place all the strings through their respective holes in the same way. With one person holding the puppet at the correct height, each string must be adjusted then tied off and each knot secured with dabs of adhesive. The following information should assist the reader to obtain the correct balance and order of stringing for the puppet.

(1)   The main weight of the puppet is borne by the shoulder strings, so start with these. Hold the control at the correct level, ie just above waist level. Measure the dis-

tance from the puppet's shoulders to the control, adding an extra 28cm (11in) to the length to allow adjustment and tying off. Cut two lengths of thread to this measurement and stitch firmly to the shoulders where indicated on Fig 69 (1). Secure each string temporarily to the control as already described. At this stage the puppet should be standing with its feet flat to the ground and the legs and body extended; the arms should be lying either side of the body and the head flopped forward. Keeping the body and legs thus described and the controls at the correct height, tie off and secure the strings making sure that both the strings are of equal length and taut. Whatever the tying off on other strings, these shoulder strings must be kept taut and the controls level.

(2)   The head strings support and move the head. Measure two lengths of thread in the same way as for the shoulder strings, measured from just behind and above where an ear might be placed. See Fig 69 (2) for placing. These strings will be shorter than the shoulder strings. Attach the head strings where indicated and, still keeping the puppet feet flat to the ground and the body stretched, pass them through their respective holes and buttons. With the neck fully extended and the eyes looking straight ahead, tie off as already described.

(3)   The back string assists the shoulder strings to control the body and is also used for bowing movements. It is often placed at waist level in puppetry, but for Miss Muffet it is placed below the waist where indicated on Fig 70 (3). Attach to the body as for the other strings and take up through the correct hole, allowing an extra 30.5cm (12in) to the measurement; the reason for this is that the back string in comparison to the others should hang slightly loose, and when the puppet is hanging from the control, it

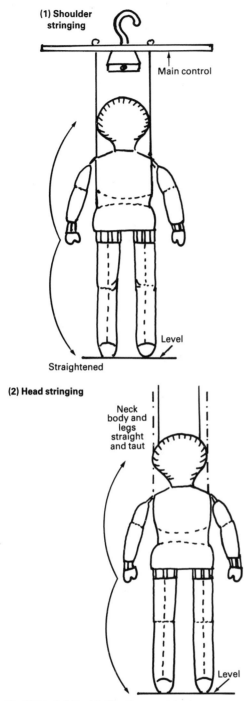

(1) Shoulder stringing

Main control

Straightened

Level

(2) Head stringing

Neck body and legs straight and taut

Level

Fig 69 Little Miss Muffet: Puppet stringing

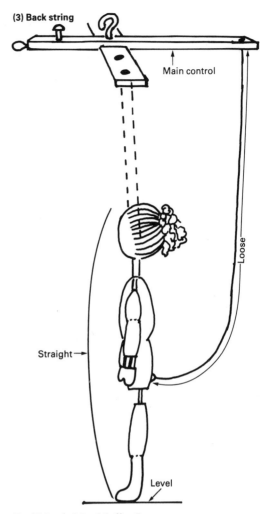

(3) Back string

Main control

Loose

Straight →

Level

Fig 70 Little Miss Muffet: Puppet stringing

should be slack. Tie off as the other strings.

(4)   The knee strings control the leg and foot movements; they are tied to a detach- able control bar, which rests on the main control when not in use. To measure the correct string length, hold the main control bar in one hand and the detachable control bar in the other hand about 15.3cm (6in) in front. Measure from the knee to control adding 28cm (11in) to the measurement. Cut two strings to this length. Attach a string to each knee where indicated. Pass each string through the skirt, to the detach- able control bar and secure as for the other strings. These strings should be very taut to produce good control; however, the feet must still be flat to the ground. See Fig 71(4).

(5)   The hand strings control all arm and hand movements. On a horizontal control the hands are usually strung on a running

cord which passes through the screw eye on the front of the control. The hands should be slightly raised from the sides of the body. Attach the string to the back of the hand where indicated, pass the other end of the string through the screw eye and attach to the other hand, adjusting the string to raise both hands slightly, Fig 71(5).

Spider The spider has a black-thread string coming from the top centre of his body and measured from ground level to the height of the control when Miss Muffet is sitting down. The thread is taken up through the screw eye on the side of the control and secured to a curtain ring. A string is taken from the centre of the hat crown up through the same screw eye hole and secured to another curtain ring; a small piece of coloured tape or thread should be bound round this curtain ring to enable the manipulator to distinguish between spider and hat.

Manipulation Practise by pulling on the various strings to discover what the puppet is capable of doing. Lower the spider on his string and at the same time pull on the hat string and he will raise his hat to Miss Muffet – less frightening for a child in this way. As the spider descends, raise the hand strings on Miss Muffet, then work the extension bar to enable her to run away. When Miss Muffet realises the spider is friendly, pull on the back string and tip the controls to enable her to bend down and stroke the spider. A mirror is most useful to practise any form of puppetry; it will show up faults in manipulation very quickly. A long black skirt or dark background will show this puppet to advantage.

Storing the Control Holding the controls in a horizontal position, twist the main puppet then secure with some ribbon in one or two places, spaced apart. Place the puppet in a large bag and tie the neck of the bag under the controls. If possible, hang the puppet by the controls in a cupboard, or a place where it can remain undisturbed until required. Care should be taken as, once a puppet has become tangled, often the only solution is to restring, which is a lengthy process.

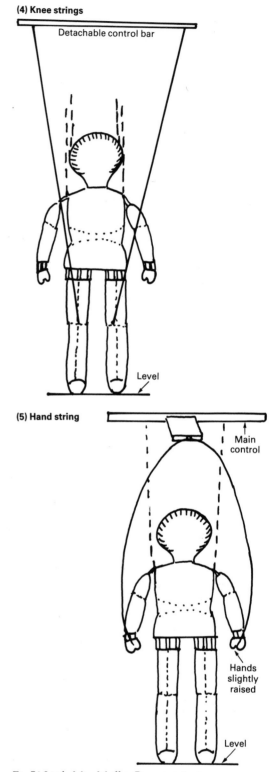

(4) Knee strings

Detachable control bar

Level

(5) Hand string

Main control

Hands slightly raised

Level

Fig 71 Little Miss Muffet: Puppet stringing

116

Pussycat, Pussycat

Pussycat, Pussycat,
Where have you been?
I've been to London
To look at the queen.

Pussycat, Pussycat,
What did you there?
I frightened a little mouse,
Under a chair.

* * *

Toy type: String-puppet cat and mouse (colour picture page 89)

Size of toy: Cat length from tip of tail to the head 45.7cm (18in); height from front foot base to ear tip 30.5cm (12in)

This toy is constructed from gathered fabric circles, based on the principle of Suffolk Puff patchwork, and is an excellent way of using oddments of material. Do take care, however, to choose materials of a similar weight and texture. Pay attention to the colouring. Fabric-circle toys are very suitable for string puppetry due to their flexibility.

The Cat

Oddments of black fabric for the body and leg circles

Small quantity of lightweight toy filling for the head, tail and feet

111.8cm (44in) of black rolled elastic

6 buttons about the size of a 2p piece

Pink felt for the ears, nose, tongue and pad markings, 10.3 x 10.3cm (4 x 4in)

White felt for the feet, the four half circles, the chin, nose piece and face shaping, 22.9 x 35.5cm (9 x 14in)

Black felt for the ears, ear markings, eyelids and eye pupils, 10.3 x 10.3cm (4 x 4in)

Grey felt for the pads, 10.3 x 12.7cm (4 x 5in)

Two different green tones of felt for eyes

Four dressmaking weights

Terylene thread or horsehair for whiskers

Thin card to make the circle templates

The Mouse

Fur-fabric 15.3 x 15.3cm (6 x 6in)

Oddment of leather for the tail

Scraps of felt for the ears to tone with the body fabric

Scraps of pink felt for the ear linings

Black felt for the eyes

Toy filling

Horsehair or black thread for the whiskers

To make the fabric circles, first cut out the template circles in card in the following diameter sizes: 8cm (3⅛in), 10.3cm (4in), 12.1cm (4¾in), 14cm (5½in), 16cm (6¼in), 17.8cm (7in) and 20.2cm (7⅞in). Make a hole in the centre of each circle and mark each with its size. It is not necessary to cut out each material circle separately. Cut one circle first then pin this on to several thicknesses of material (the number you will be able to cope with at one cutting will be determined by their thickness) and cut round. Mark the centres of the material circles through the hole pierced in each card template. If using light-coloured material, a pencil can be used for marking; on dark colours use tailor's chalk.

Each front leg requires twenty-one 8cm (3⅛in) diameter circles. Each back leg required twenty-one 8cm (3⅛in) diameter circles, two 10.3cm (4in) diameter circles and one 12.1cm (4¾in) diameter circle.

The body requires (from the tail end) one 8cm (3⅛in) diameter circle, one 10.3cm (4in) diameter circle, one 12.1cm (4¾in)

diameter circle, one 14cm (5½in) diameter circle, one 16cm (6¼in) diameter circle, two 17.8cm (7in) diameter circles and ten 20.2cm (7⅞in) diameter circles, plus four 17.8cm (7in) diameter circles, each one half black material and half white.

To obtain a half-black/half-white circle, cut out the black circles and white circles, cut each one in half, then stitch one black half to one white half and gather in the normal way, making sure the join is on the inside of the circle. By using a lightweight but firm material for the main body circles and then using white felt for the half-colour circles, you add shaping to the cat's chest by virtue of the felt being thicker which pushes the chest upwards at the front. This also helps to support the head when puppet is not in use.

Making each circle Make a hole at centre of each circle, then with strong thread gather round outside edge of the circle 0.7cm (¼in) from the outside edge. Pull up the gathers firmly until tightly pulled at centre and fasten off; flatten with palm of hand.

Body Take a length of rolled elastic 45.7cm (18in) long and fold in half. Thread a button on one end securely, place at centre of folded elastic and thread the circles on the free ends, starting at tail and stringing one 8cm (3⅛in) circle, one 10.3cm (4in) circle, one 12.1cm (4¾in) circle, one 12.7cm (5in) circle, one 16cm (6¼in) circle, one 17.8cm (7in) circle, ten 20.2cm (7⅞in) circles, one 17.8cm (7in) circle and lastly the four 17.8cm (7in) circles in half black material and half white felt. Knot the elastic ends and hold in place with a safety-pin until next stage is completed.

Head Cut two 14cm (5½in) circles from the body material, cut away chin piece, see pattern for size, and substitute a piece of white felt; stitch across as for half circles. With right sides facing, backstitch all round outside edge inserting side face pieces E and F, and leaving an opening at one side to enable the head to be turned to the right side. Stuff firmly and close the opening. When shaping the head make sure the white under chin

piece is at the back of the head at the base. Stab stitch each ear lining to each ear piece; do not turn to the other side, the ear obtains a sharper look stab stitched on right side. Stitch the ears and features into place where indicated on the graph.

Make a small slit at centre of the black and white circle at back of the head just below the sewn join. Undo the knot at the chest end of the body and insert the elastic ends into a button; tie and secure firmly, then insert this button into the slit at back of head. Insert more stuffing at this stage to pad all around button, especially at the button back, then close the slit firmly.

Front Legs Knot one end of a piece of 30.5cm (12in) rolled elastic and thread on the first twenty-one 8cm (3⅛in) circles. Place the end of the elastic through the double body elastic between the fifth and sixth circles back from the head, then thread on twenty-one more 8cm (3⅛in) circles and knot the end of the elastic.

Back Legs Knot the end of a 35.5cm (14in) piece of rolled elastic and thread on twenty-one 8cm (3⅛in) circles, two 10.3cm (4in) circles and one 12.1cm (4¾in) circle. Then apply to the body as per front legs, inserting the end of the elastic through the body elastic between body circles seven and eight from the tail end. Thread on the remaining back leg circles in reverse order and knot the end of the elastic.

Obviously, when making the body and legs, there may be a variation between the materials used in the illustrated puppet and those used by the reader. As a general gauge, pull the elastic until the circles are held firmly but not too tightly together. If they are strung too tightly, the puppet will not be flexible; if too loose, the elastic will show and the cat will lose its body shaping. If using thicker material than dress weight (cotton), allow longer lengths for the elastic when threading.

Feet Cut four sets of feet according to the pattern. Before sewing each foot together, stitch the pad markings on to the grey felt foot bases – this is easier than adding them

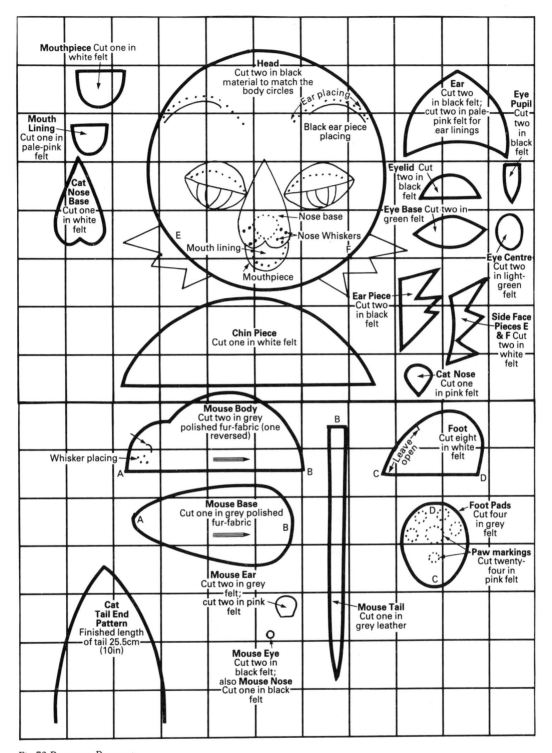

Fig 72 Pussycat, Pussycat

afterwards. The feet are stab stitched on right side. Stitch then stuff the four feet, adding a dress weight in each. Tie a button on to each leg end elastic, then insert into each foot, stuffing firmly round the button as for the head. Close the openings, then stitch the circle immediately above each foot firmly to the top of the foot. This adds strength and is a double check against the buttons being pulled out.

Tail With right sides facing, backstitch down the seam. Turn to the right side and lightly stuff. Gather the end, turning in a 0.7cm (¼in) hem, and stitch to centre of smallest circle at bottom end.

The Mouse This can be made out of an oddment of fur-fabric, preferably a smooth pile to look more realistic. Cut out according to the pattern. With right sides facing, backstitch around the body from nose A to tail end B. Insert the base, matching A to A and B to B. Stitch all round, leaving open where indicated on the pattern. Turn to the right side and stuff with lightweight filling; ladder stitch to close the opening. Stitch the leather tail piece at base B. Glue a pink lining to each ear, fold each ear in half lengthways to add shape and stitch in place. Stitch felt circles for the eyes and nose. Add whiskers.

Puppet Controls

The materials required for these controls are obtainable from most DIY stores. The beads and button thread come from handicraft shops or drapers.

Cat:
One strip of wood 29.2cm long x 3.3cm wide x 0.7cm deep (11½ x 1¼ x ¼in)
Two pieces of wood each 20.4cm long x 3.3cm wide x 0.7cm deep (8 x 1¼in x ¼in) for cross bars
Seven small beads
Button thread for stringing the puppet
Two closed eye hooks

Mouse:
One strip of wood 22.9cm long x 2cm wide x 0.7cm deep (9 x ¾ x ¼in)
One small cup hook
Three beads
Button thread
Rolled elastic

For the cat, insert a closed eye hook into each end of the 29.2cm (11½in) long strip of wood. Drill small holes in this strip of wood where indicated on Fig 73, and also in the two 20.4cm (8in) cross bars. Attach the cross bars at right angles to the main 29.2cm (11½in) strip, again using Fig 73 for exact placing.

For the mouse, drill small holes where indicated. Screw the small cup hook at the centre of the top, see Fig 73. Make sure both the cat and mouse controls are well rubbed down; they can be varnished at this stage if desired.

Stringing the Cat The strings on the puppet can be adjusted to fit the child's height, so when attaching strings to the cat and mouse allow plenty of length. Measure approximately from the ground to the manipulator's waist to give some idea of the length required.

Starting at top centre of the head, attach string (a) by sewing it firmly to the cat. On circle nine, counting from the front foot upwards, secure string (b). Counting nine from the front foot upwards on the other front leg, stitch and secure string (c). Moving along the control, sew body string (d) five circles in from the neck and body string (e) fourteen circles in from (d). Back leg string (f) is sewn to circle eighteen from the back foot and back leg string (g) is sewn to circle eighteen from the other back foot. The string for the tail (h) is sewn to the tip of the tail.

Stringing the puppet to the wooden control is a two-person job unless there is a means of securing the control to a beam or a hook from a door frame or similar. Both hands must be free. Assuming you have someone to hold the control first thread the end of head string (a) up through hole (a), then thread it through a bead and back through hole (a) again. Just tie once to hold as you will need to adjust the string length later. Follow down the control, fixing each string to its respective hole, (b) to (b), (c) to (c) etc, until the front leg, body and back leg strings are all attached. Bring the tail string up through the closed ring at (h), thread through a bead large enough not to be pulled back through the ring and tie.

Ask your helper to hold the wooden control horizontal and steady, then adjust the strings before the final tying off. The cat must be evenly balanced, with the strings holding him to the control without pulling the whole balance of the toy out. The tail should be touching the ground without the string hanging loosely from the control. Having obtained the required balance to the cat, secure the strings at the beads and cut off any excess thread.

Stringing the Mouse Sew strong (rolled) elastic to the top of the head at the centre between the ears. Attach two threads on either side of the body, approximately 2.5cm (1in) in from the tail end and 2.5cm (1in) up from the mouse base. Bring the elastic up through the closed circle hook at front of the cat control and tie it on to a bead. Bring the right-hand body string up through the hole on one side of the mouse control, thread it through a bead and tie. Treat the left-hand body string in the same way, threading it through the opposite hole on the mouse control. Balance, then tie the strings securely. The cup hook at centre of the mouse control enables it to be clipped on to the closed hook at front of the cat control when not in use.

Manipulation Hold the cat control in the left hand at approximately the centre between (d) and (e). Do not grip too tightly; hold it in a horizontal position. To walk the cat, move the control from side to side in a rocking movement. To make the cat pounce

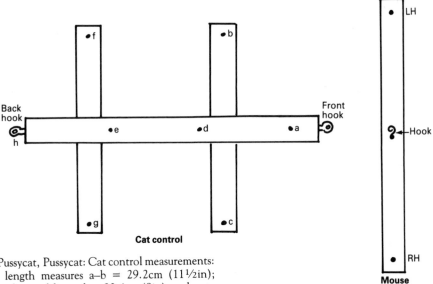

Cat control

Fig 73 Pussycat, Pussycat: Cat control measurements: overall length measures a–b = 29.2cm (11½in); cross bars b–c and f–g each = 20.4cm (8in); each outside hole for strings at b, c, f and g are 0.7cm (¼in) in from the outside edge at each end; distances between stringing holes measured from the front hook of the main control 3.8cm (1½in) to 'a', 8.3cm (3¼in) to 'd', 10.9cm (4½in) to 'e', 6.4cm (2½in) to 'h' at the back hook. Mouse control measurements: overall length measures 22.9cm (9in); the stringing holes either end are 0.7cm (¼in) in from the outside edge; the hook is placed in the centre, this enables the mouse control to be hooked on to the cat control when not in use. LH indicates that the string is attached to the left hand side of the mouse body; RH indicates the string is attached to the right hand side of the mouse body. Placing of the cat strings: (a) top of head at centre; (b) front left leg string; (c) front right leg string; (d) body string; (e) body string; (f) back left leg string; (g) back right leg string; (h) tip of the tail string

121

bring the control quickly up at front then lower well down. Individual legs can be moved by lifting the corresponding bead. If children are going to work this puppet, they can put a great deal of movement and life in the puppet by working it together – one working the controls, another the beads to raise the tail or move the legs and head. The back will arch if these strings are pulled. The mouse, as already described, is secured to the cat control by elastic, the actual wooden mouse control can be held out with the right hand whilst the cat control is held in the left hand. The mouse control then pulls the mouse away from the cat.

Provided it is explained to children that the strings on the puppets will become tang-led if not treated carefully, then this is an excellent way of amusing them, especially if an older child manipulates the cat and a young one the mouse. However, if the controls become tangled then it can be a lengthy business restringing them. After use, hook the mouse control on to the cat control, gently turn the puppets in one direction until strings are held firmly, then tie at the centre of the strings between the controls and the cat with a wide piece of ribbon. Place the cat and mouse in a bag with the controls outside; this helps to avoid tangling. When next required, remove the bag and untie the ribbon, then hold the controls in a horizontal position and allow the strings and puppets to unwind.

The Farmer's In His Den

The farmer's in his den,
The farmer's in his den,
E – I – E – I,
The farmer's in his den.

The farmer wants a wife,
The farmer wants a wife,
E – I – E – I,
The farmer wants a wife.

The wife wants a child,
The wife wants a child
E – I – E – I,
The wife wants a child.

* * *

Toy type: Glove puppets – Farmer, Wife and Child (colour picture page 107)
Size of toy: Height, Farmer 40.6cm (16in), Wife and Child 30.5cm (12in)

Farmer
Pale-pink felt 92.1 x 35.5cm (36¼ x 14in) for the puppet glove, head and legs

Tweedy material for the hat; the crown 10.3 x 17.8cm (4 x 7in), the brim a 15.3cm (6in) diameter circle
One 15.3cm (6in) diameter circle of felt for the brim lining
Oddments of white or grey fur-fabric for the beard and eyebrows
Thin plastic-coated wire approximately

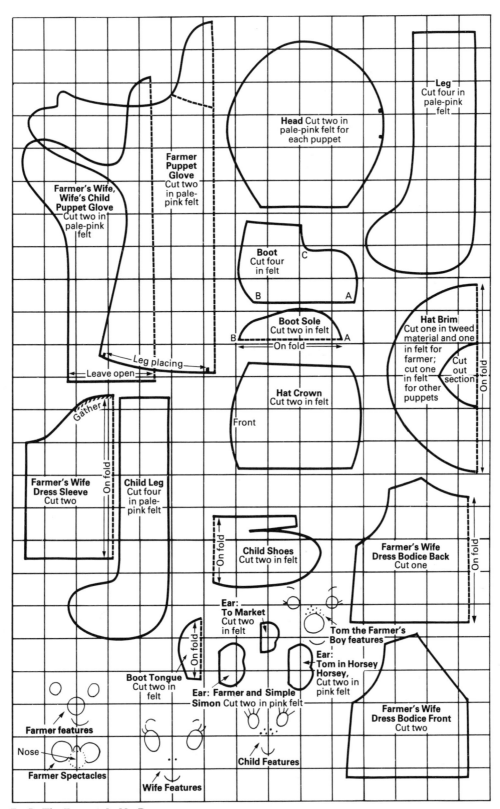

Fig 74 The Farmer's In His Den

11.5cm (4½in) long for the spectacles

Patterned material 7.6 x 43.7cm (3 x 17in) for the scarf

Plain cotton material for the smock (natural-coloured curtain lining is suitable) 68.5 x 20.4cm (27 x 8in)

A piece of material 17.8 x 33cm (7 x 13in) for the trouser leg; dark-brown velvet was used for the original model

Dark-brown felt 20.4 x 15.3cm (8 x 6in) for the boots

Thin cord or strong thread for the bootlaces

One small feather for the hat decoration

A length of soft leather, or any suitable substitute, for the belt, 35.5cm long x approximately 2cm wide (14 x ¾in)

A 2cm (¾in) oval bead on a 3.3cm (1¼in) piece of cane for the pipe; if not available a matchstick would do

Oddments of felt for the features

A roll of white lampshade binding tape; this will be sufficient for many puppets

Toy filling

Cut out all the pattern pieces. Pin then stitch the two main glove pieces together around the outside edge, leaving the bottom straight edge open. Turn up a narrow hem at the bottom edge and stitch in place with narrow tape; this will add stiffening and prevent fraying. Turn inside out.

Head Place the two head pieces together, pin and stitch around the outside edge, leaving the bottom straight edge open. Turn inside out and lightly stuff. Holding the glove with your left hand inserted – ie if you are right handed, if not reverse – place the head on to the top area of the glove and lower it until the neck edge on the head reaches the line indicated on the pattern. Stuff further if necessary, then stitch the head to the glove.

Stitch an ear on either side of the head where indicated on the pattern, pulling the stitches up slightly to curve each ear lobe. Glue eyes into place. If the puppet is for a very young child, stitch rather than glue the eyes. Add bushy eyebrows where indicated on Fig 75.

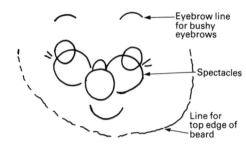

Fig 75 The Farmer's In His Den: Farmer, feature placing

Cut a 2cm (¾in) diameter circle in pink felt for the nose. Gather around the outside edge, stuff, and pull the stitches up tightly to form a ball. Ladder stitch the nose in place.

Embroider the mouth using two strands of stranded embroidery cotton and stem stitch, or a comparable stitch would do. Using pink lipstick or fabric paint, add colouring for cheeks and extra colouring to the tip of the nose. Glue the beard into place where indicated.

Smock In natural-coloured material, cut a piece measuring 50.8 x 20.4cm (20 x 8in). With the right sides facing, stitch together the 20.4cm (8in) seams. Turn a narrow hem at one long edge. Lay this tube on a table with the stitched seam at the centre back. Down either side, from the top edge, cut a 15.3cm (6in) slit for the armholes. Turn in a narrow hem around each armhole. Turn to the right side and place on the puppet glove. Turn a narrow hem along the top edge and pull to gather firmly around the puppet's neck. Fasten off.

Cut two arm pieces in the smock material, each measuring 17.8 x 9cm (7 x 3½in). With the right sides facing, form the first piece into a tube and stitch the 9cm (3½in) seams together. Turn to the right side. With the 9cm (3½in) seam under the arm, top stitch the sleeve into place in the armhole. Turn a narrow hem at the open end and gather tightly to fit the puppet glove wrist;

Goosey, Goosey, Gander, a pull-along toy

take care not to pull too tightly as this would obstruct the passage in the glove for the manipulator's fingers. Treat the other sleeve in the same way. If preferred, the sleeves can be inserted on the wrong side of the garment as with dressmaking, and then turned to the right side. However, glove puppets are purely for effect, and the top stitching is easier in a sleeve that is not shaped; it also adds interest to the smock if done in a decorative way.

Stitch the bottom front of the smock to the front of the glove in a curve, measuring 7.6cm (3in) at the centre front from the bottom hem, curving upwards to each side. Insert toy filling as you stitch the curve, to produce the effect of a rotund stomach. Fasten off and apply the belt strip over the stitching line; stitch to hold in place.

Legs Place together in pairs. Pin and then stitch around the outside edge, leaving the top straight edge open. Turn to right side and stuff firmly, leaving about 2.5cm (1in) at the top free from any filling. With the front seam of the leg facing, press the front seams to the back seam and stitch across where the toy filling ends. Then overstitch across the top straight edge. Treat the other leg in the same way. Ladder stitch to the glove where indicated on the pattern.

Trouser Legs With the right sides facing, fold the material into a tube measuring 17.8 x 16.6cm (7 x 6in). Stitch the 16.6cm (6in) seams together. Turn a narrow hem at one long side. Turn to the right side. Place on to a leg. Turn and gather a hem at the top. The trouser leg length should be, at the ankle, approximately 6.4cm (2½in) from the base of the foot. Stitch the top of the trouser leg to the puppet glove just above the top of the leg to secure it to the body. From the bottom of the trouser leg on the outside, fold the material in evenly to fit the leg firmly, and stitch from the bottom hem upwards for 4.5cm (1¾in). Fasten off. Treat the other trouser leg in the same way. This produces a

---

The Teddy Bears' Picnic, a musical drum

jodhpur effect to the trouser outline.

Boots Place together in pairs. Pin then back-stitch together the front seam A–C and also the back seam from B to the top edge, leaving the top and bottom straight edges open. Turn inside out. Insert the boot sole and stab stitch into place. Insert the boot tongue to C and stab stitch across the bottom straight edge to the inside front of the boot, making sure the sewing thread used matches the boot colouring to hide any stitches. Place the boot on a foot and stuff to shape. Lace the open boot fronts together over the boot tongue as you would lace up a real boot or a shoe. Treat the other boot in the same way.

Hat Cut one brim pattern in tweed material and one in felt. Using an all-purpose adhesive, glue the two pieces together. Place the two crown pieces right sides together and, leaving the bottom straight edge of the crown open, stitch around the outside edge to join. Turn to the right side and stitch to the opening on the crown. Trim around the brim edge if necessary to neaten. Stitch to the farmer's head at an angle, and press in the crown of the hat to shape.

Finishing Touches Add a feather to the side of the hat and stitch into place. Hem around the outside edge of the scarf and tie into place around the neck. Glue the bead to the end of the cane or matchstick for the pipe. Glue a small amount of coloured toy filling into the end of the bead to simulate smoke. Push the pipe stem through the felt skin and into the stuffing at one side of the mouth. Using a clear all-purpose adhesive, glue around the outside edge where the pipe enters the mouth; this will dry and help to support the pipe in the mouth. Shape the spectacles as shown in Fig 74 and stitch to the bridge of the nose.

Wife

Pale-pink felt 53.3 x 25.4cm (21 x 10in) for the puppet glove
Scraps of ginger-brown felt for the eyes
Oddments of ginger-brown long-pile acrylic fur-fabric for the hair

A piece of fine white terylene net 66 x 15.3cm (26 x 6in) for the mob cap

A piece of narrow velvet ribbon 15.3cm (6in) long for around the neck

A small-patterned cotton material 88 x 40.6cm (35 x 16in) for the dress

A piece of fine white terylene net 68.5 x 24.1cm (27 x 9½in) for the apron

109.2cm (43in) narrow lace trimming

91.5cm (36in) narrow tape for the apron ties

A 28cm (11in) length of 3.8cm (1½in) wide lace for around the shoulders (lace ready-gathered on to a band was used for the original model)

Cut out all the pattern pieces. See Fig 74. The basic puppet glove is made as for the Farmer, page 124, although the legs are omitted.

Hair Cut the shaggy long-pile acrylic fur-fabric, still leaving the pile on its backing, to a length measuring 28 x 25.4cm (11 x 10in) width. With right side uppermost, lay the length around the front of the puppet face from one side to the other and ladder stitch into place. Then take the fur-fabric over the head, gather it into the nape of the neck at the centre back and stitch to hold. Gently comb and smooth the hair. Stitch the fur-fabric to the top of the head by making a centre parting in the pile and backstitching the fur-fabric backing to the puppet head.

Cut a strip of the fur-fabric measuring 20.4cm wide x 5cm long (8 x 2in). Stitch the shorter ends together on the wrong side. Gather one long end and pull up tightly; fasten off. Turn to the right side; this gathering makes the centre of the bun. Fold the loose pile on the open end inwards to form a circular bun. Stitch to the head over the gathered fur-fabric at the nape of the neck. The diameter of the bun is approximately 7.6cm (3in). Comb a little of the pile around the top of the face into a fringe across the forehead of the puppet. Fur-fabric varies considerably and if the long-pile acrylic chosen for the puppet's hair has a

very firm backing it may be necessary, to make it easier to apply, to remove some of the backing.

Features Apply the ginger-brown felt eyes, adding embroidered eyelashes and eyebrows in single-strand brown embroidery cotton. The mouth is embroidered using pale-pink embroidery cotton. The nose consists of two pale-pink French knots.

Mob Cap With the right sides of the material facing, hem the long top and bottom edges. Stitch together the two shorter 15.3cm (6in) edges. Turn to the right side. Gather one long edge as tightly as possible. Fasten off. Gather around the opposite open edge 2.5cm (1in) in from the hemmed edge. Before pulling the stitches to gather, place the mob cap on the puppet head, with the joined seam at the centre back. Gather to fit the puppet head, put in a holding stitch, then stitch the cap to the puppet head.

Neck Band Using clear all-purpose adhesive, glue the piece of narrow velvet around the puppet neck to cover the stitching line where the head was applied to the glove body. Overlap the ends of the ribbon neatly at the back.

Dress With the right sides of the material facing, join the shoulder seams of the bodice together. Turn a narrow hem at the short straight end of one sleeve. Gather at the head of the sleeve where indicated, and insert the sleeve into the armhole. Fold the sleeve with right sides facing, and stitch the sleeve and bodice side seams together in a continuous seam. Make and insert the other sleeve in the same way. Return to bodice and turn a narrow hem around the neck edge, down each front piece and along the bottom edge. Turn to the right side and place on the puppet. Fold the front edges over one another until the bodice loosely fits the puppet glove. Stitch the front seams together inserting a narrow piece of lace between the edges.

Cut a piece of the patterned material to measure 88.9 x 26.7cm (35 x 10½in) for the skirt. Turn a narrow hem along one long edge. With the right sides facing, fold the

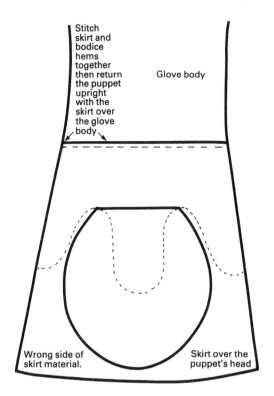

Labels on figure:
Stitch skirt and bodice hems together then return the puppet upright with the skirt over the glove body.

Glove body

Wrong side of skirt material.

Skirt over the puppet's head

Fig 76 The Farmer's In His Den: Wife, glove puppet
Applying the dress shirt to the bodice

material and join together the two shorter edges. Turn a hem at the top edge and gather to fit the bottom of the bodice. Fasten off. Turn the puppet upside down, and with the right sides of the bodice and skirt matching, lower the skirt over the bottom of the puppet glove until the top gathered edge on the skirt is in line with the bodice bottom hem; make sure the seam on the skirt is at the back of the puppet, then stitch the skirt to the bodice (see Fig 76). Return the puppet to an upright position and pull the skirt to the right side over the puppet glove.

Gather around each sleeve 2.5cm (1in) from the hem, pull up the stitches to fit the puppet arm. Fasten off. Lay the shoulder lace around the puppet neck and stitch the two ends to the bodice at the base of the front centre seams.

Apron Cut a piece of terylene net or any suitable material 60.9 x 22.9cm (24 x 9in).

Turn a narrow hem on the one long and two short edges. Trim with narrow lace. Gather the top straight edge to measure 20.4cm (8in). Fasten off.

Take a piece of matching material measuring 20.4 x 7.6cm (8 x 3in). Hem the two shorter ends. With the right sides of the material facing, lay one long edge of the waistband to just below the gathering on the apron. Stitch the band and apron together. Fold the other long edge of the waistband over the gathering to the back of the apron, turn a narrow hem and stitch to the apron. Insert an apron tie 45.7cm (18in) long into each hemmed open end on the waistband. Close the ends of the waistband and at the same time stitch the apron ties into place. Hem each end of the apron ties.

If you choose the same type of material for the shoulder lace and the apron, then the shoulder lace will double as shoulder straps for the apron and, when the apron is removed, as decoration for the dress.

Child

Pale-pink felt 41.9 x 47cm (16½ x 18½in) for the puppet glove, head and legs

Small pieces of dark-brown felt for the eyes

A bought doll's wig for the hair. Length from one end of a plait over the head to the end of the opposite plait 38.1cm x depth at the top parting 10.3cm (15 x 4in). (When purchasing a doll wig it is easy to choose one which is too large. Ideally, providing it has a stretchy backing, the wig should look on the small size to the subject it is intended for; it can then be stretched on to the doll or puppet head, for a firm fit.)

Cotton material with a small pattern 116.8 x 53.3cm (46 x 21in) for the dress and hat. To allow the use of oddments of materials the sizes of the component parts are as follows – dress skirt: 116.8 x 25.4cm (46 x 10in); bodice: 25.4 x 15.3cm (10 x 6in); hat: 40.6 x 28cm (16 x 11in)

Terylene ribbon 3.8cm wide x 60.9cm long (1½ x 24in) for the hat ties

A piece of 25.4cm (10in) wide broderie-anglaise trimming cut to 31.7 x 20.4cm (12½ x 8in) for the apron. This is a wide trimming which has a finished pattern edge and is useful for doll's clothes as it requires very little stitching

Two small buttons for the back fastening decoration

Broderie-anglaise trimming 121.9cm long x 25.4cm wide (48 x 10in) for the waist slip and pantaloon legs

A piece of felt 17.8 x 12.7cm (7 x 5in) for the shoes

Two small buttons

Toy filling

Cut out all the pattern pieces (see Fig 74). Make the puppet glove, head and legs as for the Farmer, page 124; at this stage do not attach the head or the legs to the glove body.

Stitch the wig securely into place on the puppet head. Using Fig 77, apply the features.

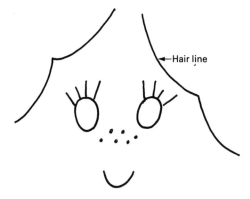

Fig 77 The Farmer's In His Den: Child, feature placing

Pantaloon Legs Cut two pieces of the broderie-anglaise trimming to measure 25.4 x 25.4cm (10 x 10in). With the pattern edge at the bottom and right sides facing, fold into two tubes and join the open seams on each tube. Turn to the right side. These are the two pantaloon legs. Slip a pantaloon leg piece on to each leg, and with the feet facing to the front and the stitched seam of

each pantaloon to the inside of each leg, stitch the top of each leg to the front and back of the pantaloon pieces 15.3cm (6in) up from the bottom patterned edge of the broderie anglaise. Fold the top of each pantaloon leg inwards, then gather and stitch to the front of the puppet glove 7.6cm (3in) up from the bottom edge and with the outside folded edges of the pantaloons lining up with the side seams of the puppet glove.

Shoes Take one pattern piece. Fold where indicated and stitch around the outside edge, leaving the top straight edge open. Turn to the opposite side. Place on the feet and fold each strap over to fit the puppet leg. Stitch to secure and add a small button at the end of each strap as decoration.

Waist Slip Take a piece of the broderie-anglaise trimming 71.2cm long x 25.4cm wide (28 x 10in). Fold in half and stitch together the 25.4cm (10in) seams. Turn to the right side. Turn a hem along the top edge of the material and gather to fit the puppet glove. Stitch to the glove to hold it in place.

Dress See Fig 78. In the patterned material, cut a piece measuring 25.4 x 15.3cm (10 x 6in) for the bodice. Hem both 15.3cm (6in) ends. With the right sides facing, fold the width in half to 7.6cm (3in). Stitch the bottom open edges together at each side from the hemmed edge for 5cm (2in); this will be the underarms. Turn a narrow hem along the raw edges in-between. On the top folded edge cut a curved piece out for the neck, measuring to 0.7cm (¼in) from the top edge and leaving 7.6cm (3in) still folded either side for the shoulders. Turn to the right side and place on the puppet glove. Gather at both hemmed edges to fit the glove wrist.

Depending on the width of material available for the skirt, it may be necessary to join the material to measure 116.8cm long x 25.4cm wide (46 x 10in). Turn a hem along one long edge. With the right sides facing, stitch together the 25.4cm (10in) edges. Turn to the right side. Fold a top hem and gather. Stitch to the bodice. Stitch the

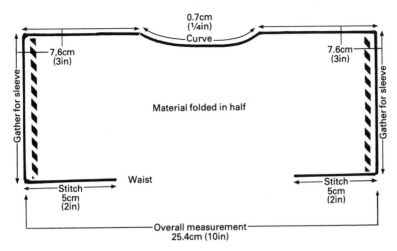

Fig 78 The Farmer's In His Den: Child Dress bodice construction

prepared head on to the puppet glove. Fold a hem and lightly gather the neck edge of the bodice to shape to the puppet neck. Fasten off.

Apron Cut a piece of broderie anglaise to measure 31.7 x 15.3cm (12½ x 6in) for the skirt. Hem down both shorter sides. Turn a hem at the top edge and gather; pull up to measure 15.3cm (6in).

Cut a piece of material 9 x 5cm (3½ x 2in) for the apron bodice. Hem the two shorter sides and one long edge. With the right sides of the bodice and apron skirt facing, lay the raw edge of the bodice on to the centre of the gathered top edge of the skirt. Turn the raw edge of the bodice under and stitch to the apron skirt.

Cut a piece of material 15.3cm long x 5cm wide (6 x 2in) for the back fastenings. With the right sides facing, fold in half to 2.5cm (1in) wide and stitch the 15.3cm (6in) edges togther. Turn to the right side. Tuck in each end and stitch one end to one side of the apron skirt at the top. Gather two separate 20.4cm (8in) pieces of 3.8cm (1½in) wide narrow broderie-anglaise trimming for the shoulder straps. Stitch a strap either side of the bodice. Take one strap and stitch to the back fastening on the joined side. Put the apron on to the puppet. Stitch the opposite end of the back fasten-

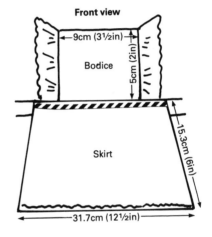

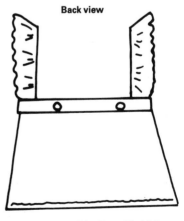

Fig 79 The Farmer's In His Den; Child Apron

ing to the other side of the apron. Sew the second shoulder strap to this so that both sides match. Stitch two small buttons to the centre of the back fastening, leaving a 5cm (2in) space in-between.

Bonnet This method of making a bonnet, whilst using more material than most, is very useful and quick. Cut a piece of material 40.6cm long x 28cm wide (16 x 11in). With the right sides facing, fold in half to measure 40.6cm long x 14cm wide (16 x 5½in). Stitch the side seams together and turn to the right side. Turn the open raw edges in, gather and pull up tightly, and secure both ends of the gathering together. This forms the back of the bonnet. Gather from one side of the bonnet to the other 7.6cm (3in) in from the front folded edge; pull the gathering up to measure approximately 20.4cm (8in). Fasten off. Cut two ribbon ties to measure 30.5cm (12in) long. Make a 7.6cm (3in) loop, by folding one end of each ribbon. Gather at the base of each loop and pull up. Stitch a tie to either side of the bonnet at the front gathering line, the loops facing upwards on to the bonnet. Tie the bonnet to the puppet head with the bow under the chin.

Simple Simon

Simple Simon went a-fishing,
For to catch a whale,
All the water he had got,
Was in his mother's pail.

* * *

Toy type: Glove puppet (colour picture page 107)
Size of toy: Height approximately 38.1cm (15in)

Flesh-coloured felt 92.1 x 35.5cm (36¼ x 14in) for the puppet glove, head and legs
Oddments of dark-brown felt for the eyes
Oddments of ginger-brown long-pile acrylic fur-fabric for the hair
Light-brown felt for the hat; the crown 10.3 x 17.8cm (4 x 7in), the brim a 15.3cm (6in) diameter circle
A triangular piece of material for the scarf, 35.5cm along the top edge x 17.8cm to the centre-back point (14 x 7in)
One 1.3cm (½in) curtain ring
Plain cotton material in light green 68.5 x 20.4cm (27 x 8in) for the smock
Dark-brown material 17.8 x 33cm (7 x 13in) for the trouser legs

Dark-brown felt 20.4 x 15.3cm (8 x 6in) for the boots; the boot laces can be made of thin cord or strong thread
Toy filling
Material quantities for the bucket as for Jack and Jill; the colouring is red and green; omit the Velcro
A piece of 0.7cm (¼in) dowel rod 21.5cm (8½in) long for the fishing rod
Strong cotton thread for the fishing line
A small open screw hook
Adhesive tape
A 17.8cm (7in) square of spotted material for the handkerchief
A twig 22.9cm (9in) long from a tree

Cut out all the pattern pieces – see Fig 74. The puppet glove, hat, trouser legs and boots are made in the same way as for the Farmer from the 'The Farmer's in his Den', page 123.

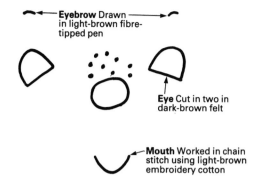

Eyebrow Drawn in light-brown fibre-tipped pen

Eye Cut in two in dark-brown felt

Mouth Worked in chain stitch using light-brown embroidery cotton

Fig 80 Simple Simon: Actual size features

Head Apply the ears where indicated on the pattern. Apply the hair all over the head, brought well down on either side of the head and in the front of the ears so that the ears are protruding.

The eyes are appliquéd. The nose is a 2cm (¾in) gathered-and-stuffed circle. The mouth and freckles are embroidered using light-brown stranded embroidery cotton, two strands only.

Scarf and Smock These are made in the same way as for Tom in 'Horsey, Horsey', page 104. The scarf is secured with a 1.3cm (½in) diameter curtain ring which is stitched into place.

Fishing Rod Cut a narrow slit into the top of the rod and tie a piece of strong cotton measuring 30.5cm (12in) in length into the slit; knot to secure. Tie the small screw hook on to the other end of the cotton and bind for 1.3cm (½in) with a small piece of adhesive tape. If for a very young child, omit the hook and tie a knot at the end of the cotton.

Handkerchief and Stick Make a ball of toy filling and place in the centre of the handkerchief. Knot the corners diagonally, tying the centre knot around the top of the twig to secure.

Bucket Make as for Jack and Jill's bucket, page 50, omitting the Velcro. Place the bucket on the puppet's right arm. Stitch Simple Simon's right hand around the fishing rod; stitch the twig with lunch handkerchief into the left hand.

To Market, To Market

To market, to market,
To buy a fat pig,
Home again, home again,
Jiggety-jig.

To market, to market,
To buy a fat hog,
Home again, home again,
Jiggety-jog.

* * *

Toy type: Glove puppet and pig (colour picture page 107)
Size of toy: Height about 40.6cm (16in)

Beige-coloured felt 92.1 x 35.5cm (36¼ x 14in) for the puppet glove, head and legs

Small pieces of black felt for the eyes
Oddments of black long-pile acrylic fur-fabric for the hair
Navy-blue felt for the hat; the crown 10.3 x 17.8cm (4 x 7in) the brim a 15.3cm (6in) diameter circle

133

A triangular piece of material for the scarf, 35.5cm along the top edge x 17.8cm to the centre-back point (14 x 7in)

Plain cotton material in dark red 68.5 x 20.4cm (27 x 8in) for the smock

A piece of medium-blue material 17.8 x 33cm (7 x 13in) for the trouser legs

Navy-blue felt 20.4 x 15.3cm (8 x 6in) for the boots

Thin cord or strong thread for the boot laces

One single piece of dried grass

Toy filling

A piece of wire about the gauge of a No 12 knitting needle for the hay fork, 30.5cm (12in) long

Grey wool for binding

Pig: As for Tom, Tom, the Piper's Son page 135, with the addition of embroidered hairs on his back in various tones of pink, beige and brown stranded embroidery cottons

Cut out all the relevant pattern pieces. See Fig 74. The puppet glove, hat and boots are as for the Farmer in The Farmer's in his Den, page 123, and are made in the same way.

Head The hair is applied all over the head with a spiky effect and stitched to hold. Glue the eyes in place. Draw the eyebrows using black fibre-tipped pen. The nose pieces are stitched together round the curved edges and lightly stuffed, then ladder stitched to the face.

Work the mouth in chain stitch using a pale-brown embroidery cotton. An unkempt appearance is achieved by working a variety of straight stitches in differing lengths over the chin area, to simulate the effect of a beard beginning to grow. The single strand of dried grass is inserted into the lower corner of the mouth and stitched to hold it in place.

Scarf and Smock These are made in the same way as for Tom in Horsey, Horsey, page 104, with the exception that the trouser legs are left hanging loosely and just turned up at the bottom.

Hay Fork Cut a piece of the wire measuring

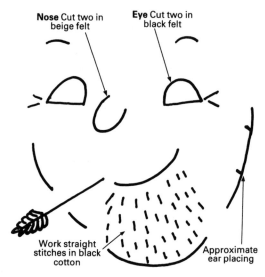

Fig 81 To Market, To Market: Actual size features

20.4cm (8in). Cut a second piece measuring 10.3cm (4in). Curve the 10.3cm (4in) piece in half and hook the top of the 20.4cm (8in) piece over the centre. Twist the wire to secure the two pieces together. Bind all the wire with either narrow pieces of sheeting or narrow tape, gluing in place as you bind. Fasten off. Bind the whole of the hay fork with grey knitting yarn, being very

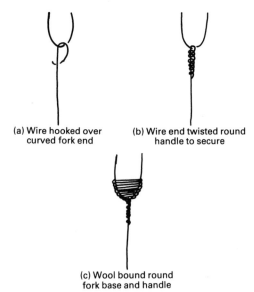

Fig 82 To Market, To Market: Hay fork construction

careful to produce an even surface. Add extra binding over the central join of the fork, taking the wool a short way on to the tines. Place in the puppet's right hand, stitch the thumb around the fork and secure to the hand.

Pig Make as for the pig in Tom, Tom, the Piper's Son. Work straight stitches all over the top of the body, using one strand of stranded embroidery cotton in various tones of pink, beige and brown. See photograph as a guide to placing.

DESIGN NOTE: Tom in Horsey, Horsey, Simple Simon, and the puppet from To Market, To Market are all basically the same puppets, but variations of colouring, feature placing, choice of hair and, when appropriate, the addition of highlights to the eyes using small shiny beads, make them into individual characters. The mature and sensible Tom; the young, fresh faced Simple Simon; and the puppet from To Market, To Market who is inclined to have a slightly spivvy, unkempt appearance.

Tom, Tom, The Piper's Son

Tom, Tom, the piper's son,
Stole a pig and away did run,
The pig was eat, and Tom was beat,
And Tom went crying down the street.

*   *   *

Toy type: Wooden-spoon arm puppet and pig (colour picture page 108)
Size of toy: Height 45.7cm (18in)

Flesh-coloured felt 60.9 x 50.8cm (24 x 20in) for the head, body, arms and legs
Blonde-coloured long-pile acrylic fur-fabric for the hair, 17.8 x 9cm (7 x 3½in)
A pair of 20mm safety-lock goggle eyes
One large wooden spoon with a handle length of approximately 25.4cm (10in). The handle should protrude sufficiently from the base of the body to enable it to be held comfortably by the manipulator
Black felt for the arm tube and shoes, 38.1 x 40.6cm (15 x 16in)
White felt for the jabot, 15.3 x 10.3cm (6 x 4in)
Oddments of lace for the jabot
Lace for the sleeve frills 6.4cm wide x 68.5cm long (2½ x 27in)
Yellow felt for the waistcoat 17.8 x 30.5cm (7 x 12in)

A 5cm (2in) square of spotted material for the handkerchief
Red felt for the jacket, beret band and sock ribbons, 40.6 x 20.4cm (16 x 8in)
Green tartan material with a small pattern for the kilt, beret and arm plaid, 88.9 x 40.6cm (35 x 16in)
A small brooch to secure the scarf at the shoulder
Seven small gold buttons: six for the jacket, one for the cap
Three small feathers to tone with the tartan for the beret decoration
Two small pearl buttons to secure the waistcoat
White long-pile acrylic fur-fabric 17.8 x 6.4cm (7 x 2½in) for the sporran
Scraps of black long-pile acrylic fur-fabric for the sporran detail
A 15.3cm (6in) piece of narrow gold cord for the sporran trimming
A 7.6cm (3in) piece of narrow gold-coloured chain for the sporran attachment

A 3.8cm (1½in) safety-pin for the kilt

A 7.6cm (3in) length of narrow leather for the kilt strap

A small buckle for the kilt attachment

Two small buckles for the shoes

Dark-fawn felt for the bagpipes, 20.4 x 20.4cm (8 x 8in)

A piece of small dowelling for the bagpipes approximately 43.7cm (17in) long (or wooden meat skewers would do)

A piece of tartan ribbon 1.3cm wide x 30.5cm (½in x 12in) for the pipe decoration

A pair of first-size children's socks in colours to tone with the tartan

Pink felt for the pig, 22.9 x 44.4cm (9 x 17½in)

One pair of blue 10mm safety-lock eyes for the pig

Scraps of black felt for the trotters and nostrils

One pipe cleaner for the tail

Stranded embroidery thread in beige and brown for the puppet's features and black for the pig's mouth

Toy filling

Cut out all the pattern pieces as given.

Head Insert the head gusset between two of the head pieces with the short ends open under the chin, and neatly overstitch in place. Insert the safety-lock eyes. Using the toy filling, stuff firmly but retain a smooth flat surface. Overstitch the opening under the chin to close. Needle-model the nose and ears using Fig 83 feature placing as a guide. Work the mouth using two strands of the beige embroidery cotton and a straight stitch. Work the eyebrows using one strand of brown embroidery cotton and small straight stitches. Lightly colour the cheeks using powder rouge.

Partly overstitch the third head piece to the back of the head, leaving the base open; this will cover the needle-model indentations and make a channel for the bowl of the wooden spoon. Insert the wooden spoon with the curve of the bowl facing the back of the head, and continue overstitching the back head piece into place, which will at the same time secure the wooden spoon.

In the blonde long-pile acrylic fur-fabric, cut a piece to fit across the puppet head from one side just above the ear to the opposite side above the ear and of a depth to cover the back of the head. If the backing on the fur-fabric is rather stiff, it may be necessary to apply the hair in several pieces rather than one complete piece, stitching firmly to the head. Comb the pile into shape.

Body Place the two body pieces together and overstitch around the outside edges, leaving the top neck edge and bottom straight edges open. Slip this on to the handle of the wooden spoon and stitch the neck neatly in place to the base of the head. Stuff the body firmly and close the bottom open edges using overstitching; the handle will protrude from the base of the body.

Arms Take a pair of arm pieces and overstitch together around the outside edges, leaving the top straight edges open. Stuff firmly. Overstitch to close. Make the second arm in the same way. Using stab stitching and matching flesh-coloured cotton, stab stitch on each hand to indicate the fingers. Ladder stitch an arm in place on either side of the body where indicated. Run a gathering thread up the inside of each arm from the wrist to the top and pull up gently to curve each arm. This will assist in the holding of the pig and bagpipes.

Arm Tube In the black felt, cut a piece to measure 28 x 40.6cm (11 x 16in). Fold in half lengthways and overstitch the long edges together to form a tube. Place the tube over the wooden spoon handle with the seam at the back and then ladder stitch the front and the back of the tube at the top edges to the bottom of the body, pleating slightly to fit body base.

Legs Take one pair of leg pieces and overstitch around the outside edges to join, leaving the top straight edges open. Stuff firmly to within 2.5cm (1in) of the top. With the seam to the front and the foot facing forwards, stitch across to hold the filling in place, still leaving the top 2.5cm (1in) free

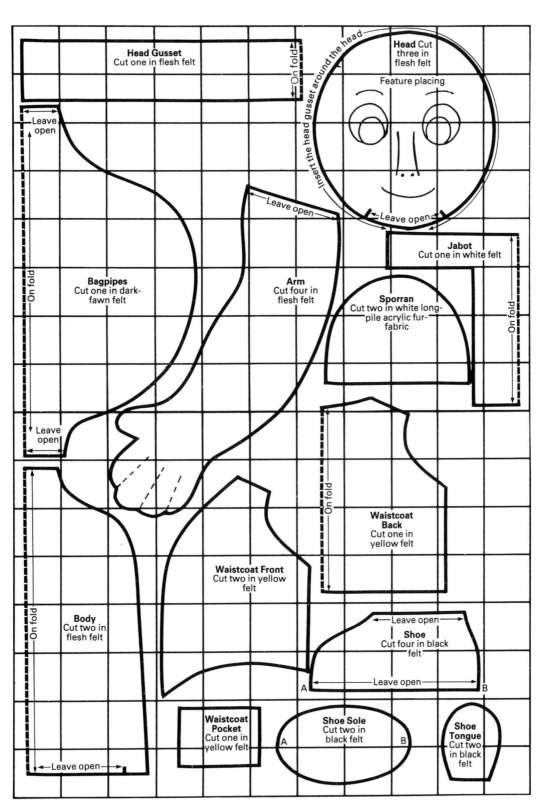

Head Gusset
Cut one in flesh felt

On fold

Insert the head gusset around the head

Head Cut three in flesh felt

Feature placing

Leave open

Jabot
Cut one in white felt

Leave open

On fold

Bagpipes
Cut one in dark-fawn felt

Arm
Cut four in flesh felt

Sporran
Cut two in white long-pile acrylic fur-fabric

Leave open

On fold

Waistcoat Back
Cut one in yellow felt

Waistcoat Front
Cut two in yellow felt

On fold

Body
Cut two in flesh felt

Leave open

Shoe
Cut four in black felt

Leave open

A

B

Leave open

Waistcoat Pocket
Cut one in yellow felt

Shoe Sole
Cut two in black felt

A

B

Shoe Tongue
Cut two in black felt

Fig 83 Tom, Tom, The Piper's Son

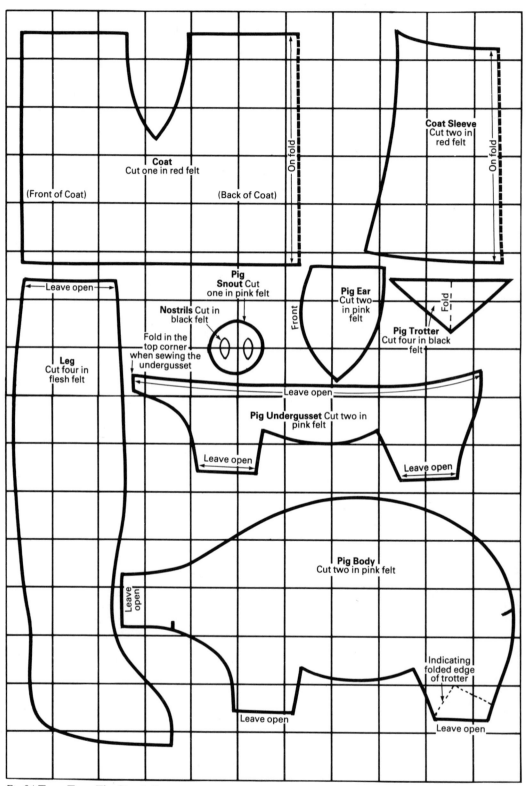

Fig 84 Tom, Tom, The Piper's Son

from any toy filling. Overstitch the top edges to close. Make the second leg in the same way. Ladder stitch a leg into place on either side of the body base and in front of the black arm tube piece.

Socks Cut the toe piece off each sock, if necessary, to obtain a neat fit, and turn the socks inside out. Gather each open end, pull up and close. Turn to the right side and place on the puppet.

Shoes Cut out the pattern pieces as given. Take two side pieces and overstitch the front seams, and then the back seams, to join where indicated. Insert the sole and overstitch in place. Insert a tongue and stitch in place. Make a second shoe in the same way. Stitch a buckle to each shoe.

Sock Ribbons Cut two pieces of red felt to measure 1.3 x 12.7cm (½ x 5in). Take one piece, fold it in half and stitch to the outside of a sock just below the top edge. Fold the sock top edge over. Trim the ends of the felt to a point. Treat the second piece in the same way.

Waistcoat Cut out the patterns in yellow felt. Join the shoulder seams together and then the side seams. Turn to the opposite side. Overstitch the pocket in place on the left front of the waistcoat. Carefully fold in the raw edges of the handkerchief and stitch this in the pocket; pull a point of the handkerchief down over the outside of the pocket and stitch to hold.

Jabot Cut the pattern in white felt. Stitch strips of gathered lace across the base of the jabot, leaving the neckband free. Place the neckband around the neck of the puppet and stitch to join at the back. Place the waistcoat on the puppet and stitch two small buttons to the centre-front edges of the waistcoat; pull up to join the edges together.

Jacket Cut the pattern pieces in red felt. Join the shoulder seams together and turn to the opposite side. Take one sleeve piece, fold it in half and overstitch to join the underarm seams. Insert the sleeve into the armhole of the jacket, matching the edges of the sleeve and armhole, and overstitch in place. Treat

the second sleeve in the same way.

Cut two pieces of the 6.4cm (2½in) lace to measure 34.3cm (13½in). Take one piece and join the shorter edges. Gather one long edge, place it on to the arm until the bottom ungathered edge of the frill is to the wrist placing, pull up the gathers to fit the arm and fasten off. Treat the second frill in the same way. Put the jacket on to the toy, pulling the sleeves down over the gathered frills. Stitch three buttons down either side of the jacket at the front edges as decoration.

Kilt Using the selvedge edge if possible as the hem, cut a piece of the tartan material to measure 73.7 x 14.6cm (29 x 5¾in); add 1.3cm (½in) to the measurement if turning a hem. For the waistband, cut a strip of the material to measure 44.4 x 5cm (17½ x 2in). Fold in the kilt material 2cm (¾in) on one short end to the right side and stitch 1.3cm (½in) from the fold. Fray the remaining 0.7cm (¼in) to make a fringe at the side of the kilt. Press the material away from the fringe.

Measure 13.4cm (5¼in) from the edge of the kilt, and mark with a pin. Measure 2.5cm (1in) from the pin. To make a pleat fold the second pin to the first pin. Tack from the top to the bottom of the kilt. For the second and remaining pleats, measure 3.8cm (1½in) from the first pleat and bring the pin to the fold of the pleat. Make ten pleats in this way. Go to the fringe end of the pleating and measure 1.3cm (½in) from the pleat; make a small pleat to face the pleating and tack down as before. Turn under a small hem on the remaining short raw edge and neaten. Steam press the pleats but leave in the tacking. Stitch down the pleats for about 2.5cm (1in); this will ensure that they stay in. Remove the tacking stitches.

Take the waistband piece and with a 1.5cm (⅝in) seam, stitch the waistband to the right side of the kilt, turning in the raw ends of the waistband to the seam side. Press the waistband up then fold it to the wrong side, enclosing the raw seam. Making the

139

waistband approximately 1.3cm (½in) deep, stitch to close the seam. Cut a small piece of leather or felt to measure 5.7x 1.3cm (2¼ x ½in) and cut a point at one end. Stitch the straight end to the top of the kilt at the front, 2cm (¾in) in from the frayed kilt edge. Stitch a small buckle over the first pleat on the unfringed edge of the kilt level with the leather piece. Stitch a small piece of Velcro on the waistband to secure the underlap of the kilt in place. Place the kilt on the puppet, securing the leather strap through the buckle, and fasten the front of the kilt to the underlap using a 3.8cm (1½in) safety-pin lying parallel to the side fringe.

Beret Cut a 22.9cm (9in) diameter circle of the tartan material. Gather around the outside edge and pull up to a circle of gathering measuring approximately 6.4cm (2½in) in diameter. Cut a strip of red felt to measure 40.6 x 3.8cm (16 x 1½in). Form into a circle from the centre of the piece to a diameter of 7.6cm (3in) and stitch to join, leaving the tails free. Place over the gathered 6.4cm (2½in) circle and stitch the top edge of the band to the gathered crown, encasing the 6.4cm (2½in) circle. Place on the puppet's head with the two felt-band tails hanging down the back. Place three small feathers together and stitch them at their base to the right hand of the beret at the front. Stitch a small gold button over the base of the feathers as decoration.

Bagpipes Cut the bag pattern piece in dark-fawn felt. Fold in half and overstitch the outside edges together, leaving divisions where indicated for the insertion of the dowelling and also a small stuffing opening. Stuff firmly and overstitch the stuffing opening to close. Cut dowel rods to the following lengths: two at 11.5cm (4½in), two at 6.4cm (2½in) and one at 7.6cm (3in). Insert the dowel rods in place, see Fig 85, adding some all-purpose adhesive to the openings on the bag and pressing the felt around the base of each dowel rod to secure. Place point A between the thumb and first

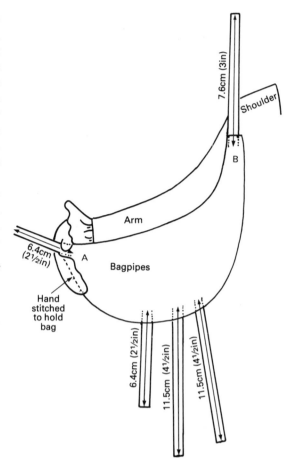

Fig 85 Tom, Tom, The Piper's Son: Diagram (not to scale) of bagpipes, front view

finger of the puppet's right hand and over-stitch right around the hand shape to attach it to the bagpipes, leaving a gap around the inside of the thumb. Place point B on the bagpipes to the front of the same arm near the shoulder of the jacket and stitch to hold. Add 1.3cm wide x 30.5cm (½ x 12in) tartan ribbon to the pipes as decoration.

Sporran Cut two pattern pieces in the white shaggy fur-fabric. Place together wrong sides facing and overstitch around the outside edges to join. Using all-purpose adhesive, glue a strip of narrow gold-coloured cord around the top curve of the sporran, making a small loop at the top centre. Cut three small pieces of black long-pile acrylic fur-fabric, each backing piece to measure

140

approximately 1.3 x 0.7cm (½ x ¼in). Part the pile of the white fur-fabric, insert one piece of the black fur-fabric and stitch in place towards the top of the sporran at the centre. Stroke the white fur-fabric over the black fur-fabric to mask any joins.

Insert the other two pieces of the black fur-fabric on either side of the sporran at the front, slightly lower than the centre black piece. Stitch these into place in the same way. Cut two pieces of gold-coloured chain, each measuring 3.8cm (1½in), and stitch a piece to either side of the gold-braid trimming on the sporran. Stitch the end of each gold chain piece to the kilt side just under the waistband: one just in from the fringed edge of the kilt and the other just in from where the pleating on the kilt starts.

Arm Plaid Cut a piece of the tartan material 12.7 x 40.6cm (5 x 16in). Fringe the short ends. Fold both long edges to the back of the piece and hem. With the hemmed edges together, place the plaid over the right shoulder and stitch to secure under the arm. Add a small brooch as decoration on the plaid at the shoulder level.

Pig Leaving the snout open, pin the two body pieces together and insert the under-body gusset pieces where indicated. Over-stitch around the outside edges to join, leaving the snout, base of legs and under-body seams open. Insert the snout and over-stitch into place. Insert the trotters into the base of each foot with the points to the front (see Fig 86). Insert the safety-lock eyes where indicated.

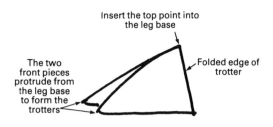

Fig 86 Tom, Tom, The Piper's Son: Diagram of pig trotter

With the exception of the snout, which is lightly stuffed, stuff the toy firmly paying careful attention to attaining a smooth toy skin. Ladder stitch to close the underbody. Push the snout inwards towards the body to form wrinkles and stitch these to hold by running the sewing thread through the base of each wrinkle, pulling up to hold and fastening off. Stitch the nostrils in place and work a smiling mouth using stem stitch and single strand black embroidery thread.

Take one ear piece. Fold the front edges to the centre at the base and stitch to join for approximately 0.7cm (¼in). Ladder stitch to the head with the join at the base of the ear underneath, facing the body. Treat the second ear in the same way.

Cover the pipe cleaner with an oblong of pink felt and overstitch all around the outside edges to make the tail. Overstitch one short end in place on the body. Take a pencil and wind the pipe cleaner round and round it to form the tail curls; remove the pencil.

SOFT TOYS INVOLVING OTHER MEDIUMS

Fiddle De Dee

Fiddle de dee,
Fiddle de dee,
The fly has married the bumble bee.

* * *

Toy type: Mobile (colour picture page 53)

Please refer to 'Mobiles' in the techniques section. This mobile can be constructed as the original, in the given sizes; however, extra bees and flowers can be made to enlarge the content of the mobile, and the reader may wish to alter the mobile's size to fit a specific location.

Mobile wires, sold in sets at crafts shops
A rich-yellow felt for the bees, 22.9 x 17.8cm (9 x 7in)
Black felt for the bride's body, bridegroom's morning coat and hat, and the vicar's cassock, 28 x 10.3cm (11 x 4in)
White felt for the vicar's surplice, collar on bridegroom and daisy petals, 20.4 x 22.9cm (8 x 9in)
Oddments of yellow felt for the daisy centres; light- and dark-green felt for the leaves
A piece of fine white net for the bridal veil, fly's wings and bridesmaid bees' wings, 12.7 x 17.8cm (5 x 7in)
A piece of Vilene for the bridegroom's wings 7.6 x 6.4cm (3 x 2½in)
A piece of ribbon for the vicar's stole,

17.8 x 1.3cm (7 x ½in)
Covered flower wire for the bride and bridegroom's legs, 121.9cm (48in)
A skein of black stranded embroidery cotton for the bridesmaid bees' legs and for covering the bride and bridegroom's legs also oddments of pink and lilac embroidery cotton for the features
Scraps of very narrow ribbon in yellow and green for the bridesmaids' head dresses, and blue for the bridegroom's hat band
Four broderie-anglaise flowers cut from narrow broderie-anglaise trimming, for the bridesmaids' head dresses
A scrap of narrow red ribbon for the bridegroom's buttonhole
A scrap of pale-blue ribbon for the bride's garter
A scrap of fine green silk material for the bridegroom's cravat
¼m (10in) narrow lace for the bride's head dress and dress trimming
½m (19¾in) very narrow pink ribbon for the bride's dress trimming

Hush-a-bye Baby

A piece of very fine white material for the bride's dress, 20.4 x 8.3cm (8 x 3¼in)

Fine nylon sewing thread for stringing the mobile

Toy filling

A few small pieces of everlasting or artificial flowers for the bouquet

Six black brocatelle beads for the vicar and bridesmaids' eyes and the bride's front legs

A small piece of fast-drying white modelling compound for the bride's shoes

Clear all-purpose adhesive

A black fibre- or felt-tipped pen

A piece of white notepaper, 6.4 x 2.5cm (2½ x 1in) for the marriage service sheet

Cut out all the pattern pieces.

Bridegroom Bee Fig 89 (a)

Place the two body pieces together and stab stitch around the outside edge to join, leaving open where indicated. Stuff and close the opening with stab stitching.

Eyes Fig 87 (a). Cut two 0.7cm (¼in) diameter circles and stitch to the head where indicated. Add white highlights using embroidery cotton. Draw in the mouth (Fig 87 (b)) with the pen and add four stripes around the body, working from the tail end and leaving approximately 0.7cm (¼in) spaces between the stripes.

Legs Cut three 15.3cm (6in) lengths of the wire. Push each piece through the side seam of the body and out the other side where indicated. Bind each wire with black stranded embroidery cotton, working from the base to the tip of each leg. Fasten off with a knot and add a drop of glue to secure, but leave approximately 1.3cm (½in) of the stranded cotton at the end of each leg dangling.

Collar and Cravat Cut a piece of white felt to measure 7 x 0.7cm (2¾ x ¼in). Place around the bridegroom's neck and fasten at the front (the underbody). Fold a piece of green silk material into a loop to fit between

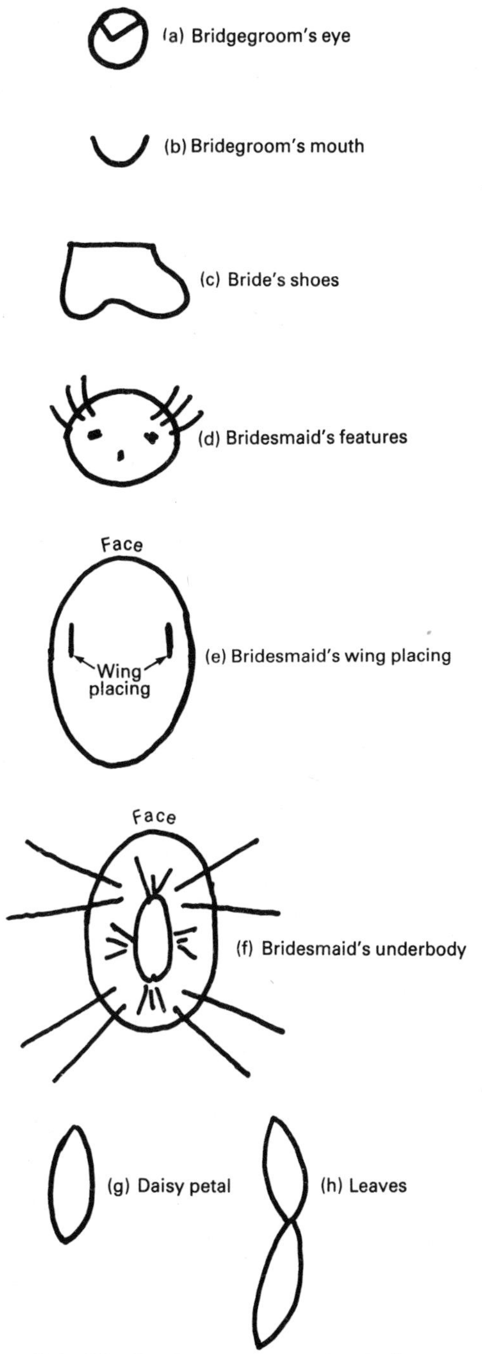

Lavender's Blue

Fig 87 Fiddle De Dee: patterns. (a) Bridegroom's eyes: cut two in felt; (b) Bridegroom's mouth shape; (c) Bride's shoes: side view; (d) Bridesmaid's features; (e) Bridesmaid's wing placing on top of body; (f) Leg placing on bridesmaid's underbody; (g) Daisy petal: cut seven in white felt for each flower; (h) Leaves: cut two in dark-green felt and two in light-green felt for each flower

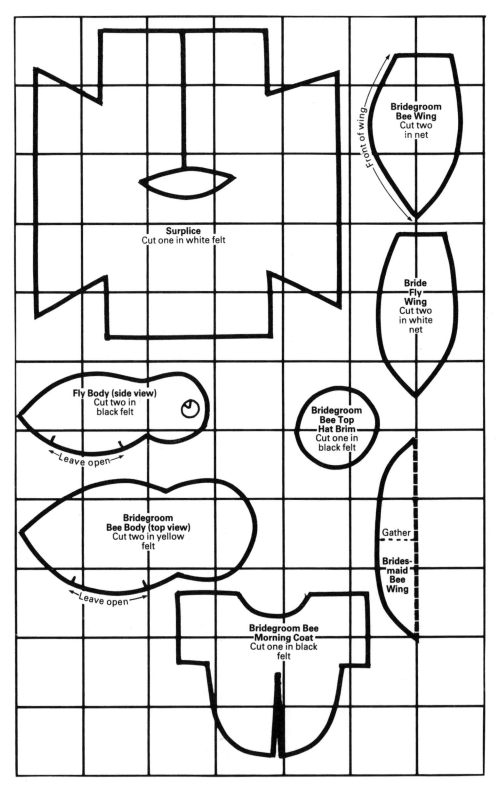

Bridegroom Bee Wing Cut two in net

Front of wing

Bride Fly Wing Cut two in white net

Surplice Cut one in white felt

Fly Body (side view) Cut two in black felt

←Leave open→

Bridegroom Bee Top Hat Brim Cut one in black felt

Bridegroom Bee Body (top view) Cut two in yellow felt

←Leave open→

Gather

Bridesmaid Bee Wing

Bridegroom Bee Morning Coat Cut one in black felt

Fig 88 Fiddle De Dee

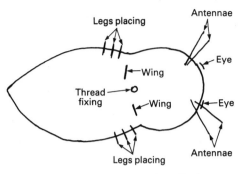

(a) Bridegroom Bee, top view of body

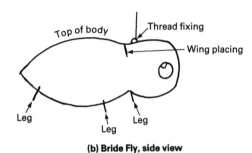

(b) Bride Fly, side view

Fig 89 Fiddle De Dee: (a) Bridegroom Bee: top view of body; (b) Bride Fly: side view

the collar points and stitch into place.

Morning Coat and Buttonhole Place the morning coat around the bee's shoulders and stitch to the top front (the underbody) to cover the base of the cravat. Gather a small length of narrow red ribbon on the edge only, pull up to form a tiny rosette, stitch to hold, and secure to the lapel of the coat for the buttonhole. Cut a 1.3cm (½in) square of black felt for the coat pocket and stitch to the left side of the coat at the front. Cut a 0.7cm (¼in) square of white felt and place it in the pocket as a handkerchief.

Wings Stitch the straight edges of the wings in place where indicated.

Top Hat Cut a 3.8cm (1½in) diameter circle for the brim in black felt. Cut a 3.8cm (1½in) square of black felt for the crown. Roll the crown into a tight tube and stitch to hold. Cut a circle of black felt to fit the diameter of the top of the crown and glue in place. Glue the base of the crown to the centre of the brim. Place a piece of very nar-

row blue ribbon around the base of the crown for the band; stitch to secure.

Bride Fly Fig 89 (b).

Place the body pieces together. Stab stitch to join, leaving open where indicated. Stuff and close. Cut two 0.7cm (¼in) diameter circles in white felt for the eyes. Stitch to the body where indicated, then stitch a black brocatelle bead into the centre of each eye.

Legs and Shoes The bride's legs are 10.3cm (4in) long and applied in the same way as the bridegroom's where indicated in Fig 89 (b). Cut the ends of the stranded cotton binding short and glue a black brocatelle bead to the ends of the two front legs.

Using white modelling compound, form a tiny shoe to the given size (Fig 87 (c)) and press on to the ends of the remaining four legs.

Dress Cut one long edge of the dress material piece using pinking shears. Trim both the short edges with narrow lace. Turn in the top raw edge and gather to fit around the bride's neck, securing at the top centre front. Tie a small bow in the narrow pink ribbon, making sure the ribbon tails are long enough to be stitched down both lace-trimmed front edges of the dress. Stitch in place to hold.

Veil Cut a piece of white net to measure 12.7 x 3.8cm (5 x 1½in). Gather one long edge and pull up. Stitch to the top of the bride's head with the short open edges to the back of the head. Gather a strip of the narrow lace to form a rosette of approximately 1.3cm (½in) diameter. Stitch to the top of the head over the veil gathering. Tie a tiny bow in the narrow pink ribbon to match the dress trimming and stitch to the centre of the head dress.

Garter Gather a small piece of narrow pale-blue ribbon, and pull up and stitch around the top of one of the bride's legs.

Wings Apply to either side of the body where indicated, stitching the straight edges only.

Bouquet Place a few small flowers in a spray

147

to measure not more than 3.8 (1½in). Bind together then stitch to hold to the bride's front left leg, tying a piece of narrow pink ribbon to hide the stitching.

Vicar Bee Fig 90

Gather a 9cm (3½in) diameter circle of yellow felt, pull up slightly and stuff into an elongated shape measuring approximately 7.6cm (3in). Lay the gathered edges parallel and stitch together; this stitched line is to the front of the body. Draw black lines around the body as for the bridegroom bee.

The vicar has only four legs, applied as for the bridegroom, where indicated on the pattern.

Features Work the nose and mouth using two strands of embroidery cotton. Apply two small brocatelle beads for the eyes. The antennae are worked using six strands of stranded embroidery cotton; they are approximately 2cm (¾in) long.

Cassock, Surplice and Stole Cut a strip of black felt to measure 15.3 x 5cm (6 x 2in). Gather one long edge and pull up to fit the bee's neck, with the open edges at the back of the body. Cut two small arm holes either side at the top and place the arms through these.

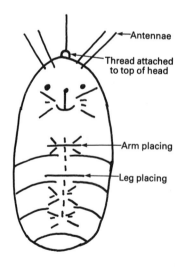

Fig 90 Fiddle De Dee: Vicar Bee. Front view of the vicar's body. The 9cm (3½in) diameter circle, gathered and stitched into an oblong.

Place the white-felt surplice over the vicar's head with the opening at the back. Stitch at the top of the back to join.

Take the piece of ribbon for the stole and fringe each end. Place around the vicar bee's neck and fold his front legs to the front of the body.

Marriage Service Sheet Fold the piece of paper in half. Write on the outside 'Marriage Service', and on the inside: 'Dearly beloved we are gathered together in the sight of God to join together this bee and fly in holy matrimony.' Glue in place for the vicar to hold.

Bridesmaid Bee

Gather a 5cm (2in) diameter circle of yellow felt and form into an oblong measuring 2.5cm (1in). Construct as for the vicar. Cut an oval to fit the body base, and to cover the gathering, and stitch into place. Draw black lines around the body as for the other bees, leaving one end free from stripes for the face.

Features Using Fig 87 (d) work, in embroidery cotton, a small pink nose and black eyes and eyelashes, leaving the eyelashes free to stand out either side, sewing them at their base to the head.

Wings Cut two wings in white net. Take one wing and gather across the centre. Pull up the gathering and stitch to one side of the body, Fig 87 (e). Make and apply the second wing to the opposite side of the body.

Legs Using stranded embroidery cotton, add the legs either side as shown on Fig 87 (f), each front leg to measure 1.3cm (½in) and each back leg 2cm (¾in). Secure to the body.

Head Dress Cut an individual flower from broderie-anglaise trimming and glue to the top of the head. Tie a tiny bow in the very narrow ribbon to measure 2cm (¾in), in either green or yellow, and glue to the back of the broderie-anglaise flower.

Make three more bridesmaid bees.

Daisies Fig 87 (g) and (h)

Cut a 2cm (¾in) diameter circle in bright-yellow felt for the centre. Gather around the outside edge, stuff and form into a ball, then fasten off. Place the bases of seven white-felt petal shapes over the gathering on the flower centre, and stitch to hold. Cut two leaves in dark green and two leaves in light green and stitch to the back of the flower. Make a further five daisies.

Mobile Construction

Start with the main mobile wire which measures 25.4cm (10in). Add a thread with a loop to the centre of the wire for hanging. Do not glue in place at this stage. Thread two bridesmaid bees and two daisies spaced approximately 7.6cm (3in) apart on one nylon thread measuring 45.7cm (18in); knot to hold each one in place. Thread two daisies and a bridesmaid bee on another piece of nylon thread measuring 73.7cm (29in); knot to hold each one in place. Tie these threads to either end of the main mobile wire.

Suspend a second wire measuring 20.4cm (8in) from the centre of the main wire with a 17.8cm (7in) drop. From the centre of the second wire suspend the vicar on a nylon thread measuring 16.6cm (6½in) secured to the top of his head. Suspend the bridegroom from one end of the second wire on a nylon thread measuring 17.8cm (7in), and the bride from the opposite end of the same wire on a thread measuring 19.2cm (7½in). Finally, suspend a bridesmaid bee and daisy from the main wire on a thread measuring 28cm (11in). All the thread lengths are given as an approximate guide only. Many elements can effect the balance of the mobile, for example the weight of the materials used. When a good balance has been obtained, glue each knot in place on the wires. The whole construction should move freely.

A pretty addition to this mobile would be butterflies in a variety of colours to tone with the figures, made according to the butterfly in The Teddy Bears' Picnic, scaled down in size, and glued to the flower centres or flying with the mobile thread placed through the body.

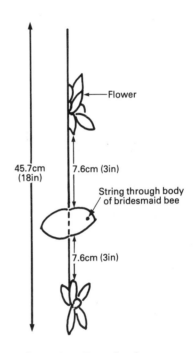

Fig 91 Fiddle De Dee: Example of stringing method – construction of bee and flowers on to thread. The thread is tied through the back of each daisy and knotted to hold. The thread passes through the top and base of the bee's body and is knotted underneath to secure

Goosey, Goosey, Gander

Goosey, Goosey, Gander,
Whither shall I wander?
Upstairs and downstairs,
And in my lady's chamber.
There I met an old man,
Who would not say his prayers,
I took him by the left leg,
And threw him down the stairs.

* * *

Toy type: Pull-along toy or sit-and-ride toy (colour picture page 125)

Size of toy: Height from ground level to top of head 59.7cm (23½in); length 60.9cm (24in)

Whilst this toy was designed as a pull-along toy, with a few adaptations it can be made as a sit-and-ride toy. Before making the toy in the latter form please refer to the section on safety factors in toymaking, page 16.

1m (39½in) of 1.37m (54in) wide white polished fur-fabric for the body and wings

Yellow felt for the feet, 35.5 x 22.9cm (14 x 9in)

Orange felt for the beak, 36.8 x 15.3cm (14½ x 6in)

One pair of 22mm brown safety-lock eyes

Ten pipe cleaners

Black stranded embroidery cotton

A 76.2cm (30in) piece of Velcro for attaching the body to the base

Toy filling

Light-green felt for covering the base, 48.2 x 22.9cm (19 x 9in)

Braid to cover the sides of the base, 121.9cm (48in), the braid to be wide enough to cover the thickness of the plywood

A piece of plywood 48.2 x 22.9 x 1.3cm (19 x 9 x ½in)

Four good-quality castors; sixteen screws to attach the castors (these are usually supplied with the castors)

One 22.9cm (9in) square of bright-blue felt for the flowers

Yellow felt 7.6 x 7.6cm (3 x 3in) for the flower centres

One 22.9cm (9in) square of green felt for the leaves

Three 3.8cm (1½in) diameter circles of felt oddments to construct the flowers and leaves on

Four 1.3cm (½in) squares of the soft halves of Velcro to attach the flowers to the baseboard

A 33cm (13in) piece of 1.3cm (½in) dowel rod

One wooden ball with a hole to fit the dowel rod

One small screw hook and eye

One black fibre- or felt-tipped pen

Cut out all the pattern pieces

Body With the right sides facing, pin then backstitch the side body pieces together from A at the base of the neck, over the head to B at the tail end. Insert the underbody gusset matching A–A and B–B, and pin then backstitch into place, leaving open on one side for a stuffing opening where indicated on the pattern. Turn to the right side. Insert the safety-lock eyes. Stuff the body firmly. It is advisable to leave the toy filling to settle overnight, then add more toy filling if necessary and close the opening using ladder stitching.

Wings Place together in pairs with the right sides facing. Take one pair and pin then backstitch together, leaving open C–D.

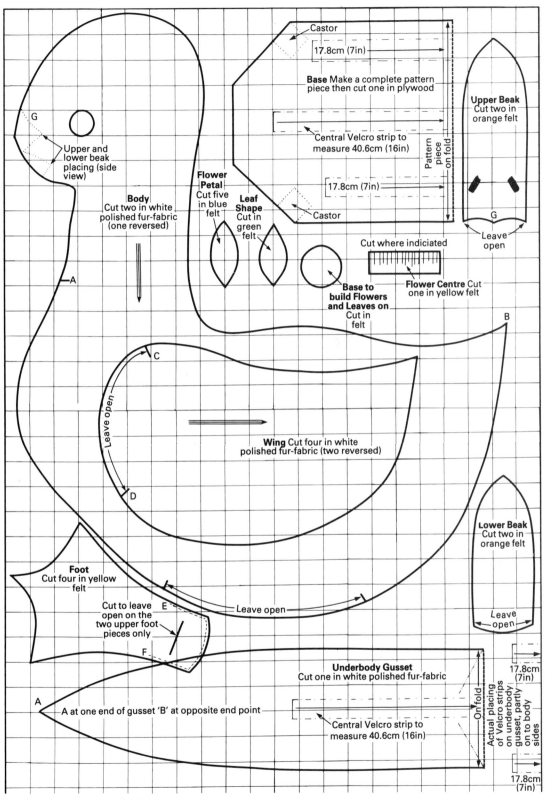

Castor

17.8cm (7in)

Base Make a complete pattern piece then cut one in plywood

Central Velcro strip to measure 40.6cm (16in)

Pattern piece on fold

17.8cm (7in)

Castor

Upper Beak Cut two in orange felt

G

Leave open

G

Upper and lower beak placing (side view)

Body Cut two in white polished fur-fabric (one reversed)

Flower Petal Cut five in blue felt

Leaf Shape Cut in green felt

Cut where indiciated

Base to build Flowers and Leaves on Cut in felt

Flower Centre Cut one in yellow felt

A

C

Leave open

B

Wing Cut four in white polished fur-fabric (two reversed)

D

Lower Beak Cut two in orange felt

Foot Cut four in yellow felt

Cut to leave open on the two upper foot pieces only

E

Leave open

Leave open

F

A

A at one end of gusset 'B' at opposite end point

Underbody Gusset Cut one in white polished fur-fabric

On fold

17.8cm (7in)

Central Velcro strip to measure 40.6cm (16in)

Actual placing of Velcro strips on underbody, gusset, partly on to body sides

17.8cm (7in)

Fig 92 Goosey, Goosey, Gander

Turn to the right side and lightly, but evenly, stuff. Treat the second wing in the same way. Take a wing and place on the body where indicated on the pattern, and backstitch the C–D half of the wing nearest the body into place, following the open curve on the wing. Add more toy filling if necessary to shape, and then ladder stitch the outer half of the wing to the body just in front of the previously stitched inner piece. Attach the second wing in the same way.

Beak Place the two upper beak pieces together and overstitch around the outside edges to join, leaving the top curved edges open. Insert a pipe cleaner to one outside curve of the beak shape, and stitch in place at the top to hold. Insert a second pipe cleaner into the beak on the opposite outside curve of the beak, and attach at the top to hold in place. Overstitch the top curve of the beak to close. Lay this upper beak aside.

Place the lower beak pieces together and treat in the same way as the upper beak. Overstitch the upper beak in place first on the head, then line up the under beak with the points on the beak pieces matching, and overstitch in place. Using three strands of black stranded embroidery cotton, work the beak markings in irregular straight stitches.

Feet Place together in pairs. Take one pair and overstitch around the outside edges to join, leaving the top curved end open. Insert a pipe cleaner in line with an outside edge and stab stitch in place. Insert a second pipe cleaner in line with the opposite edge and stab stitch in place. Insert a third pipe cleaner in the centre of the foot at the centre point, and stab stitch in place. Overstitch the open end of the foot to close. Treat the second foot in the same way.

Stitch both feet from E to F into place where indicated on the underbody gusset pattern, then backstitch across each foot from side to side to attach to the body, approximately 3.8cm (1½in) measured from the top curve of each foot. Attach the soft halves of the strips of Velcro to the underbody gusset (see pattern), laying the hooked halves of each piece to one side.

Base Cut the plywood base to the given size. Attach the castors where indicated.

Handle Glue the wooden ball on to the end of the dowel rod. Screw the small hook into the opposite end of the rod. Screw the eye into the centre front of the wooden base. Hook the handle on to the eye and press the hook to close and securely attach.

Cover the top of the plywood base with light-green felt, using a latex-based adhesive. When dry, trim the edges of the felt flush to the top edges of the base. Trim the outside edges with lampshade braid or similar, using adhesive to apply. When the covering and braid are completely dry, glue the hooked halves of the Velcro strips in place, first making sure they are in line with the Velcro strips on the underbody gusset. Any slight variation in placing the strips on the underbody gusset could mean the strips will not match up to the pattern placing on the base. Allow to dry, and attach the goose to the base by matching the Velcro strips on the body to the Velcro strips on the felt-covered base.

Flowers There are four flowers, each comprising one yellow centre, five blue petals and four leaves. Cut out the necessary pieces. To construct one flower, roll up a yellow centre firmly and stitch to hold. One by one, stitch the five petals around the yellow centre by their base points. Cut a 3.8cm (1½in) diameter of felt as the base. Glue the tips of three leaves to this base, each meeting at the centre of the circle. Glue the flower, lying on its side, to the centre of the leaves. Glue a leaf to the back of the flower to cover the stitching. Using the black fibre- or felt-tipped pen, add the veins on three leaves only, leaving the one on the flower unmarked. Make another three flower and leaf constructions in the same way.

Glue a 1.3cm (½in) square of the soft half of a piece of Velcro to the base of each flower construction. When completely dry, attach one flower to the centre Velcro strip at the front of the base, and one each to the ends of the Velcro strips at the back base.

Finally groom the goose using a teasel brush. *Adjusting to a Sit-and-Ride Toy* The plywood base should be much thicker to take the weight of a child. It should be reduced slightly in size to enable it to be inserted into the base of the toy. Then the toy should be stuffed very firmly using wood wool (often available from china shops) encased in terylene or nylon toy filling to produce a smooth feel to the toy skin. After the stuffing has been inserted, close the opening using ladder stitching, then attach the castors through the toy skin and firmly into the plywood base. The handle which is applied to this toy for the pull-along version would be omitted on the sit-and-ride toy.

The Teddy Bears' Picnic

If you go down to the woods today,
You're sure of a big surprise,
If you go down to the woods today,
You'd better go in disguise,
For every bear that ever there was,
Will gather there for certain because,
Today's the day the teddy bears have their picnic.

* * *

Toy type: A musical-drum observation toy (colour picture page 126)
Size of toy: 25.4 x 9.6cm (10 x 3¾in)

This musical drum is designed to teach a child to observe the many small detailed items. It will be fun to discover all the tiny creatures which are sharing the picnic with the bears. On the board are the following: six teddy bears of varying sizes, a bull, a squirrel, a rabbit, a ladybird, a spider, a butterfly and ducks. There is a picnic hamper containing cups, plates and serviettes; a picnic cloth is laid on the grass with sandwiches, cottage loaf, honey and bee, hot cross buns, jam tarts, Swiss roll, plates, cups and saucers, sugar bowl, cream jug, teapot and spoon. At the top of the tree there are three blackbirds in a nest. One bear has his kite caught in the tree. A bear is feeding a jam tart to a squirrel. Another bear sits in a boat on the river. On the bridge a bear is fishing and has caught a fish which the ducks are trying to eat. The bull leans over a gate eating a hot cross bun. Around the side of the drum life under the stream is depicted, with fish and weeds. A frog nestles in the mud. Under the field where the bears are picnicking worms and beetles are shown in the earth, and hidden in the roots of the tree is a tiny dormouse asleep. Once the child tires of looking for the various items then stories can be made up around the bears and their friends.

All the patterns for this musical drum are very small and an excellent way of using oddments of materials. When cutting out tiny items, it is essential to use a small pair of sharp pointed scissors to obtain a clear outline. It is easier to cut out the felt pieces if the pattern is first pinned on to the felt and then that portion of felt removed from the main piece; it is then much easier to manipulate. Cut around the pattern shape turning the felt to the scissors, with the scissor blades facing ahead to 12 o'clock. If the scissors are constantly turned, the outline shape can easily be spoiled.

153

This musical drum was designed as a stationary musical box which can be turned from time to time to show a different view. However, if desired it could be placed on a turntable. A word of caution: whilst a toy which can be turned easily might appear to be a good idea, once a child discovers something will move it might mean that the drum will be constantly spun round, defeating the object of it being an observation toy.

THE DRUM

Two round 25.4cm (10in) cake bases, the heavier type with the deeper sides

Five pieces of 3.8cm (1½in) diameter strong cardboard tubing, each measuring 7.6cm (3in)

Oddments of card to tubing diameter

One plastic shelled 1/12SE key-wind musical unit, tune the Teddy Bears' Picnic

One 30.5cm (12in) diameter circle of light-green felt for top of the drum

One 30.5cm (12in) diameter circle of light-brown felt for base of the drum

Blue felt 35.5 x 12.7cm (14 x 5in) for the side panel river scene

A piece of card 35.5 x 10.3cm (14 x 4in)

Brown felt 38.1 x 12.7cm (15 x 5in) for the side panel underground scene

A piece of card 35.5 x 10.3cm (14 x 4in)

A piece of blue felt for the stream a slightly lighter tone than the panel side, 25.4 x 10.3cm (10 x 4in)

UNDERWATER SCENE

Scraps of orange and grey felt for the fish

Black felt for the beetles

Green felt for the weeds

White felt for the air bubbles

UNDERGROUND SCENE

Wool oddments in varying tones of brown for the tree roots

Grey, beige and black felts for the worms and beetles

An oddment of beige-coloured polished fur-fabric for the dormouse

Green felt for the frog

Black marker pen

Copydex adhesive

Uhu adhesive

SCENE ON TOP OF THE DRUM

Tree: Oddments of wool of varying shades of brown; two packets of pipe cleaners; a small roll of narrow lampshade binding; a packet of yellow drop stamens, the type used in making artificial flowers; oddments of green felt for the leaves

Blackbirds' nest: Scraps of fine wool, length approximately 35.5cm (14in)

Blackbirds: Black and yellow felt

Bridge: Dark-brown felt 22.9 x 7.6cm (9 x 3in); card for base 22.9 x 7.6cm (9 x 3in)

Gate: Dowelling for the posts, 11.5 x 0.7cm (4½ x ¼in); dowelling for the bars, two pieces slightly thinner than the posts each measuring 7.6cm (3in)

Boat: Tan-coloured felt 19.2 x 6.4cm (7½ x 2½in); tan-coloured stranded embroidery cotton; two pieces of card 2.5 x 1.3cm (1 x ½in) for the seats

Ducks: Scraps of yellow and orange felt

Bullrushes: Brown and green felt; two pieces of thin wire 5cm (2in) long; green stranded embroidery cotton

Bull: Medium-brown felt 10.3 x 19.2cm (4 x 7½in); scraps of pink, black, white and beige felt; a small curtain ring; a piece of fine chain 15.3cm (6in) long

Butterfly: Scraps of black and orange Vilene

Rabbit: Beige felt 5 x 5.7cm (2 x 2¼in)

Squirrel: Oddments of ginger-coloured felt; two small black brocatelle beads

Ladybird: Red and black felt

Flowers: Scraps of yellow, red and green felt

Picnic hamper: A small box to measure approximately 5 x 2.5cm (2 x 1in) (separate lid and base); sufficient tiny red-check gingham material to cover the top, base and sides of the box; two pieces of red felt for the lining

Picnic cloth, cushion and honey-pot cover: Check gingham to match the picnic basket 14 x 11.5cm (5½ x 4½in)

Swiss roll, jam tarts and sandwiches: Yellow, red, cream, white and brown Vilene or Funtex

Cottage loaf and hot cross buns: Beige felt; beige stranded embroidery cotton; a piece of greaseproof paper 7.6 x 7.6cm (3 x 3in)

Honey pot: Honey-coloured Vilene or Funtex 6.4 x 5cm (2½ x 2in); small piece of white paper for honey label; 5cm (2in) diameter circle of gingham material for the top

Crockery: The original was made from Fimo; any quick drying modelling compound could be used

Spider: A scrap of black felt; fine white nylon sewing thread; a piece of white toy filling

Rug: A piece of woven woollen material 7.6 x 7.6cm (3 x 3in)

Kite: Red, yellow and blue Vilene or Funtex; a 2.5cm (1in) piece of fine wire for the handle; stranded embroidery cotton

Fishing rod: Wire 7.6cm (3in) long; black stranded embroidery cotton

Windmill: Scraps of blue and pink Vilene or Funtex; one dressmaker's pin; a piece of fine wire 5cm (2in) long; stranded embroidery cotton

Bumble bee: Yellow felt; fine white net for wings

Larger bear: Light-fawn felt 10.3 x 14.6cm (4 x 5¾in); scraps of medium-brown felt for the foot pads

Medium-size bear: Light-fawn felt 11.5 x 11.5cm (4½ x 4½in); scraps of dark-brown felt for the foot pads

Tiny bear: Light-fawn felt 10.3 x 6.4cm (4in x 2½in); scraps of ginger-brown felt for the foot pads

Toy filling for the three bears

Small pieces of very narrow ribbon in red, yellow, green, pink, light blue and dark blue for neck bows

Dark-brown stranded embroidery cotton

The Drum Preparation Cover one side of one cake board with Copydex adhesive spread thinly and evenly. Leave until nearly dry. Lay the board on to the centre of the light-green felt circle. Apply adhesive to the side drop of the board and when nearly dry, press the excess felt from the top covering down

all around the side drop. Trim to neaten. Treat the second cake board in the same way, covering with the light-brown felt. Lay this board to one side.

Tree Take ten pipe cleaners. Bind them together with the narrow tape to within 3.8cm (1½in) of one end, leaving the top of the pipe cleaners on the opposite end exposed for 1.3cm (½in). Divide the 3.8cm (1½in) pipe cleaners to four at the centre and three sets of two pipe cleaners , see Fig 93. Bind the three sets of two pipe cleaners with wool (these are the roots), leaving the four central pipe cleaners free. Make a hole right through the green-covered cake board, see Fig 96 for placing, insert the four central pipe cleaners and then fan these out on the underside of the cake board and glue to hold. Lay one end of the wool parallel to the base of the bound pipe cleaners and stitch to hold, then bind with the wool up to the 1.3cm (½in) exposed ends of the pipe cleaners, covering the tape-bound section of the pipe cleaners. Add a second layer of wool binding if necessary to

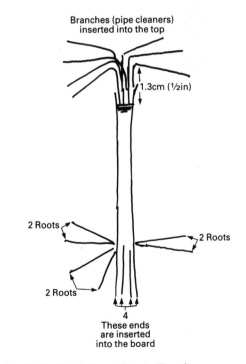

Fig 93 The Teddy Bears' Picnic: Tree diagram

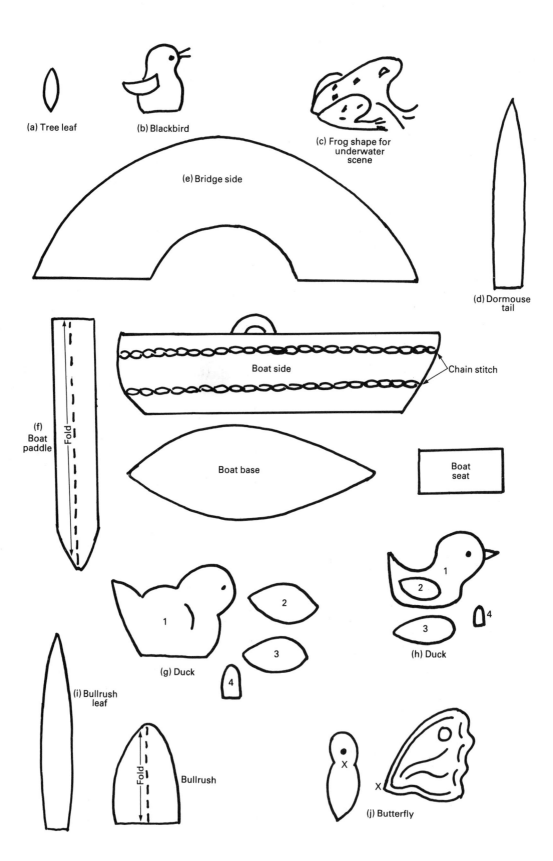

(a) Tree leaf

(b) Blackbird

(c) Frog shape for underwater scene

(e) Bridge side

(d) Dormouse tail

(f) Boat paddle

Fold

Boat side

Chain stitch

Boat base

Boat seat

(i) Bullrush leaf

1

2

3

4

(g) Duck

1

2

3

4

(h) Duck

Fold

Bullrush

X

X

(j) Butterfly

cover them completely. Bind seven more pipe cleaners with wool to within 1.3cm (½in) of each end. Insert these ends into the centre of the top of the tree where the 1.3cm (½in) of exposed pipe cleaners of the trunk remain; these inserted pieces are the branches of the tree. Fan out as for the branches of a weeping willow tree. Bind with wool to cover the pipe cleaner ends. Take six stamens and stitch to secure to the end of a branch. Treat all the branches in the same way. To cover the area where the stamens are stitched, cut out the leaf Fig 94 (a) in varying sizes and glue to the branches.

Nest Using fine wool in three tones of brown, plait a 35.5cm (14in) length. Coil and stitch this into a circle approximately three plaits high and with a top measurement of 2.5cm (1in). Glue to the top centre of the tree.

Blackbirds Fig 94 (b). Cut two body pieces in black felt. Overstitch around the outside edge, leaving the base open. Stuff and close. Stitch the beak in place and embroider tiny dots for the eyes. Overstitch the wings in place. Make three birds and place in the nest previously lined with a small amount of toy filling. Stitch to hold.

The Drum Construction Space four of the five 7.6cm (3in) cardboard tube pieces evenly

---

Fig 94 The Teddy Bears' Picnic: Actual size patterns. (a) Tree leaf: cut shape in varying shade of green felt to requirements; (b) Blackbird: cut two bodies and two wings in black felt, cut beak in yellow felt; (c) Frog shape: cut in light-green felt, add markings in black using a fibre-tipped pen; (d) Dormouse tail: cut one in beige fur-fabric – the dormouse body is a 3.8cm (1½in) diameter circle; (e) Bridge side: cut two in dark-brown felt, cut two slightly smaller in card; (f) Boat paddle: Cut two in brown felt, Boat side: cut two in medium-brown felt, Boat base: cut one in medium-brown felt, Boat seat: cut two in brown felt, cut two in card; (g) and (h) Ducks: both the same – (1) Body: cut two in yellow felt, (2) Wing: cut two in yellow felt, (3) Base: cut one in yellow felt, (4) Beak: cut two in orange felt; (i) Bullrush leaf: cut four in green felt varying the size, Bullrush: cut two in dark-brown felt; (j) Butterfly – Body: cut two in black felt, Wing: cut two in orange Vilene or Funtex and mark pattern with a black fibre-tipped pen

---

around the uncovered side of the brown cake board approximately 1.3cm (½in) in from the outside edge. Glue into place. Locate the fifth piece of tube in the centre of the cake board. Glue into place. Add a circle of card to the top of each tube and glue into place; when dry, add adhesive to the top of each tube circle and press the uncovered side of the green cake board on top of the tubes, making sure the cake boards are lined up to one another exactly.

Underwater Scene Cover the card panel with the blue felt using adhesive, turning in the felt over the long edges. Using Fig 95 as a guide, cut out the fish, weeds and beetles and glue into place. Glue the panel into place where indicated on Fig 96.

Underground Cover the card with brown felt, turning in the felt over the long edges. Cut out the worms, frog (Fig 94 (c)), beetles, dormouse (Fig 94 (d)) and tree roots. Apply with adhesive using Fig 95 as a guide to placing. Glue panel in place where indicated on Fig 96.

For the panel containing the musical unit, cover one side with brown felt, turning the longer edges over the card. Make a hole in the card to the level of the key, measured when the musical unit is standing on one side on top of the base unit with the back of the movement facing the outside. Remove the key. Glue the edge of the musical unit to the inside of the card. Add adhesive to the base board and top and bottom edges of the boards. Press the side panel and musical unit into place, see Fig 96. Replace the key.

Stream Glue the blue-felt pattern piece into place where indicated, leaving the cut pieces free.

Bridge Fig 94 (e). Cut the pattern pieces in brown felt and the card linings slightly smaller. Glue the felt to the bases leaving the edges of the felt free from the adhesive. Cut a piece of brown felt for the bridge top 14 x 3.8cm (5½ x 1½in). Overstitch the bridge sides to the bridge top, and glue the bridge into place.

Gate Cut the 0.7cm (¼in) piece of dowelling in half. Glue the 7.6cm (3in) bars

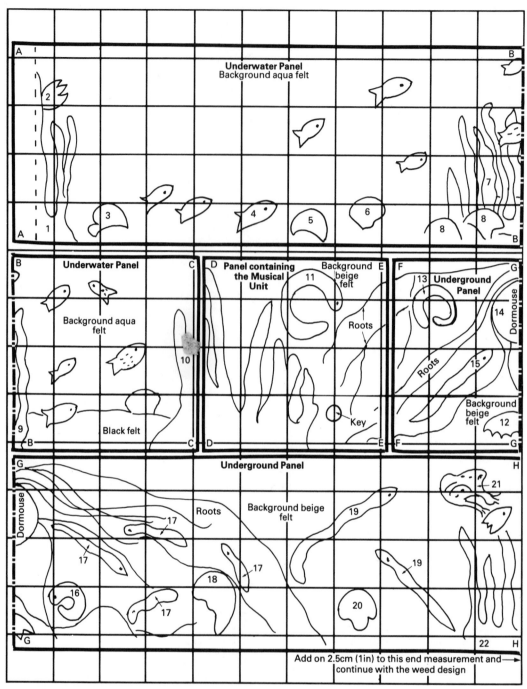

The figure contains the following labels:

A ... **B**
Underwater Panel
Background aqua felt
2

3 4 5 6 7 8 8

A 1 ... **B**

B Underwater Panel ... **C** **D** Panel containing the Musical Unit ... Background beige felt **E** **F** 13 Underground Panel **G**

11

Background aqua felt

Roots

Dormouse

14

10

Key

Roots

15

Black felt

Background beige felt 12

9

B ... **C** **D** ... **E** **F** ... **G**

G ... **H**
Underground Panel

21

Dormouse

Roots   Background beige felt   19

17

17

17   19

18

16

17

20

G 22 **H**

Add on 2.5cm (1in) to this end measurement and → continue with the weed design

Fig 95 The Teddy Bears' Picnic: Side panel design. To allow the fitting of the panel designs on to the graph it has been necessary to divide them into sections. If the reader starts at the top panel on the graph at A and follows through to the next solid line at C–C this is the complete *Underwater Panel.* D–D to E–E is a complete panel containing the musical unit. The *Underground Panel* starts at F–F to the extended measurement at H–H. The colouring of the original model felts is as follows: 1 lime green; 2 medium green; 3 light green; 4 the fish are varied – silver, gold, orange, grey and beige; 5 light green; 6 black; 7 lime green; 8 black; 9 lime green; 10 medium green; 11 grey; 12 black; 13 grey; 14 brown fur-fabric; 15 grey; 16 beige; 17 beige; 18 black; 19 grey; 20 black; 21 light green; 22 lime green

158

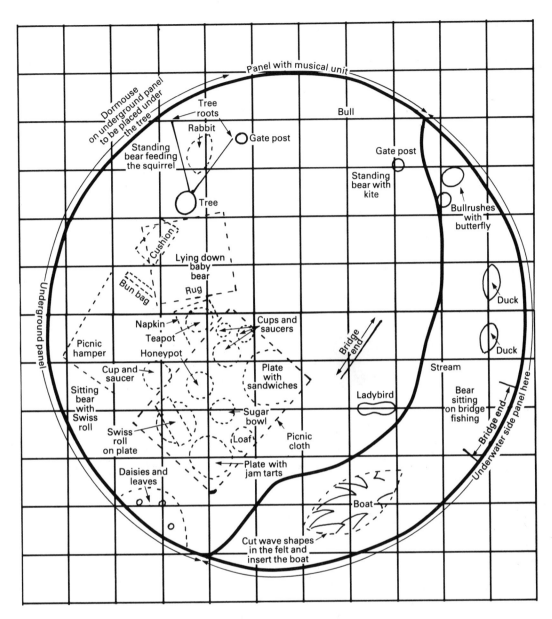

Fig 96 The Teddy Bears' Picnic: The thicker lined outline to the circle, and the stream are the actual pattern shapes. The thinner lines and dotted lines indicate the approximate placing of the items on the covered top of the cake board. These are not to scale. Spaces have been left to show the individual items clearly; when the bears and other models are placed on to the board they almost entirely fill the surface. Match the side panels Fig 95, placing the underwater scene under the stream and follow round until the side is completely encased; A–A should meet H–H

evenly between the thicker pieces. Allow to dry then glue into place.

Boat Fig 94 (f). Overstitch the open ends of the side pieces to join. Insert the base and overstitch to secure. Work two lines of chain stitching down either side of the boat. Make two loops of felt either side to hold the oars in place. Cover the card pieces with brown felt for the seats and glue into place in the boat, spaced apart. Using small lettering, write 'The Bruin' on the white piece of paper, cut out and glue to the front of the boat. Glue the boat in place on the stream. Cover two pieces of pipe cleaner each measuring 5.7cm (2¼in) with the felt pattern paddle pieces, overstitching along the edges to join and leaving the curved ends free. Place a paddle through each loop.

Ducks Fig 94 (g) and (h). Place two body pieces together. Overstitch around the outside edges to join, leaving the bottom straight edges open. Stuff and insert the

base using overstitching. Stitch a wing in place on either side of the body. Apply the beak. Embroider the eyes. Glue the base of the duck to the water. Make the other duck in the same way and glue to the water.

Bullrushes Fig 94 (i). Bind the two 5cm (2in) pieces of wire with green stranded embroidery cotton. Fold the bullrush pattern in half and overstitch to join. Stuff slightly and place on top of a bound wire piece. Stitch in

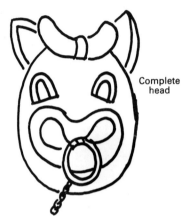

Complete head

Fig 97 The Teddy Bears' Picnic: Actual size bull pattern. (1) Mouthpiece: cut one in pink felt; (2) Nostrils: cut two in dark-brown felt; (3) Eyes: cut two in white felt; (4) Pupils: cut two in black felt; (5) Horn: cut one in beige felt; (6) Horn centre: cut one in brown felt; (7) Head: cut two in brown felt; (8) Body: cut two in brown felt; (9) Hoof (for feet): cut two in beige felt; (10) Leg: cut four in brown felt; (11) Ear: cut two in brown felt; (12) Arm: cut four in brown felt; (13) Tail: cut two in brown felt; (14) Hoof (for hands): cut two in beige felt

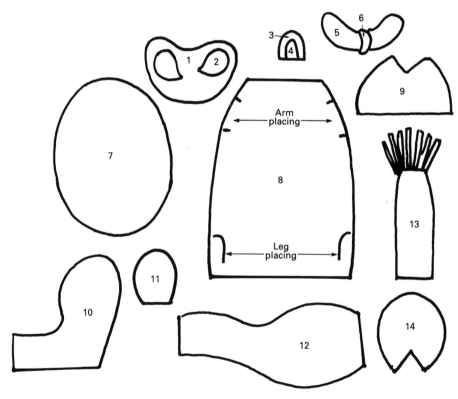

place. Treat the second wire in the same way. Cut several bullrush leaf shapes in varying sizes and stitch to the base of the covered wires. Glue to the stream piece where indicated.

Butterfly Fig 94 (j). Glue a wing base on either side of the body piece and glue the base of the body to the gate post.

Bull Fig 97. Place the body pieces together and overstitch around the outside edges, leaving the base open. Stuff and overstitch to close base. Place the head pieces together, overstitch to join, then stuff and close. Glue the features to the face. Stitch the horns to the top centre front of the head. Ladder stitch an ear in place on either side of the horns. Place two arm pieces together. Overstitch to join. Stuff and close. Fold a hoof piece in half and place around the shorter straight end of the arm. Stitch to secure. Treat the second arm in the same way. Stitch an arm on either side of the body. Place two of the leg pieces together and construct as for the arms. Make a second leg. Stitch to the body on either side. Stitch the curtain ring to the face just below the nostrils. Stitch the end of the chain to the ring. Tie the opposite end of the chain around the gate post and stitch into place. Glue a hot cross bun to the bull's right hoof.

Spider and Web Work strands of the nylon thread across from the tree trunk to the underside of a branch; as you stitch, place a small ball of nylon toy filling at the centre and take the nylon strands through this. Secure. Cut a tiny black circle of felt not more than 0.7cm (¼in) diameter, glue to the centre of the toy filling and stitch single-strand black legs from the circle outwards, cutting each leg separately and rejoining the thread to the spider's body to work the subsequent legs. Work eight legs.

Squirrel and Nest Fig 98 (a). Place the squirrel head/body pieces together. Overstitch around the outside edge, leaving the bottom straight edge open. Stuff and close. Stitch an ear in place either side of the head. Stitch the paws in place. Stitch a small black brocatelle bead in place on either side

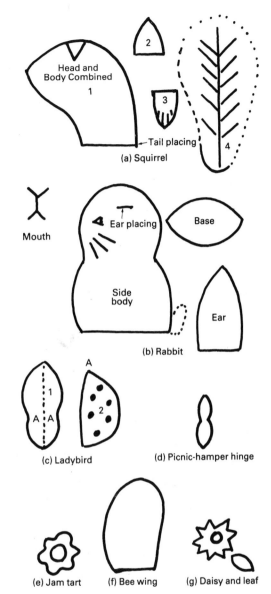

(a) Squirrel

Mouth

Ear placing   Base

Side body   Ear

(b) Rabbit

(c) Ladybird   (d) Picnic-hamper hinge

(e) Jam tart   (f) Bee wing   (g) Daisy and leaf

Fig 98 The Teddy Bears' Picnic: Actual size patterns. (a) Squirrel – (1) Head and body combined: cut two in ginger-brown felt, (2) Ear: cut two in ginger-brown felt, (3) Paw: cut two in beige felt, (4) Tail: cut one in ginger-brown felt and cut where indicated to shape; (b) Rabbit – (1) Body: cut two in beige felt, (2) Base: cut one in beige felt, (3) Ears: cut two in beige felt; (c) Ladybird – (1) Body: cut two in black felt, (2) Wing: cut two in red felt and add markings using black fibre-tipped pen; (d) Picnic hamper hinge: cut two in red felt; (e) Jam tart: cut fluted shape in cream or beige felt or Vilene and the centre circle in red felt for the jam; (f) Bee wing: cut two in white net; (g) Daisy and Leaf: cut the daisy shape in yellow felt or Vilene, cut the leaf shape in green felt

of the head as eyes. Stitch the tail to the back of the body where indicated. Using brown wool to match the tree trunk, make a nest shape as for the blackbird's nest. Place the squirrel into the nest shape and stitch to hold. Glue the base of the nest to the trunk of the tree at the back and place it approximately 5cm (2in) down from the top of the tree; this should appear to be part of the tree trunk.

Rabbit Fig 98 (b). Place the side body pieces together. Overstitch around the outside edges to join, leaving the bottom straight edges open. Stuff, insert base and close. Line the ear pieces with thin white interfacing, fold in half lengthways at the base and stitch an ear to either side of the head facing outwards sideways not to the front of the body. Work the eyes and features in single-strand cotton. Add three white whiskers either side of the mouth. Form a small ball of white toy filling for the tail and glue into place. Glue the rabbit between the tree roots.

Ladybird Fig 98 (c). Fold the black body piece in half lengthways and overstitch to join, adding a small amount of toy filling prior to closing. Place a wing piece, with the markings drawn in black marker pen, on either side of the body and stitch into place. Glue the ladybird to the base as indicated.

Picnic Hamper Cover the small box lid and base with the gingham material, turning the raw edges into the inside of the lid and base. Line the inside of the lid and base with red felt. Add small red felt hinges, Fig 98 (d), to join the lid and base together at the back edges. Add a handle and straps cut in red felt to the front edges of the box. Glue a piece of very narrow ribbon across the inside of the lid; this will eventually hold the plates in place.

Crockery In the modelling compound form tiny cups, saucers and plates. A pencil or piece of dowelling is useful for forming the cups around. The flat end of the pencil is also useful for marking indentations for the centre of the cups and plates. Make a small sugar bowl and add tiny cubes for the sugar.

Make a teapot and spoon. Bake or dry the models according to the compound being used.

Jam Tarts Fig 98 (e). These are cut from either Vilene or Funtex. The red centres are glued to each tart and then the tarts are glued to a plate. Make six tarts.

Sandwiches Place a piece of brown Funtex between two 1.3cm (½in) pieces of white Funtex; glue to hold. Cut in half diagonally and glue to a plate. Make several sandwiches in this way.

Swiss Roll Cut one piece of red and one piece of yellow Funtex to measure 5 x 4.5cm (2 x 1¾in). Roll up together lengthways and glue to hold. Cut off a piece one end; a bear will hold this.

Honey Pot Cut a piece of honey-coloured Vilene or Funtex to measure 6.4 x 2.5cm (2½ x 1in). Join the shorter edges. Insert the base and overstitch to hold. Write 'Honey' on a small label and glue to the jar. Gather just in from the outside edge of a 5cm (2in) diameter circle of tiny checked gingham, and pull up to fit the top of the jar. Fasten off.

Bee Fig 98 (f). Gather a 2.5cm (1in) diameter circle of yellow felt, but do not pull up. Press into an oblong and stitch the opposite edges together. Bind one end to form a small knob head. Attach a net wing to either side of the body. Work two small eyes in black cotton with two feelers above. Glue the bee to the honey pot.

Cottage Loaf Cut one 3.8cm (1½in) diameter circle and one 2.5cm (1in) diameter circle in beige felt. Gather around the outside edge of the larger circle, stuff and fasten off. Make the smaller circle in the same way and glue the small circle on to the larger one over the gathering.

Hot Cross Buns Cut both 2cm (¾in) circles and 3.3cm (1¼in) circles, then gather and stuff. Using stranded embroidery cotton, work a cross on the top of each bun. Make eight buns. Cut the piece of greaseproof paper in half and glue together on three sides. When dry, place some of the hot cross buns in the bag.

162

Large bear

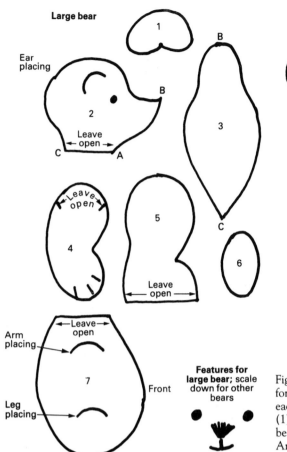

Ear placing

1

B

B

2

Leave ← open →

C   A

3

Leave open

4

5

Leave ← open →

C

6

Arm placing

Leave ← open →

7

Front

Leg placing

Features for large bear; scale down for other bears

Small bear

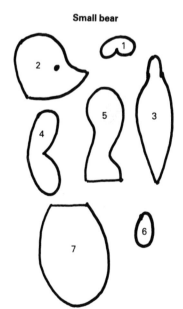

2

1

5

3

4

7

6

Medium size bear

1

2

5

3

4

7

6

Fig 99 The Teddy Bears' Picnic: Actual size patterns for bears. Due to the smallness of the pattern pieces, each has a number. Cut out as follows for each bear: (1) Ear: cut two in beige felt; (2) Head: cut two in beige felt; (3) Head gusset: cut one in beige felt; (4) Arm: cut four in beige felt; (5) Leg: cut four in beige felt; (6) Foot pad: cut two in dark-brown felt; (7) Body: cut two in beige felt

Picnic Cloth Cut a piece of the tiny check gingham to measure 7.6 x 10.3cm (3 x 4in). Turn in a narrow hem and glue to hold. Glue the picnic cloth to the base board. Place the sandwiches, honey, cottage loaf, Swiss roll, sugar bowl, cups, saucers and teapot on to the picnic cloth and glue in place. Place some cups and saucers into the picnic hamper and cut small 2.5cm (1in) squares for the serviettes. Glue the picnic hamper to the base board.

Flowers Fig 98 (g). Cut several yellow flowers in felt and glue in a group, adding small felt leaves.

Rug Fray the edges of the woven rug piece then glue the centre only to the base board.

Cushion Cut two 3.8cm (1½in) squares of gingham. With right sides facing, join three

163

sides. Turn to the right side. Stuff. Turn in
the open edges and overstitch to close. Glue
along the overstitched edge to the rug, laying the top of the cushion against a tree
root.

Bears These are all made in the same way
and are glued into place on the base board.
There are three larger bears, two medium
size bears and one baby bear.

Place the side head pieces together.
Overstitch A–B together. Insert head gusset
matching B–C. Overstitch in place. Stuff.
Gather neck base, pull up and close.

Overstitch body pieces together leaving
the straight edge open. Stuff. Gather the
top of the body. Pull up and close. Ladder
stitch the head to the top of the body.

Place arms together in pairs. Take one
pair and overstitch together, leaving open
where indicated. Stuff and overstitch to
close. Treat the second arm in the same
way. Overstitch to the body.

Place legs together in pairs. Take one pair
and overstitch together, leaving open
where indicated. Stuff. Insert a foot base
and overstitch in place. Treat the second
leg in the same way. Overstitch to the body.
Make two larger bears sitting down, and the
baby bear, one medium size bear and a larger
bear standing up.

Fold the ears at the base to curve, and
ladder stitch on either side of the head
where indicated. Work the features using
dark-brown stranded cotton. Tie a narrow
ribbon around the bear's neck. Work three
claws on each hand in brown cotton.

Place one larger bear sitting beside the
picnic, with the previously cut piece of
Swiss roll glued to his left hand. A medium
size sitting bear is placed in the boat with a
hot cross bun in the front of the boat. A
larger bear sits on the bridge holding a
fishing rod, which is a piece of wire measuring 7.6cm (3in) long bound with black
stranded embroidery cotton. A length of
black cotton is tied to the top of the rod
dangling to the water, with a small piece of
thin wire as the hook, tied to the end. A fish

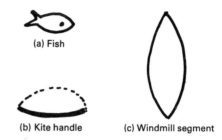

(a) Fish

(b) Kite handle   (c) Windmill segment

Fig 100 The Teddy Bears' Picnic: Actual size patterns.
(a) Fish: cut two in orange felt or Vilene; (b) Kite
handle: this is the actual size required; make as per
written instructions; (c) Windmill segment: cut one
in blue and one in pink Vilene

Fig 100 (a), is glued to the wire and the fish
and line hang between the ducks on the
stream who are also trying to catch it. A
medium size bear holds a string on the end
of which is a kite (see below) caught in a
branch of the tree. Place a larger bear, holding a jam tart in his right hand, behind the
tree under the squirrel's nest. The bear is
offering the squirrel the jam tart. The baby
bear is tired so he is having a sleep, lying on
the rug and cushion. Beside him lies a windmill (see below) that he has been playing
with.

Kite Handle, Fig 100 (b). Gently curve the
2.5cm (1in) piece of wire to the given
shape. Bind with stranded embroidery
cotton then take the cotton straight across
from one end to the other. Stitch to hold.
Cut out the kite shape, and using the black
marker pen draw in the detail. Cut tiny bow
shapes in blue and yellow. Tie a cotton
thread measuring 12.7cm (5in) to the base
point of the kite, and string on the bows
spacing well apart. Fasten off. Tie a cotton
thread from the centre back of the kite to
the handle and knot to secure. Place the
kite in the tree and the handle in the bear's
left hand.

Windmill Fig 100 (c). Cut two pattern
pieces, one blue and one pink. Place on to
the dressmaker's pin at the centre of each.
Lay the end of the pin against the 5cm (2in)
length of wire and bind with the stranded
cotton. Fasten off.

Hush-A-Bye Baby

Hush-a-bye baby, on the tree top,
When the wind blows the cradle will rock,
When the bough breaks the cradle will fall,
Down will come baby, cradle and all.

* * *

Toy type: Felt mouse in a cradle (colour picture page 143)
Size of toy: Height 12.7cm (5in)

This toy requires considerable neatness and care during construction. The pattern pieces must be cut out with smooth edges. Tiny overstitching must be used. When stuffing, use small amounts of toy filling at a time and gradually fill the toy. A small toy requires everything to be scaled down in size; the toymaker should 'think small' in relation to the materials being used and the finished article will then reflect the care taken. Felt is a very useful medium when working on a small item, as fraying of materials can be a hazard to the toymaker. If using materials which are inclined to fray, it can sometimes be useful to glue the edges lightly prior to cutting.

A purchased or handmade basket approximately 25.4cm long x 15.3cm across x 6.4cm deep (10 x 6 x 2½in)
Felt oddments for the mouse
2 pipe cleaners
Small amount of toy filling
Lightweight material or 9cm (3½in) wide broderie-anglaise trimming for making the nightgown
Narrow ribbon 20.4cm (8in) long for neck decoration on nightgown
Cotton material for the pillow, eiderdown and frill around the basket, to tone with the mouse colouring
Material to tone with the cotton material for the mattress and sheet
Dainty trimming
NOTE: See overleaf for calculating the amounts required

Cut out all the pattern pieces.
Head Place two side head pieces together and sew seam a–b together using stab stitching. Sew the head gusset to each side of the head b–c, remembering to sew one side first then go back to b and sew the second side. Sew the seams c–d together and stuff the head firmly without putting too much pressure on the seams.

Gather the nose circle and ladder stitch to the head at b. Stitch the eyelids in place on their curve, leaving the bottom straight edge open. Using black thread embroider eyelashes, starting just under the eyelid. See Fig 102. Using a single horsehair strand, apply two whiskers on either side of the head just below the nose.
Body Place two body pieces together – the seams are at each side of the body – overstitch around the outside edge leaving the neck edge open. Stuff firmly. Gather the neck edge to close. Ladder stitch the head to the body.
Legs and Feet For each leg, place two pieces together and overstitch around the outside edge leaving the bottom straight edges open. Stuff firmly. Using ladder stitching, sew on to the body where indicated on Fig 102. Overstitch the feet pieces together in pairs and attach to each leg base.
Ears For each ear, place one ear piece and one lining together. Using overstitching sew together. Fold inwards along the straight bottom edge to form a slight curve, then stitch to hold. Ladder stitch the ears to the head where indicated on the pattern.
Arms and Paws The arms are made in one continuous strip. Cut a piece of a pipe cleaner 12.7cm (5in) long. Cover it in felt, overstitching down the long edge. Attach

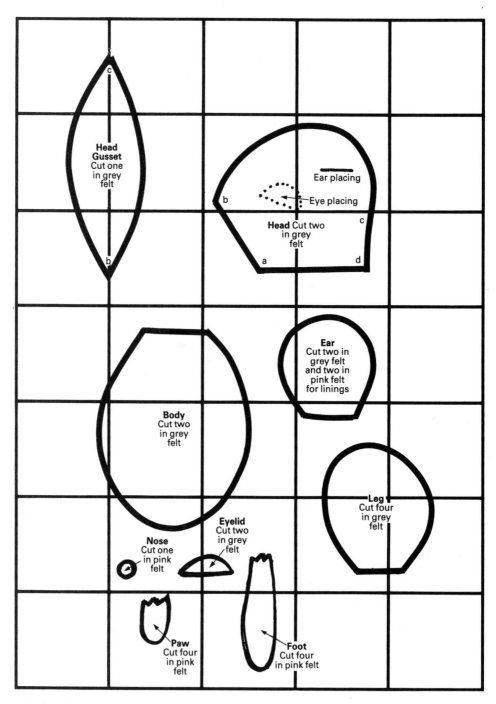

Fig 101 Hush-A-Bye Baby: Mouse

the centre of the covered pipe cleaner to the back of the mouse level with the shoulder. Overstitch the paw pieces together in pairs. Stitch a paw to the end of each arm.

Tail Cut a piece of felt 12.7cm (5in) long and wide enough to cover a pipe cleaner cut to the same size. Oversew along the length and taper the end to a point. Stitch the tail

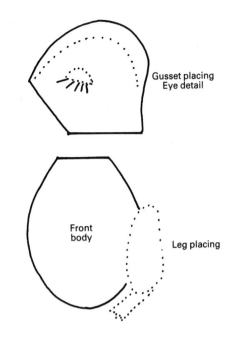

Gusset placing
Eye detail

Front body

Leg placing

Sample of rocker shape for cradle
Measurement a–b adjusted to width of underbase of cradle

a   b

Front view

Fig 102 Hush-A-Bye Baby

to the body at the back between the legs, approximately 0.7cm (¼in) up from the body seam at the base.

Nightgown As this toy is not designed to have the clothes removed, it is not necessary to make a miniature garment with set-in sleeves – the nightgown is constructed on the body. Using a lightweight material or broderie-anglaise trimming, cut a piece 25.4 x 12.7cm (10 x 5in). Turn a 0.7cm (¼in) hem on one long edge. (This will not be necessary if using the broderie-anglaise trimming.) Fold the material to form a tube and stitch the seams together. Turn in a narrow hem for the neck edge, gather to fit the neck of the mouse and fasten off. Cut two small arm holes either side and bring an arm out each side of the body.

For each nightgown sleeve, cut a piece of material 10.3 x 5cm (4 x 2in). Turn a

narrow hem at the wrists and shoulders if necessary. With right sides facing, sew down each sleeve seam to form a tube. Turn to the right side. Gather at each wrist to fit the arms and fasten off. The wrists can have the gathering placed to leave a frill if you are using the broderie-anglaise trimming. Gather at each shoulder and stitch around the armholes, covering any raw edges.

Mouse Basket
There are many different types of inexpensive baskets available in stores and crafts shops. The basket in the photograph is one example: it measures 25.4cm long x 15.3cm across x 6.4cm deep (10 x 6 x 2½in). The original was draped in an attractive cotton material in pale lemon with a design of tiny mice. Whilst most work baskets are capable of producing material and trimming oddments, sometimes it is nice to purchase a material which is particularly suitable for the subject being made. The bedding is in lemon-coloured flannelette material trimmed with lemon broderie-anglaise daisy trimming. Colours which complement or match one another look a more professional article.
Mattress Measure the bottom of the chosen basket. Cut two pieces of material 1.3cm (½in) larger all round than the finished size required; this will allow for the width taken up by the stuffing. Place right sides together and stitch round the outside edge, leaving one narrow end open. Turn to the right side and lightly stuff, stitch to close.
Pillow If the basket is oval, cut two pieces of the patterned material to the width and depth of the top end of the basket. Curve both the top corners. Place the two pieces together, right sides facing, and stitch around the curved outside edge, leaving the bottom straight edge open. Turn to the right side and stuff. Turn in the bottom straight edge and stitch to close. Stitch a piece of pretty trimming to one side of the pillow; this will be the front.
Sheet Cut a piece of material to match the mattress 3.8cm (1½in) larger all round than the size of the basket to enable the

sheet to be placed over the mouse and tucked under the mattress. Turn and stitch a narrow hem all around the outside edge. Trim the top edge to match the pillow.

Eiderdown This is made in the same way as the pillow with one end curved to fit the curve on the basket front. Obtain the dimensions by measuring the width and the length of the cradle, adding 3.8cm (1½in) all round to allow for the volume of stuffing. After stitching, trim to match the pillow including the top straight edge.

Basket Frill (optional) Some baskets look attractive showing the woven canework sides – sometimes all that is required is a bow at the front of the basket on the outside. If a frill is required, it should match the eiderdown and pillow material. A small article can look very cluttered if too many different materials are used. Measure from under the top rim of the basket to the base level; add 2cm (¾in) for the top and bottom hem of the frill. The frill length is the measurement taken around the basket and doubled. Turn up and stitch the bottom hem, then, using strong thread, hem and gather the top edge to fit the basket circumference, and place a holding stitch. Neatly stitch the top hem to the cane upright stakes of the basket or, if the canework is closely woven, attach to the weave. Either stitch the narrow open ends of the frill together or turn a hem to neaten the raw edges. Trim with narrow ribbon bows if desired.

Basket on Wooden Rockers A rocking cradle can be made using an oblong basket which has a canework lip around the underneath of the base. Cut two rockers to the shape given (see Fig 102) and insert one at either end of the basket into the lip; glue into place. Ribbons can be attached if a cradle is required to hang.

Lavender's Blue

Lavender's blue, diddle, diddle,
Lavender's green,
When I am king, diddle, diddle,
You shall be queen.

* * *

Toy type: Felt doll with laminated mask face (colour picture page 144)
Size of toy: Height 38.1cm (15in)

The doll has a laminated face formed on a doll mask measuring at the back 5.7 x 7cm (2¼ x 2¾in) – see Fig 104. Any suitable doll head could be used as the base, provided it is of comparable size and in proportion to the body. This design is an excellent subject for using oddments of materials; however, when selecting for the dress and trimmings choose toning shades from dark to light. The veil and the top layer of the dress are in the lightest tone.

Flesh-coloured felt for the head, hands and legs, 38.1 x 25.4cm (15 x 10in)
Dark-mauve felt for the body, arms and shoes, 17.8 x 22.9cm (7 x 9in)
Two different tones of 0.7cm (¼in) wide ribbon for the dress and crown decorations, four lengths each of 28cm (11in)
A 106.7cm (42in) length of narrow pale-mauve ribbon for the shoe ties
½m (19¾in) narrow light-mauve broderie-trimming for the dress and crown. Try to choose a design suitable for a crown, possibly with raised loops
Narrow light-mauve lace trimming for the dress front, 55.9cm (22in)

168

Four small silver bells

Patterned or plain nylon material for the panties, 17.8 x 16.6cm (7 x 6½in)

Plain nylon (or if not available use a fine flimsy material) for the skirt: dark mauve for the two underskirt layers 101.6 x 50.8cm (40 x 20in); pale mauve for the top skirt layer, the veil and bodice trimming 101.6cm x 48.2cm (40 x 19in)

Mohair yarn for the hair. The hair for this doll requires plenty of bulk although the actual strands must not be too thick for the fringe

A 5cm (2in) piece of narrow white tape

Black, blue and red fibre-tipped pens for drawing the features

A 12.7cm (5in) circle of nylon cut with pinking shears for the lavender bag

A very narrow piece of pink or mauve ribbon to tie around the neck of the lavender bag

A small amount of dried lavender

A small sprig of artificial lavender, or mauve heather

Toy filling

Head Make the face mask as per the laminating process described in the toy techniques section, page 13. Using flesh-coloured felt, cut two of the back head pattern pieces. Construct as shown on Fig 106. Stuff the head firmly, taking the toy filling well into the face mask feature indentations. Lay the stuffed head aside.

Body (bodice) Cut a piece of dark-mauve felt to measure 9 x 17.8cm (3½ x 7in). Fold where indicated on Fig 107. At either side of the fold, curve slightly to form the shoulders, (Fig 107). Overstitch the outside edges together, leaving the bottom straight edges open. Turn to the opposite side. Stuff evenly and firmly without putting too much strain on the overstitching. Overstitch the bottom straight edges to close, inserting more toy filling prior to closing completely. At the top fold of the stuffed body, snip open along the fold to the width of the neck measurement of the prepared head.

Insert the neck into the opening and neatly stitch around the neck base, using

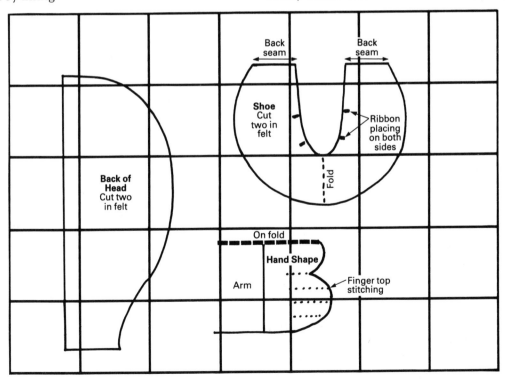

Fig 103 Lavender's Blue

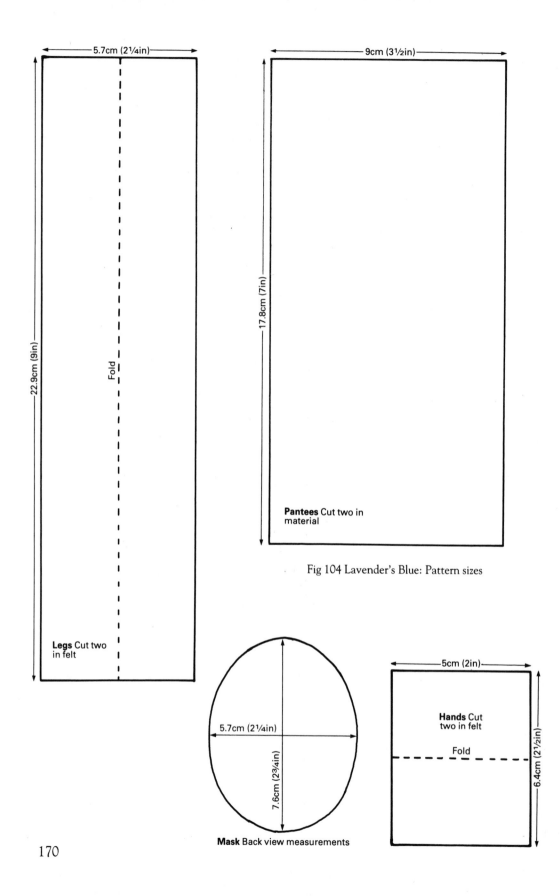

5.7cm (2¼in)

Fold

22.9cm (9in)

Legs Cut two in felt

9cm (3½in)

17.8cm (7in)

Pantees Cut two in material

Fig 104 Lavender's Blue: Pattern sizes

5.7cm (2¼in)

7.6cm (2¾in)

Mask Back view measurements

5cm (2in)

Hands Cut two in felt

Fold

6.4cm (2½in)

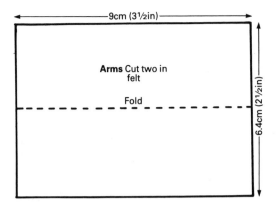

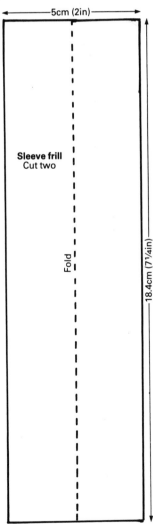

either a running stitch or overstitch, to join the head to the opening on the body. Make sure you do not distort the mask. It will be easier to stitch through the laminating if a fine sewing needle is used. Draw in the features with the fibre-tipped pens, using the original mask as a copy.

Arms Using the same dark-mauve felt as the body, cut two pieces of felt each measuring 9 x 6.4cm (3½ x 2½in). Cut two flesh-coloured pieces of felt for the hands to measure 6.4 x 5cm (2½ x 2in). Place one mauve arm piece and one flesh hand piece together, matching the 6.4cm (2½in) measurement; overlap by approximately 1.3cm (½in) the pink piece behind the mauve. Backstitch to join. Repeat for other arm and hand.

Fig 105 Lavender's Blue: Pattern sizes

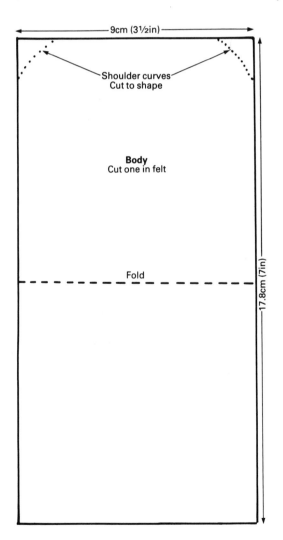

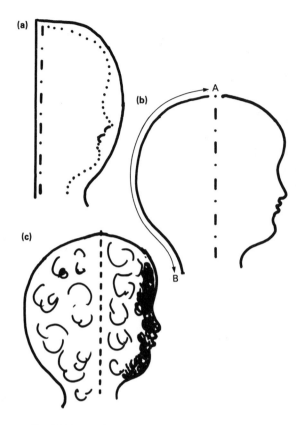

Fig 106 Lavender's Blue: Applying head back pieces to a laminated mask. (a) Lay a back of head piece to either side of the laminated mask, covering the mask and lining up the straight edges, and backstitch in place; (b) Take the attached side pieces to the back of the laminated mask and ladder stitch to join from the top of the head 'A' to the back of the neck 'B'; (c) Stuff the head firmly, paying particular attention to the feature indentations

Fold one arm piece in half lengthways and overstitch the mauve-felt edges together using matching thread. Cut the hand shape given, on the pink felt, then, changing to matching flesh-coloured thread, overstitch around the outside edge. Do not turn to the opposite side. Stuff firmly without adding strain to the seaming. Overstitch the open ends to close. Stab stitch on the hand to indicate fingers. Treat the other arm and hand in the same way.

Ladder stitch an arm to either side of the body just below the shoulder level, with the overstitched arm seam at the back of the arm, and the thumb to the front.

Legs In the flesh-coloured felt, cut two pieces measuring 5.7 x 22.9cm (2¼ x 9in). Take one piece and fold it in half lengthways and pin to hold. Cut one end to curve for the heel. Overstitch around the outside edges, leaving the top straight edge open. Do not turn. Stuff firmly and evenly. With the overstitched edge of the leg at the back, overstitch the open top edges together to close. Press the toe of the foot upwards slightly (see Fig 108) and take a line of ladder stitching across the foot to join it to the leg; this is similar to adding a dart. Treat the other leg in the same way. Stitch the legs to the base of the body so that each is in line with the sides of the body – use ladder stitching across the front of each leg and overstitching across the back.

Panties Cut two pieces of the material each measuring 17.8 x 8.3cm (7 x 3¼in). Turn in a narrow hem top and bottom of each piece on the longer edges. With the right sides facing, join the shorter side seams. Join the centre of the long edges together at the base for 2.5cm (1in) to make the crutch. Turn to the right side. Place on to the doll. Gather the top edge and pull up to fit the body. Fasten off. Gather one leg opening, pull up to fit the leg. Fasten off. Treat the other leg opening in the same way.

Shoes Cut two of the shoe pattern shapes in the dark-mauve felt. Take one piece and fold it in half. Overstitch around the curved edges to join, and also join the back seams. Fasten off. Do not turn. Make the other shoe in the same way. Cut four pieces of narrow mauve ribbon each to measure 26.7cm (10½in). Stitch a ribbon to either side of each shoe as shown on the pattern. Place a shoe on each foot. Cross the ribbons at the front, take them round the back of the leg, cross at the front higher up the leg than the previous cross, take to the back of the leg and tie a tiny bow. Cut off any excess ribbon. Treat the ribbons on the other shoe in the same way.

Neckband Measure around the neck of the doll and add 1.3cm (½in) to the measurement; cut the neckband in the lighter-tone

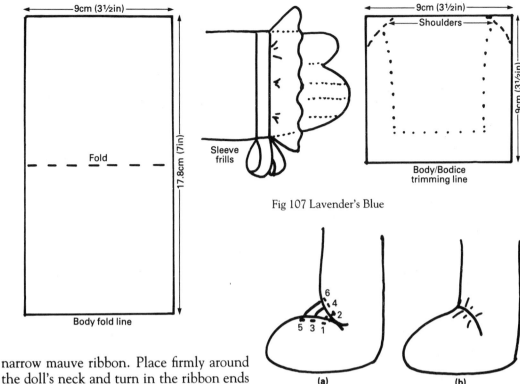

Fig 107 Lavender's Blue

Fig 108 Lavender's Blue: Leg darting (side view). (a) Press inwards to form a dart and stitch; the toe to foot dart is approximately 2cm (³⁄4in) measured at the top of the foot. (b) Pull up the stitches to dart, and fasten off

narrow mauve ribbon. Place firmly around the doll's neck and turn in the ribbon ends neatly to join at the back of the neck; stitch securely in place.

Arm (sleeve) Frills (Fig 107) Cut two pieces of the pale-mauve nylon material, each to measure 5 x 18.4cm (2 x 7¼in). Take one piece and fold it in half lengthways. Gather the 18.4cm (7¼in) edges together and pull up the gathering to fit around the doll's wrist. Join the edges and then stitch the frill to the wrist with the open short edges underneath the arm. Measure around the wrist over the frill gathering and add 2.5cm (1in) to the measurement. In matching ribbon to the neckband, cut a piece to the required measurement. Place around the wrist over the frill gathering. Fold the ribbon ends into two loops and stitch together under the hand. Treat the other wrist in the same way.

Bodice Trimming (Fig 107) Cut a piece of the broderie-anglaise trimming to measure 26.7cm (10½in). Stitch to the bodice starting at one side of the back, then going over the shoulder, down 5cm (2in) to the waist, across the front of the bodice, up and over the shoulder and down the back to the opposite side. Fasten off.

Hair The mohair yarn is referred to as hair in the following instructions. For the fringe, cut a piece of narrow white tape to measure 5cm (2in). Stitch 2.5cm (1in) strands of the mohair yarn to the top edge of the tape only, making sure that the tape is completely covered. Lay to one side. The length of the hair is 38.1cm (15in). Cut as many strands as are necessary to produce bulk and thickness in relation to the size of the doll. Place the cut strands across the top of the head to a depth as shown in Fig 109 (a). The actual size of the parting will vary slightly according to the base size used for the head. Backstitch to secure the hair to the top of the head. Lay the prepared fringe across the forehead and stitch to hold either side, Fig

173

109 (b). Lay some extra lengths of the hair across the head to hide the top edge of the fringe; stitch in line with the centre parting. Lay a final long strand of the yarn across the parting division.

Making sure the individual strands lie parallel and neatly placed, take the hair from one side of the parting and, holding the hair together in a bunch, stitch to one side of the base of the head. Treat the opposite side likewise. Take six strands of hair at the front (side face), twist then fold at the centre to form a curl, see Fig 109 (c). Stitch to the head under the hair at the side. Take another six strands of hair and form another curl and stitch to the head under the hair. Treat the opposite side of the head in the same way. Place the doll face downwards, taking care not to flatten the laminated features; take the remaining hair from the left-hand side of the doll, fold it across the back of the head and then tuck it under the right-hand hair, curving and spreading out the hair at the top – Fig 109 (e). Stitch across to hold in place. Fasten off. Take the right-hand remaining hair, fold it across the back of the head and place it over the previous fold, then tuck it under the top of the left-hand hair; stitch to hold in place – see Fig 109 (f). Cut varying lengths of the hair six strands thick and form curls in the same way as the front side curls. Stitch to the centre back of the head, see Fig 109 (g), to cover the stitching on the back pieces. The finished length of the longest curls should not be more than 5cm (2in). Trim the fringe to the required length.

Skirts Two in dark-mauve nylon material; one in pale-mauve nylon material. Cut each piece to measure 101.6 x 25.4cm (40 x 10in). Gather a dark-mauve piece along one long edge and pull up to fit the doll's waist just below the bodice broderie-anglaise decoration. Join at the top only at the centre back of the doll, stitch to hold, then backstitch around the top of the gathering to secure to the waist. Treat the other dark-mauve piece in the same way, stitching it to secure just above the line of the first skirt. Turn in a narrow hem on one long edge of the pale-mauve piece, gather and pull up. Place around the doll's waist just above the second dark-mauve skirt-waist gathering, with the opening at the front of the doll. Pull up to fit the doll, leaving a 5cm (2in) gap at the centre front of the waist to show the darker-mauve skirts. Place a holding stitch, then stitch this skirt to the bodice around the waist. Trim down the front edges of the pale-mauve skirt with the narrow pale-mauve lace to neaten them. Using pale-mauve ribbon and ribbon matching the neck and wrist trimming, cut four pieces of ribbon (two in each colour) to measure 28cm (11in). Turn in a narrow hem at one end of each ribbon and attach a bell, making a shank with the sewing thread to secure each bell in place. Make a 2.5cm (1in) loop on one of the pale-mauve ribbons and one of the toning ribbons, and stitch to the bodice to one side of the bodice trimming at the waist. Treat the other pair of ribbons in the same way and attach to the opposite side of the bodice at the waist. Cut a 63.5cm (25in) length of the pale-mauve ribbon, tie a small bow at the centre of the ribbon and stitch to the centre front of the waist, leaving the ends of the ribbon dangling.

Crown and Veil Cut a 17.8cm (7in) piece of the mauve broderie-anglaise trimming and stitch the ends together to form a circle. Lay to one side.

Cut a 28 x 22.9cm (11 x 9in) piece in the pale-mauve nylon material. Place on the doll's head slightly at an angle so that the folds do not hang evenly. Work a circle of stitches to secure to the top of the head to the size of the broderie-anglaise crown. Fasten off. Turn the veil back from the face. Lay the prepared crown on top of the turned-back veil and on top of the circle of stitching, and pin to hold. Stitch in place and remove the pins. Cut a 35.5cm (14in) length of ribbon to match the bodice ribbon. Fold in half then form three loops at the centre, each loop to measure approximately 1.3cm (½in). Stitch to hold, then

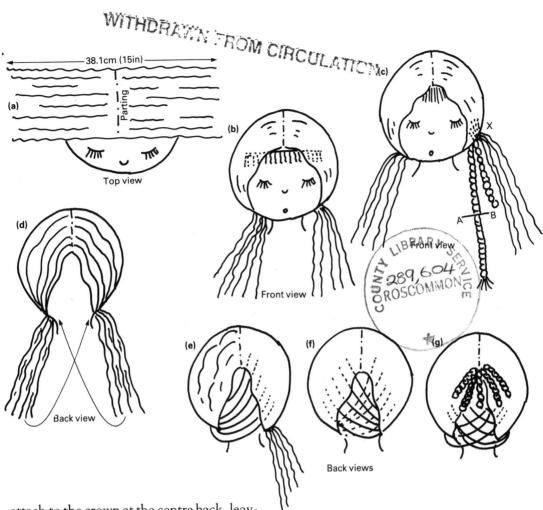

Fig 109 Lavender's Blue: Hair diagram. (a) Top view: hair laid across the top of the head; (b) Front view: fringe inserted each side; (c) Front view: to form curls twist strands together, fold at A–B and let the bottom half twist upwards on to the top half to form the curl, and stitch the ends under the side hair piece at 'x'; (d) Back view: arrowing indicates the direction of the side hair pieces; (e) Back view: hair taken from the left-hand side and tucked under the right-hand hair piece, and stitched to hold; (f) Back view: hair taken from the right-hand side over the previously draped hair and tucked under the left-hand side, and stitched; (g) Back view: form several small curls measuring not more than 5cm (2in) long and attach to cover any joins in the draped hair pieces

attach to the crown at the centre back, leaving two ribbon tails hanging down the back of the head. Gather along one edge of a 5.7cm (2¼in) piece of matching ribbon and pull up until the gathering measures approximately 2.5cm (1in). Fasten it to hold, then stitch to the crown ribbons just below the loops, following the line of the ribbon tails.

Bouquet and Lavender Bag Cut a 12.7cm (5in) circle of nylon using pinking shears. Place a small quantity of dried lavender, with stalks removed, in the centre of the circle. Gather and pull up the circle approximately 2.5cm (1in) from the outside edge. Fasten off. Tie a very narrow ribbon around the gathering and finish with a bow. Cut a 10.3cm (4in) length of narrow mauve ribbon and stitch one end to the lavender bag in line with the gathering and at the opposite side to the ribbon bow. Turn in a narrow hem at the other end of the ribbon; place this end over the fingers of the doll's left hand and stitch in a loop to hold. Stitch a small sprig of the artificial lavender or heather just below the hand loop, following the line of the ribbon.

175

APPENDIX: SPECIALIST MATERIALS

Brocatelle beads also called Rocailles Beads
Tiny beads mainly used in embroidery.

Copydex This is a latex adhesive excellent for fabrics. Available from craft stockists, DIY stores and stationers.

Funtex This is a non-woven material made of 100 per cent Polyester. Hand-washable; crush-resistant; colour-fast; firm and crisp; easy to stitch and glue; and in a range of sixteen colours.

Manufactured by The Vilene Organisation, P.O. Box No 3, Greetland, Halifax, West Yorkshire HX4 8NJ, England. Available in America and Canada from: Pellon Corporation, 119 West 40th St, New York, NY10018, USA; Pellon Chemotextiles Ltd, 1020 Montreal Road, Cornwall, Ont, K6H 5V7, Canada. In both these countries it is known as Phun-phelt.

Furmofelt Furmofelt is stiffened felt. The texture, range and depth of colour of superfine felt is retained in Furmofelt. It is non-fray and simple to stitch or glue. This product is only sold in the UK and is available direct from the manufacturers: Bury and Masco, Hudcar Mills, Bury, Lancashire, BL9 6HD, England. At time of going to press, the price is £1.75 per pack of ten colours each 20.4 x 25.4cm (8 x 10in). Include £1.00 carriage plus 15 per cent VAT (cheque with order).

Also available from craft material stockists.

Musical Units The Teddy Bears' Picnic and a wide range of musical units available from: W. Hobby Limited, Knight's Hill Square, London SE27 0HH, England. This firm exports to many countries.

Turabast This is a synthetic raffia available in a wide range of attractive colours from craft stockists.

Velcro Velcro consists of two nylon strips, one with loops and one with thousands of tiny hooks. When pressed together the hooks grip the loops tightly, resisting a lateral pull far greater than anything likely to be encountered in normal use. Yet, to separate them again is a simple matter: just 'peel' the two strips apart. Being woven entirely from nylon, Velcro is easy to cut precisely to any length required, and can be sewn by hand or machine to virtually any fabric.

Velcro is manufactured by Selectus Ltd, Biddulph, Stoke-on-Trent, ST8 7RH, England, who also manufacture woven edge ribbons. It is also available in the USA, Canada, Australia and New Zealand.

BIBLIOGRAPHY

Anderson, Enid *The Techniques of Soft Toymaking* Batsford (1982)

A World's Work Children's Book One, Two. (1965)

Boswell, Hilda (ed), *Treasury of Nursery Rhymes* Collins (1962)

Cope, Dawn and Peter, *Humpty, Dumpty's Favourite Nursery Rhymes*, Treasure Press (1983)

Gift Book of Nursery Rhymes, Dean (1965)

Ireson, Barbara, (ed). *The Faber Book of Nursery Stories* Faber and Faber Ltd (1966)

Lines, Kathleen, (compiled by), *Lavender's Blue* Oxford University Press (1983)

100 Nursery Rhymes Hamlyn (1980)

Opie, Iona and Peter, (assembled by) *The Oxford Nursery Rhyme Book* OUP (1955)